Reciprocity in Human Societies

Antti Kujala · Mirkka Danielsbacka

Reciprocity in Human Societies

From Ancient Times to the Modern Welfare State

Antti Kujala
University of Helsinki
Helsinki, Finland

Mirkka Danielsbacka
University of Turku
Turku, Finland

Translated by Jüri Kokkonen

ISBN 978-3-030-07141-7   ISBN 978-3-319-96056-2   (eBook)
https://doi.org/10.1007/978-3-319-96056-2

This Palgrave Macmillan imprint is published by the registered company Springer Nature Switzerland AG
The registered company address is: Gewerbestrasse 11, 6330 Cham, Switzerland

PREFACE

As long as societies have been stratified and hierarchical, there has been an unofficial reciprocal social contract of mutual obligations between rulers and subjects. In return for their contributions, taxpayers expect governments to protect them against external threats and to provide economic support in times of need. Rulers and governments neglecting their responsibilities have often suffered as a result, losing power through revolution or in elections, or the prolonged and one-sided protection of elite interests has created weak societies lagging behind others.

Reciprocity in Human Societies—From Ancient Times to the Modern Welfare State describes various manifestations of reciprocity between elites and the common people. The welfare state that emerged after the Second World War is the most recent form of this universal social contract. The economic recession of 2008, however, raised doubts whether maintaining the welfare state and its services could still be afforded. Especially in the United States but also in other developed industrialized countries there are tendencies to cut back on social security for ordinary citizens. We, however, feel that the welfare state has not yet met its end.

Our book is based on our work in Finnish from 2015 *Hyvinvointivaltion loppu? Vallanpitäjät, kansa ja vastavuoroisuus* (The End of the Welfare State? The Elites, the People and Reciprocity). The English version, however, differs from it. All the chapters have been revised and discussion of recent developments has been extended to the end of 2017.

Finnish sociologists Risto Alapuro, Heikki Hiilamo, Heikki Sarmaja and Antti Tanskanen kindly read the manuscript of the Finnish version, and we are grateful to them for their sound advice. Thanks are also due to Hiroshi Momose-sensei for information concerning Japan. Jo Rune Kristiansen Ugulen and Mari Lyssand helped clarify an obscure point of the medieval Norwegian Gulatingslag. Jüri Kokkonen skillfully translated the manuscript into English and Hugh Leburn provided assistance with translations in an earlier stage of the work. We express our thanks to all of them. We are grateful to the Sociology Unit at the University of Turku and the Otto Malm Foundation for participating in funding the translation and to Makoto Murai-sensei and Panu Pulma for their assistance. Last but not least, many thanks to our editors in Palgrave Macmillan and Springer Nature: Alexis Nelson, Kyra Saniewski, Poppy Hull and Murali Dharan Manivannan.

Helsinki, Finland   Antti Kujala
May 2018   Mirkka Danielsbacka

CONTENTS

LIST OF FIGURES

CHAPTER 1

Introduction

In an article published on the last day of 2016, *The Independent* wrote that 2016 would be remembered as "the year that the volcano of inequality exploded." There were many who felt that "the left-behinds" had struck back, causing the outcome of the Brexit referendum and Donald Trump's victory in the US presidential election. The newspaper pointed to other reasons as well, noting that an interpretation of democratic backlash against widening income inequality was "too simplistic." *The Independent's* conclusion was that "the political eruptions of 2016 were not solely a consequence of economic grievances. Yet it would surely be naïve to imagine those grievances did not help to prepare the ground for these shocks."[1]

Grave concern about the possible social consequences of increasing income inequality in the United States was already voiced at a conference of major international investors in New York in the autumn of 2013. Wealth is increasingly concentrating in the hands of the financial elite, the richest 1%, whereas the younger generation of the American middle class cannot expect to attain the living standard of their parents, which implies, without mentioning, the further impoverishment of the poor. This could eventually result in an "Arab Spring" in the United States. The message of the experts was unmistakable: "Unless the decision-makers of economic and financial policy soon stop the growth of income and wealth inequality, it will be broken by the rebellion of the middle class – either at the polls or in the street."[2]

© The Author(s) 2019
A. Kujala and M. Danielsbacka, *Reciprocity in Human Societies*,
https://doi.org/10.1007/978-3-319-96056-2_1

1

Increasing inequality undermines the legitimacy of the political system in the developed Western countries. Does the global financial elite wish to contribute to the preservation of social services, such as universal healthcare, education and social protection, which became established in the post-WW2 era, benefiting economic growth, or will the investments be outsourced overseas, and taxes avoided in the developed countries through tax havens? Will those in power allow this to happen? In the light of recent developments, it is not far-fetched to ask whether the welfare state has a future or will be dismantled, and what the repercussions of that could be.

In this book, we address the system of mutual obligations and expectations between the common people and the elites in earlier societies and present-day welfare states. Our aim is to show how deeply the notion of reciprocity is embedded as an organizing principle for society and the relations between its different strata, and the various ways in which reciprocity is present in societal relations of influence.

The book's core concept of reciprocity can be defined as a system of rights and obligations that its parties (social groups and their members) generally regard to be fair, or at least feel it is in their interest to describe as fair (the perception of "fair" varies in different periods and among cultures), and which maintains the stability of social relations. At the interpersonal level, reciprocity promotes mutual trust and positive feelings. In many traditional societies, reciprocity is part of human reproduction and relations of kinship. We maintain that the logic of reciprocity functions between members of society as well as between the ruling elites and the common people. The latter relationship is the focus of this book. We also consider, however, reciprocity between the more equal members of society, as it helps in understanding the relations between ruling elites and the people. Furthermore, we address the tension between "genuine" reciprocity and its abuse. The notion of reciprocal social relations is innate for people and its roots can be traced back to the prehistory of the human race.

EVOLUTIONARY ROOTS OF RECIPROCITY

Various interpretations of the violent nature of human prehistory have been suggested (see e.g. Pinker 2011; Hart and Sussman 2011). With reference to finds of the crushed skeletons of Australopithecine hominids, which lived millions of years ago, and Neanderthals, the parallel species of modern man dating back 30,000–250,000 years, researchers previously concluded that these species were highly violent both among themselves and to other species and practiced extensive cannibalism. This, however, has subsequently proven to be partly mistaken. Researchers observed that crushed and dismembered bones are explained more likely as the remains of hunting by other carnivorous beasts than the results of inter-human violence. Humans and hominids were without doubt violent to each other, but there is no consensus about the extent of that violence. The oldest indisputable evidence of large-scale warfare between human groups is from the period of modern humans, approximately 10,000 years ago (Fry 2006, pp. 91, 100–135, 239; Hart and Sussman 2011, pp. 28–30).

Archeologists have also found indications that the early predecessors of modern man already took care of their old and injured. Around 2000, a toothless skull of *Homo erectus*, an early hominid, dating back 1.77 million years was discovered in Georgia. The researchers claimed that this old man, who had died at age of ca. 40, had lost almost all his teeth years before his death. The lack of teeth meant high age, disease or both, and the need for assistance in order to survive. Without teeth, he could not have eaten meat or fibrous plants, which were the main source of nutrition for people in his area and would probably been offered the softer parts of game animals and crushed plants. The community appears to have fed its aged member. He may have been kept alive also because of the knowledge that he possessed. This finding appears to be the oldest known example of assisting the old and the infirm. Other researchers, however, have criticized this suggestion, since the skull cannot be unequivocally considered to be evidence of compassion (Lordkipanidze et al. 2005). Previously, only the fossils of younger Neanderthal humans were known with similar signs of nursing and care. It is also known that Neanderthals most likely buried their dead with ritual ceremonies (Valste 2012, pp. 225–240).

The prehistory of modern man (*Homo sapiens*), on the other hand, includes numerous archeological examples of demanding care and nursing. The oldest and possibly most extreme case is that of a 20–30-year-old male who lived around 4000 years ago in the present area of North Vietnam and who survived in a seriously disabled condition (possibly with quadriplegia) for at least ten years before his death. He had needed assistance and care from others in almost all things. Researchers suggest that his carers felt compassion, respect and attachment, for otherwise there would be no explanation for the care of an individual with such serious disabilities (Tilley and Oxenham 2011).

Empathy, the ability to place oneself in the position of others and to understand their emotional states, has been observed not only in humans but also in other animals. Among others, mice, dogs and elephants behave with empathy and assistance towards members of their own and other species. Chimpanzees and other primates also behave with empathy and in a helping manner towards both members of their own species and other species. Primatologist Frans de Waal (2008, pp. 279–300) believes that the ability for empathy is an evolutionary adaptation in humans and some social mammals that permits so-called direct altruism. Direct altruism is an immediate response to the pain, needs or anxiety felt by others. The ability for empathy may lead to an emotional "compulsion" to care for the well-being of others (see also Ricard 2013, especially pp. 48–66, 171–198).

The ability for empathy does not necessarily lead helping others, for the recognition of another person's emotional state can also be used maliciously. Empathy permits the feeling of benign sympathy for another person. Sympathy differs from empathy in that only it will lead to explicitly helping others. Other animals display empathy and direct altruism, but the overwhelming social abilities of humans in the animal kingdom make empathy and the sympathy that it facilitates particularly important for people. In fact, we cannot manage without our fellow humans, as seen in concrete terms in the long childhood of humans in which they are dependent on care. In the animal kingdom, human children need an exceptionally long period of close care, which means that mothers have never been able to both care for their children and acquire nutrition on their own. They have always needed others alongside them, and therefore humans are described as cooperative breeders. In earlier human societies, the mother was usually helped by the child's older siblings, her own siblings, her mother, the father of the child and other relatives (Hamilton 1964; Hrdy 1999, pp. 79, 101–109, 121, 141–143; Sear and Mace 2008). Sympathy and assistance for one's own relatives can easily be understood and argued for in the light of evolution (*kin selection theory*, see Hamilton 1964), but why do people also help non-relatives or even complete strangers?

Citing the concept of reciprocal altruism, Robert Trivers (1971) explains why people who are not closely related tend to help each other unselfishly. An act is defined as altruistic if "the benefit of the altruistic act to the recipient is greater than the cost of the act to the performer." Reciprocal altruism is based on the expectation that the return benefit will come directly—or indirectly through a third person. The grounds for an indirect return benefit are the reputation of the performer of the original altruistic act as a reliable person (Maestripieri 2012, pp. 120–121; Wilson 1995, p. 43). Trivers seeks to explain with reciprocal altruism the human ability for cooperation and benefits of collaboration. His definition, however, has been applied later in economics as an example of the basically selfish person, who helps others only in order to benefit from it later. Trivers's concept of "reciprocal altruism" has also been criticized for its use of the word "altruism," because the reciprocity that he implies could more precisely be called reciprocal cooperation, in which it can be necessary to wait for even a long while for a favor or service to be returned, but nonetheless includes its possibility (West et al. 2011, p. 242).

The benefits of reciprocity to an individual have been demonstrated by subjecting people to recurrent test situations (tournaments) based on game theories. The best strategy turned out to be the simplest one: "tit for tat," i.e. cooperating on the first move, paying the other person in his own coin, good for good, evil for evil, and never being the first to defect. The strategy is also forgiving. As soon as the other person stops defecting, the response will again be positive instead of retaliation. "Tit for tat" is a cooperative strategy based on reciprocity (Axelrod and Hamilton 1981). Reciprocity between others than relatives looking after their offspring calls for recurrent interaction and the ability to recognize other individuals and to note their behavior. This ability is exceptionally strong among humans (Ridley 1997, pp. 69–70; Trivers 1971).

Many researchers who have considered this topic have concluded that the usefulness of cooperation for the individual is the key to understanding human sociality and assistance (see e.g. Boix 2015; Hart and Sussman 2011; Ridley 1997). In early hunter-gatherer communities, cooperation with other people than relatives was vital, among other reasons, because people had to protect themselves against carnivorous beasts and later began to hunt large game animals themselves. The life expectancy of someone forced out of their community was therefore short. In addition to empathy and attachment, people thus take care of each other because everyone benefits from cooperation.

The above-mentioned earliest human communities were most likely small and egalitarian. It was only in the later stages of human history that hierarchical systems of various kinds and finally societies began to evolve (Fry 2006, pp. 91, 100–113, 135, 239), which also meant that reciprocity was realized in new hierarchical relations. Citing Adam Smith, biologist Matt Ridley suggests that underlying the birth of societies was the innate human tendency for reciprocity and bartering (Ridley 1997, p. 46; see also Smith [1759] 1982, pp. 85–91). Ridley (1997, p. 6) notes aptly that "[s]ociety was not invented by reasoning men. It evolved as part of our nature."

The evolutionary basis of reciprocal altruism helps us understand why violations of reciprocity arouse such strong reactions in people. The Finnish sociologist Edward Westermarck (1862–1939) made a distinction between two kinds of moral emotions: disapproval, or indignation, and approval. They belong to a wider group of emotions, which he called retributive emotions. People respond to the acts of other persons with retributive (rewarding or retaliating) emotional reactions. These are shared by all cultures, but the moral ideas and the views of law and justice resulting from common retributive moral reactions vary extremely widely between different cultures. The notion of duty ("ought") includes the idea that the act which should be performed will, nevertheless, possibly not be performed. This will provoke moral indignation. "Duty is a 'stern lawgiver' who threatens with punishment but promises no reward." A deed is regarded as meritorious only when it stands above average or typical behavior (Westermarck [1906–1908] 1971, pp. 21–22, 131–157, quote pp. 136–137; on Westermarck's theory of moral emotions, see also Pipatti 2017a, b).

Notions of justice and injustice also pertain to retributive moral emotions. Partiality invokes a feeling of injustice. Acting in conformity with justice leads to no praise, but an unjust deed arouses indignation. When observing laws, the chief executive officer of a major corporation acts justly, invoking no praise and without anyone paying much attention to it. Many people, however, disapprove, when the same CEO retires in good health at the age of 60, having for years expressed vociferous demands to raise the lowest retirement age from 63 to 65, including for those who have been debilitated by physically hard work. This kind of double standard can only cause indignation.

Conforming to justice or fairness does not become commendable until most others would not have done so. An example is a strictly impartial choice by a person in authority in an organization between two job applicants, one of whom is the decision-maker's acquaintance or associated with his interests in other ways, but, being less qualified, is not selected. In that situation, most people would have chosen the applicant closer to them or in accordance with their own interests. Moral gratitude and disapproval proceed from an assessment that rates average conformity with fairness.

People have a common measure of fairness that has emerged from social interaction. Behavior failing to correspond to the average moral standard will provoke indignation. People are inclined to punish each other for morally "undersized" acts, even though this can inflict harm on them as well as economic loss. This refutes the idea of people mainly pursuing their economic interests in their responses to acts by other persons.

There have been many different versions of the above-mentioned games and the procedures mainly chosen by people in them do not support the notion of man being primarily *Homo economicus*, i.e. concerned rationally only about his own interests. This model of action is typical of very few people, at the most. Instead, the predominant model of behavior that emerges is *Homo reciprocans*, reciprocating man (Bowles and Gintis 2000, pp. 37–45).

Heikki Sarmaja (2004, 2006) has discussed why people do not demand 100% performance from each other but will accept the average. Everyone has commitments to several communities starting with family and work, along with personal interests that will always conflict to some degree with the interests of others. It would be unrealistic to expect others to perform 100% in all things, and it would place them under impossible requirements. To demand "full throttle" would lead either to exploitation or coercion by a totalitarian society. Presenting this requirement aims at manipulating others or indicates self-delusion if expressed in a sincere manner. People thus accept average effort, praising what exceeds it and denouncing moral performance that fails to meet standards. In everyday life, people permit one another to display a certain degree of selfishness, but in extreme situations, such as the aftermath of a catastrophe, they will demand unselfish assistance from themselves and others alike. Mutual human benevolence decreases in proportion to distance between people.

Selfishness can be divided into ruthless selfishness arousing moral reproach in us, as it fails to meet the standard of fairness, and acceptable selfishness, which we expect from others. We feel that people have an obligation to look after themselves and to take care of their own affairs.

It is nonetheless in the common interest of everyone for society to be equally fair to everyone. The "usefulness" of reciprocity for the individual in both normal and extreme situations has made it possible to become selected, through evolution as part of human behavior. People tend to demand and expect reciprocity in social interaction. The expectations and obligations of reciprocity apply not only to relations between two or more individuals, but also to the relationship between those in power and ordinary people.

We should note that the evolutionary psychological approach described above explains *why* people have the tendency for cooperation and assistance. It does not contend that people will act in that manner in every possible situation.[3] Neither does it explain, as such, why cultures and societies differ from each other so immensely, or why human interaction can vary from reciprocity to physical annihilation. Human abilities based on evolution namely formed at a time when human societies were small and relatively egalitarian (Fry 2006, pp. 219–220). The present work, however, focuses on the common features of the preconditions and forms of reciprocity and inter-human cooperation in different periods and cultures, and therefore the evolutionary psychological notion of universal characteristics of human nature is a good starting point.

Anthropologists, sociologists and historians alike have analyzed older human communities and present society with reference to reciprocity or closely related concepts. Their approaches to reciprocity underline the different dimensions of this phenomenon: the "good" that comes from following it; the "bad" resulting from its absence or being insufficient realized; and finally, how the human predilection for reciprocity has been exploited throughout history.

MUTUAL OBLIGATIONS AND GIFT EXCHANGE

According to Barrington Moore (1978, p. 20), "[t]here are certain mutual obligations that generally link rulers and ruled, those in authority and those subject to authority. They are obligations in the senses (1) that each of the parties is subject to a moral obligation to carry out certain tasks as its part of the implicit social contract and (2) that failure of either party to perform the obligation constitutes grounds for the other to refuse the execution of its task."

The obligations of those in power can be broken down into three major tasks: protection from foreign enemies, the maintenance of peace and order, and the obligation to contribute to the material security and prosperity of the subjects. In return, the subjects are expected to obey orders serving these tasks. Traditionally, the main obligations of the people have been to provide soldiers and to pay their taxes and rents. These mutual obligations are usually not defined by any written constitution as such, and those in power and their subjects continuously test them in practice to see how much they can benefit, and to check where permitted behavior becomes a breach of the social contract, or insubordination. The parties are not equal, but the subjects, nonetheless, have recognized moral demands and requirements with regard to those in power. The violation of reciprocity or mutual obligations by elites can fatally undermine the legitimacy of their position and lead to their overthrow from power.[4] The upheaval that toppled President Viktor Yanukovych in Ukraine in 2014 is the latest example of the fate of countless rulers and elites who have violated their obligations vis-à-vis their subjects.

The British social historian E. P. Thompson, in turn, suggested the concept of the "moral economy of the crowd," which was almost synonymous with Moore's recognized moral obligations of subjects. According to Thompson, raised prices, abuses of trade (price gouging) and outright hunger led to riots in eighteenth-century England in which the masses felt they were defending fairness as recognized by society. The notion of "moral economy" implies that it is immoral to exploit human subsistence. By occasionally agreeing to the aims of the rioters, those in power reinforced the legitimacy of this model of action (Thompson 1993, pp. 185–258).

Social scientists have regarded the so-called gift form of exchange as a basis of reciprocity.[5] The French social anthropologist Marcel Mauss contended that the gift form of exchange rested on three foundations: the obligation to give, the obligation to receive and the obligation to repay. Giving a gift is a voluntary act in theory, but not in practice. The failure to make a return gift is tantamount to an offence and often leads to a conflict, at worst to war between two communities (Mauss 1954). It is not difficult to see that gift-giving and gift-receiving encompass retributive moral emotions, as discussed above. Mauss's famous essay on the gift (1925) is often considered to concern only archaic societies, but, as a matter of fact, he was interested, not merely in archaic gifts, but also in the fact that they are a primitive form of social contract. His essay deals with the origins and evolution of the modern contract (Parry 1986, pp. 453–471).

Mauss's theory was based on studies by Western anthropologists above all on indigenous communities of the Pacific islands and the north-west coast of North America. Commodities exchangeable as gifts were transferred to each other by communities (via their chiefs) or families and by individuals as in a market economy. Gift exchange in the Trobriand Islands, however, later proved to be an activity more between individuals than chiefs alone, as assumed in the 1920s. In principle, the same rules apply gift exchange between both communities and individuals. Exchange between individuals was considerably more significant than Mauss believed. The human reproduction of individuals and families (marriages, descendants and other relations of kinship) is often part of gift exchange.

Unlike in the market, the pursuit of economic advantages plays no part in exchange of this kind. The exchange of gift between communities is carried out through rituals and celebrations led by chiefs. Communities maintain mutual dependence, i.e. peace and solidarity, with the gift institution, and sometimes chiefs and communities use it for competing among themselves for power and status. Mauss pointed to the religious basis of the gift institution. It was necessary to sacrifice, i.e. to give gifts, to the gods and ancestors, so that they reciprocate by providing good crops and not cause accidents. The gift objects had a spirit that even after giving would partly belong to the giver and would lead to dire consequences for the receiver if he neglected the obligation of making a return gift. Mauss claimed that there was also the exchange of commodities based on economic motives between individuals in societies in which the gift institution predominated.[6]

Present-day anthropological research maintains that early societies did not have a gift economy with anything like the predominant role originally claimed by Mauss. On the contrary, the gift institution functioned alongside commercial exchange and, depending on the time and the situation, the same commodity or service could be a gift or a commercial commodity (or appear as neither one). Nicholas Thomas points out that people have always given things and objects different meanings depending on prevailing conditions. The gift institution itself is more complex than Mauss assumed. There are also gifts that do not generate a debt, the necessity of a gift in return. In the Fiji Islands there was debt in, among other situations, marital and family relations that was not generated by a gift but involved the permanent obligation of responding with services and company. In fact, in many places very little is known about the pre-colonial gift economy of the Pacific islands. Colonialism reinforced many of the traditional features of societies (Thomas 1991, *passim*, especially pp. 59–75, 90–92, 189–204).[7]

Writing of the gift in sixteenth-century France, Natalie Zemon Davis refers to three forms of exchange that took place via the gift, sales or coercion and were parallel rather than being consecutive or replacing each other (Davis 2000, especially pp. 3–22, 124–132). Social anthropologist Marshall Sahlins distinguishes three forms of reciprocity. In generalized reciprocity, altruistic gifts and services are passed on without defining a return gift or service, which may or may not be provided, without disturbing the relationship, as in the case of a parent and child. Balanced reciprocity means the exchange of gifts, services and commodities of approximately the same value without much delay between giving something and reciprocating in return. Mauss focused on this reciprocity because of his interest in the evolution of contractual obligations. In negative reciprocity, the receiving party deliberately fails to reciprocate (Sahlins 2004, pp. 185–230, 277–314, especially pp. 193–195).

According to Annette B. Weiner,[8] anthropological focus on the gift institution and reciprocity has overshadowed the even more important fact that people, kin groups and communities in fact aim via reciprocity and giving to keep what she calls inalienable possessions. Inalienable possessions and the symbolic meanings assigned to them by their owners create and maintain social distinctions and power. Weiner regards reciprocity as a struggle to keep one's own inalienable possessions and to gain such possessions from the opposite party. Inalienable possessions, however, ultimately belong to their original owners and should be returned. To the detriment of the original owners, this does not always happen, which is due to changes not only in relations of power but also in symbolic meanings and the destruction of possession. Inequality is masked by formally equal reciprocity (Weiner 1992).

While accepting Weiner's view, Maurice Godelier redefines her paradox of *Keeping-while-Giving* as *Keeping-for-Giving-and-Giving-for-Keeping*. He maintains that society is not based solely on exchange and agreements (i.e. reciprocity) but also on what people try keep outside them and which maintains inequality. Godelier notes several instances where Mauss referred to the existence of inalienable possessions, while maintaining that Mauss did not pay sufficient attention to them. According to Godelier, the items of gift exchange—objects or commodities and people as part of the order of family and kin relations—are at the same time both inalienable and alienable. In other words, the right of use is transferred but the obligations of the recipient, the rights of the party giving the gift, remain. In market-based exchange, on the other hand, the ownership of commodities is transferred to the buyer. All societies have imaginary sacred objects (e.g. the Jewish Ark of the Covenant or the constitution of present-day France), which are not relinquished or donated. They are the basis and justification of society. Both sacred objects and the items of gift exchange are ultimately the creations of human social relations, although people imagine them have an essence separate from and above them and their community. In principle, any object can be a sacred object or an item of gift or market exchange.

According to Godelier, gift exchange has lost its role of constructing and renewing fundamental social relations in the developed societies of the modern era. Charity is also a characteristic of capitalist societies, but the primary role of gift exchange is nonetheless to maintain interpersonal relations (Godelier 2008, pp. 49–53, 291–295 and *passim*). "Altruistic" gift exchange in modern societies[9] and human reproduction, i.e. the various forms of marriage and family relations in all periods, are not the main concern of this book, which focuses on relations between different groups and classes in society and the manifestations reciprocity and inequality in them.

Florence Weber underscores that Mauss had stated his essay presents questions to be considered by historians and ethnographers rather than complete solutions or a final model (Weber 2012, pp. 1–2; Mauss 1954, p. 76). At least from the perspective of historical research, this may be the best way to apply Mauss's and Polanyi's classic works.

According to Karl Polanyi, an economist active in 1940s and 1950s, there are three forms of exchange of commodities and services, or social integration: reciprocity between basically equal partners, redistribution based on inequality and on the presence of an allocative center (political authority) in society, and the market pattern (a market economy controlled and regulated by market prices). He maintains that his three forms of exchange were not three distinct forms of society but were partly present alongside each other. Polanyi opposed the commonly held notion that the exchange of commodities and services took place via the market at all times. Reciprocity was based on gifts exchanged among equal partners (family or kin communities) in approximately the same way as suggested by Mauss. Gifts were not given for purposes of economic gain or earning. An individual who behaved selfishly could be excluded from the community.

Polanyi claimed that redistribution was related to the presence of hierarchy and an allocative center, i.e. the inequality of a ruler and elites on the hand and subjects on the other. He noted, however, that even this kind of exchange was not based on economic interests. Rulers or the state transferred (concentrated) to their own use part of the resources produced by society, while redistributing a given proportion of them to their subjects in the form of economic assistance or services providing security. While exchange of this kind implemented reciprocity, it was not based on equality. Polanyi regarded ancient China, India and Egypt, the Greek states of antiquity, the Roman Empire and feudalism as redistributive societies of this kind. On the other hand, chieftains redistributed resources also in archaic societies.

Polanyi admitted that there was also the market-based exchange of commodities in the above European societies but individual households (manors, village settlements and families [peasant households]) mostly aimed at self-sufficiency, which was only complemented by production for sale and profit. Finally, a market economy prevailed in capitalist societies steered only by market prices, i.e. the economy regulated itself as prices were defined by supply and demand. In practice, a market economy without any outside regulation is an ideal situation that has hardly ever existed. Polanyi not only held this view but also actively spoke for the regulation of the market economy (Polanyi 2001 [1944], pp. 45–70 and *passim*; 1957, pp. 12–26, 64–94, 243–270). The weakest link of this tripartite division, however, was not the market but society in which redistribution had a leading role. This concept has been a slightly formalistic blanket term for highly different societies and the diversity of the exchange of commodities and services has been reduced to a simple model.[10]

In fact, nothing prevents us from looking upon redistribution as reciprocity between unequal parties, and this is what many historians and sociologists have done, e.g. Barrington Moore mentioned above. Reciprocity is a system of rights and obligations which is generally considered just. Reciprocity between unequal parties also involves an element of deception. Those in power often attempt to "sell" substantially unequal redistribution to their subjects as "genuine" reciprocity.

The present-day welfare state redistributes resources just like the authorities and rulers of the past. Those in power and their subjects have expectations concerning one another, stipulating that taxes must be paid, but the state must use them to produce services that are of benefit to citizens.

THE STRUCTURE OF THIS BOOK

There have been mutual expectations and obligations between those in power and the people in all periods in human communities if they have had any form of stratification and hierarchy. The indigenous communities of Peru and Bolivia before the Spanish conquest and India, Japan, Sweden and Finland in Early Modern Times are examples of societies where reciprocity functioned in one way or another. Post-conquest Peru and Bolivia, on the other hand, are examples of societies where the majority or a large part of the population, in this case the indigenous population was thoroughly oppressed. Nonetheless, indigenous communities in these countries have based their identity on reciprocity until the present day and have expected those in power to follow it with regard to them. The long-term subjugation of the majority has produced an internally weak and backward society. When the people feel that the elites have violated the principles of reciprocity and justice too blatantly, the result, especially in Modern Times, has occasionally been a rebellion, revolution or change of power in a subtler manner.

The last chapter of the historical section of the book describes the expectations of soldiers in the ranks of the conscript armies of twentieth-century Finland and France regarding their officers and their way of protesting if unofficial rules regarded as just and fair were broken.

We address the positive and negative dimensions of reciprocity at present with reference to two different models of the welfare state, the Nordic and the liberal model. Serving as the example of the Nordic model is Finland, which can still be regarded in global perspective as an egalitarian society with well-being for its members. As discussed in the chapter on the Nordic model presenting Finland, a closer look reveals various fissures eroding equality and well-being. The United States is an example of a liberal welfare state.

With regard to their relations of power and their forms of exchange for commodities and services, pre-capitalist societies were less similar to each other than Mauss originally suggested, but this does not by any means mean that his and Polanyi's approach to archaic societies would not still be relevant. When Columbus landed in the Americas in 1492, the Inca state with a population of over ten million, operating on the principle of reciprocity and with no use of money, existed on the Pacific coast of South America and in the Andes. While the Inca state can be considered as a prime example of the gift institution and redistribution sensu Mauss and Polanyi, Moore's and Thompson's perspective on the mutual expectations of those in power and the people (moral economy) applies equally well to it.

NOTES

1. *The Independent* (Ben Chu, "2016: The year that the volcano of ine-quality exploded"), http://www.independent.co.uk/news/business/news/brexit-donald-trump-2016-the-year-inequality-volcano-erupted-a7477941.html. Accessed December 31, 2016.
2. *Taloussanomat* (Jan Hurri, "Finanssikriisin yllättävä riski: tuloerojen kasvu"), http://www.taloussanomat.fi/jan-hurri/2013/9/29. Accessed September 29, 2013.
3. The New Zealand Maoris have the saying: "A relative in winter (at planting time), A son in autumn (at harvest time)." The Sirionó people of the Bolivian rain forests say: "The bigger the catch the more sullen the hunter' (because he will have to share it with others)." Similar proverbs complaining about the excess obligations of human relations can no doubt be found among many other peoples. During a famine on the island of Tikopia in the Pacific in 1953, generosity first increased, but as the crisis grew worse solidarity collapsed within the community and survived only within families. Theft and robber were common. Sahlins (2004, pp. 125—129, 202—204, 214, quote pp. 126, 204).
4. Moore (1978, pp. 3–48, 506–510). On the legitimacy of power (authority) and social order, see Weber (1972, pp. 16–20, 122–124).
5. Two interdisciplinary collections of essays on gifts and reciprocity are *The Gift* (1996) and *The Logic of the Gift* (1997).
6. Mauss (1954, pp. 1–45, introductory chapter and Chapters 1–2). Mauss also discussed extensively the *potlatch* feasts of the North-West Pacific Coast of North America, where the chief or other host not only distributed gifts but also destroyed his wealth. If an invited guest was incapable of a similar sacrifice, he would lose face and have less power in relation to his host. The *potlatch* was thus only a gift institution but also a non-violent form of social competition and subjugation. Giving gifts, however, also served as a kind of insurance for times of misfortune, when

a return gift would save its recipient from distress. Mauss maintained that the *potlatch* had originally existed in various cultures and he also assumed that the giver was still present in the gift. In addition, the gift has a spirit leading towards the original owner. Marshall Sahlins pointed out that Mauss's notion of the *spirit* of a gift object was based on a partial misinterpretation of Maori thinking. The correct interpretation would have been the *fecundity* or *yield* of the gift, which creates the obligation to return it. Sahlins (2004, pp. 149–183, originally published in 1972). Jonathan Parry, in turn, feels that Sahlins exaggerates the spirit of the gift and the connection created by its giver in Mauss's notion of the gift. Parry notes that the fecundity of the Maori gift means the increase of its value on the recipient's side, this being precisely what binds the parties of the Maori gift to each other, since the one that does not reciprocate ceases to be an acceptable partner. Parry (1986, pp. 453–471). According to Maurice Godelier, as long as social relations are organized on the basis of gift exchange, people will imagine that the objects of exchange have a spirit, although in reality this involves a total renewal of social relations via gift exchange. Godelier (2008, pp. 63–147 and *passim*).

7. In an anthropological study originally published in 1982, C. A. Gregory (second edition 2015, with a new long preface, pp. xix–lxiii) considers the exchange of gifts and commodities from the perspective of production and consumption as part of the reproduction of production and people. Things and land are exchanged as commodities in class-based societies, and also labor in capitalism. In clan-based societies, these three factors are exchanged in the gift form. This also applies to human reproduction, i.e. the forms of marriage and family relations. In Gregory's analysis, reciprocity was by no means a central term. He noted that in Papua—New Guinea, which he had studied, gift exchange still flourished alongside the colonial exchange of commodities.

8. According to Weiner, women have an important role in maintaining inalienable possessions and their symbolic meanings, which is associated with their activities in giving birth, as spouses and as siblings.

9. Carrier (1995) describes gift exchange in the modern era, which grew stronger as capitalism thrived, in other words the multifaced relationships of the personal social sphere with the impersonal economic sphere. On gift exchange in the modern era, see also Cheal (1988, *passim*) ("the gift economy is an autonomous moral economy consisting of redundant transactions"—p. 136); Godbout and Caillé (1998, especially pp. 26–97).

10. Michael Mann (2012, pp. 24, 60–62) criticizes Polanyi for focusing on exchange and ignoring production.

REFERENCES

Axelrod, Robert, and William D. Hamilton. 1981. The Evolution of Cooperation. *Science* 211 (4489): 1390–1396.

Boix, Carles. 2015. *Political Order and Inequality: Their Foundations and Their Consequences for Human Welfare.* New York: Cambridge University Press.

Bowles, Samuel, and Herbert Gintis. 2000. Reciprocity, Self-Interest, and the Welfare State. *Nordic Journal of Political Economy* 26: 33–53.

Carrier, James G. 1995. *Gifts and Commodities: Exchange and Western Capitalism Since 1700.* London and New York: Routledge.

Cheal, David J. 1988. *The Gift Economy.* London and New York: Routledge.

Davis, Natalie Zemon. 2000. *The Gift in Sixteenth-Century France.* Madison: The University of Wisconsin Press.

De Waal, Frans B.M. 2008. Putting the Altruism Back into Altruism: The Evolution of Empathy. *Annual Review of Psychology* 59: 279–300.

Fry, Douglas P. 2006. *The Human Potential for Peace: An Anthropological Challenge to Assumptions About War and Violence.* New York: Oxford University Press.

Godbout, Jacques T., and Alain Caillé. 1998. *The World of the Gift,* trans. Donald Winkler. Montreal and Kingston: McGill-Queen's University Press.

Godelier, Maurice. 2008. *L'énigme du don.* Paris: Flammarion.

Gregory, C.A. 2015. *Gifts and Commodities.* Chicago: Hau Books.

Hamilton, W.D. 1964. The Genetical Evolution of Social Behavior I and II. *Journal of Theoretical Biology* 7 (1): 1–52.

Hart, Donna, and Robert W. Sussman. 2011. The Influence of Predation on Primate and Early Human Evolution: Impetus for Cooperation. In *Origins of Altruism and Cooperation,* ed. R.W. Sussman and C.R. Cloninger, 19–40. Developments in Primatology: Progress and Prospects 36. New York: Springer Science+Business Media, LLC.

Hrdy, Sarah Blaffer. 1999. *Mother Nature: A History of Mothers, Infants, and Natural Selection.* New York: Pantheon Books.

http://www.independent.co.uk.

Komter, Aafke E. (ed.). 1996. *The Gift: An Interdisciplinary Perspective.* Amsterdam: Amsterdam University Press.

Lordkipanidze, David, Abesalom Vekua, G. Reid Ferring, Philip Rightmire, Jordi Agusti, Gocha Kiladze, Alexander Mouskhelishvili, Medea Nioradze, S. Marcia, Ponce de León, Martha Tappen, and Christoph P.E. Zollikofer. 2005. The Earliest Toothless Hominin Skull. *Nature* 434 (7034): 717–718.

Maestripieri, Dario. 2012. *Games Primates Play: An Undercover Investigation of the Evolution and Economics of Human Relationships.* New York: Basic Books.

Mann, Michael. 2012. *The Sources of Social Power: A History of Power from the Beginning to AD 1760*, Vol. 1. New York: Cambridge University Press.

Mauss, Marcel. 1954. *The Gift: Forms and Functions of Exchange in Archaic Societies*, trans. Ian Cunnison. Glencoe: The Free Press.

Moore, Barrington. 1978. *Injustice: The Social Bases of Obedience and Revolt*. London and Basingstoke: Macmillan.

Parry, Jonathan. 1986. The Gift, the Indian Gift and the 'Indian Gift'. *Man* 21 (3): 453–473.

Pinker, Steven. 2011. *The Better Angels of Our Nature: Why Violence Has Declined*. New York: Viking.

Pipatti, Otto. 2017a. The Evolution of Westermarck's Theory of Moral Emotions. In *Evolution, Human Behavior and Morality: The Legacy of Westermarck*, ed. Olli Lagerspetz, Jan Antfolk, Ylva Gustafsson, and Camilla Kronqvist, 115–128. London and New York: Routledge.

Pipatti, Otto. 2017b. *Morality Made Visible: Edward Westermarck's Moral and Social Theory*. Helsinki: Hansaprint.

Polanyi, Karl. 1957. "Marketless Trading in Hammurabi's Time" and "Aristotle Discovers the Economy" and "The Economy as Instituted Process." In *Trade and Market in the Early Empires: Economies in History and Theory*, ed. Karl Polanyi, Conrad M. Arensberg, and Harry W. Pearson, 12–26, 64–94, 243–270. Glencoe: The Free Press.

Polanyi, Karl. 2001. *The Great Transformation: The Political and Economic Origins of Our Time*. Boston: Beacon Press.

Ricard, Matthieu. 2013. *Plaidoyer pour l'altruisme: La force de la bienveillance*. Paris: NiL.

Ridley, Matt. 1997. *The Origins of Virtue. Human Instincts and the Evolution of Cooperation*. New York: Penguin Books.

Sahlins, Marshall. 2004. *Stone Age Economics*. London and New York: Routledge.

Sarmaja, Heikki. 2004. Moraalin logiikka ja tunteiden pelit. *Yhteiskuntapolitiikka* 69 (2): 113–134.

Sarmaja, Heikki. 2006. Kärsimys ja syntien sovitus. *Yhteiskuntapolitiikka* 71 (4): 341–360.

Schrift, Alan D. (ed.). 1997. *The Logic of the Gift: Toward an Ethic of Generosity*. New York and London: Routledge.

Sear, Rebecca, and Ruth Mace. 2008. Who Keeps Children Alive? A Review of the Effects of Kin on Child Survival. *Evolution and Human Behavior* 29: 1–18.

Smith, Adam. [1759] 1982. *The Theory of Moral Sentiments*, ed. D.D. Raphael and A.L. Macfie. Indianapolis: Liberty Fund.

http://www.taloussanomat.fi

Thomas, Nicholas. 1991. *Entangled Objects: Exchange, Material Culture, and Colonialism in the Pacific*. Cambridge, MA and London: Harvard University Press.

Thompson, E.P. 1993. *Customs in Common*. London: Penguin.

Tilley, Lorna, and Marc F. Oxenham. 2011. Survival Against the Odds: Modeling the Social Implications of Care Provision to Seriously Disabled Individuals. *International Journal of Paleopathology* 1 (1): 35–42.

Trivers, Robert. L. 1971. The Evolution of Reciprocal Altruism. *The Quarterly Review of Biology* 46 (1): 35–57.

Valste, Juha. 2012. *Ihmislajin synty*. Helsinki: SKS.

Weber, Florence. 2012. Présentation: Vers une ethnographie des prestations sans marché. In *Essai sur le don: Forme et raison de l'échange dans les sociétés archaïques*, 1–59. Paris: Presses Universitaires de France.

Weber, Max. 1972. *Wirtschaft und Gesellschaft: Grundriss der verstehenden Soziologie*. Tübingen: J.C.B. Mohr (Paul Siebeck).

Weiner, Annette B. 1992. *Inalienable Possessions: The Paradox of Keeping-While-Giving*. Berkeley: University of California Press.

West, Stuart A., Claire El Mouden, and Andy Gardner. 2011. Sixteen Common Misconceptions About the Evolution of Cooperation in Humans. *Evolution and Human Behavior* 32 (4): 231–262.

Westermarck, Edward. [1906–1908] 1971. *The Origin and Development of the Moral Ideas*, Vols. I–II. Freeport: Books for Libraries Press.

Wilson, James Q. 1995. *The Moral Sense*. New York: The Free Press.

CHAPTER 2

Inca and Maya Reciprocity

At the beginning of the sixteenth century, two-thirds of the inhabitants of the Inca realm of the Andes lived at altitudes of over 3000 meters (D'Altroy 2003, p. 35). The economy and culture of the period had adapted amazingly well to these severe conditions.

The Inca realm (also referred to as the Inca state or empire) expanded in the fifteenth and early sixteenth centuries to cover an area from present-day Ecuador via Peru and Bolivia to central Chile and North-West Argentina. The Incas proper were only the less than 40,000 residents of the capital, Cuzco, of real or imaginary royal ancestry, in addition to whom there were so-called Incas by privilege who had been accepted into the elite. The rest of the population of the realm were the subjects of the Incas. The ruler was known as *Sapa Inca* (Unique Inca) (D'Altroy 2003, pp. 62–108; Moseley 2001, p. 9). In theory, all the land belonged to the Inca ruler.[1] This, however, was more a point of ideology than real life. In reality, family and tribal communities had the right of tenure and use to their lands. Also, the members of the aristocracy, chieftains and the religious cults, both local ones and those extending throughout the realm had tenure over their lands.

The Inca realm subjugated individual ethnic groups through warfare or with the threat of it. In the latter case, the carrot was diplomacy and gifts. The people to be ruled and their peasant collectives and chiefs were allowed to keep their land, and the latter their status, if they agreed to recognize Inca supremacy without fighting back. The Inca ruler awarded gifts and favors to chiefs agreeing to his rule in order to bind

© The Author(s) 2019
A. Kujala and M. Danielsbacka, *Reciprocity in Human Societies*,
https://doi.org/10.1007/978-3-319-96056-2_2

them to the realm. Gifts such as precious metals were in turn expected from the chiefs. Inca dominance was mostly indirect and hegemonic.[2] Nonetheless, land in the areas of ethnic groups was set apart for maintaining the Inca realm, its aristocracy and the Incas' religious Sun cult. Rebellious peoples could be resettled in new areas to be controlled, while loyal groups were moved to the opposite end of the realm to places where they were needed not only for producing foodstuffs but also to keep the empire intact or to guard borders (Pärssinen 1992, pp. 163–170).

Based on real or imagined kinship (a shared ancestor), the *ayllu* communities or collectives controlled their respective areas of land, distributing them to the families or households within them to be farmed according to their numbers of members and needs. Herds of llamas and alpacas, local tylopoda, were part of the economy of the people of the Andes. A considerable proportion of the herds, however, belonged to the ruler. The kin communities were, in principle, self-sufficient. A single community would often have farmland and pastures and members attending to them on the lower slopes and higher up in the mountains. The latter farmed land was at elevations from **3500** to **5000** meters and included the *altiplano*, the high plateau of southern Peru and Bolivia. The communal form of agriculture benefited from the existence of different ecological zones. An environment of this kind required brief but intensive labor input to complete the scheduled work. The economic model of vertical complementarity helped reduce the risks of change in the weather. If the crop failed in one altitude zone, the same did not have to occur in another ecological zone. These colonies could occasionally be very far from their own parent communities.

The *ayllu* had a shared cult, a shrine (*huaca*) and a place of burial for the kin group. Ancestors were present in the life of the community as mummies, participating in celebrations and consulted for advice. The duty to offer food and animals to the cult and ancestors could not be neglected. When the Spanish conquered Peru and began to convert the Indians[3] to the Roman Catholic faith, the authorities and priests destroyed the mummies of the Inca kings and lesser figures. In the minds of the Indians, the Catholic saints gradually replaced the bodies of ancestors and from now on the images of the former were carried in processions.

The principle of reciprocity[4] applied to all members of the *ayllu*. When some of its adult males were carrying out their labor service to the state or at war, others would carry out their farm work. The family had to compensate for services received with labor of the same value. It was thus a question of work bank of a kind. Orphans, widows, the elderly and the sick also worked according to their ability, with the *ayllu* taking care of them, i.e. providing social security. The principle of reciprocity was also followed with regard to the ancestors by repaying the debt to them with sacrifices. But there was also asymmetrical, non-equal exchange of labor and services within the *ayllu*.[5]

The *ayllus* were divided into moieties, which were further divided in similar fashion into smaller parts. The various sectors of the community and their members were not equal, and there was instead a hierarchy within the *ayllu*. Marriages were between brides and grooms from different parts of the community, i.e. endogamy prevailed. The world was structured according to the cosmic principle of duality. Mutual unity and balance (harmony, justice) were maintained with rituals. In the visual language of the Andean cultures, there are scenes of two processions joining each other during celebrations. Solidarity was also reinforced with competitions and bloody ritual battles, a custom that has survived to the present day. They were used to prevent contradictions from turning into conflicts dangerous to the community. The merging of the processions and the ritual battles were called *tinku*. Libations following strict etiquette and intoxication with *chicha* (corn beer) were also part of the celebrations. The leaders of the *ayllu* and its parts were expected to host feasts for the members in a generous manner. The Spanish referred to this phenomenon as *cargo* (burden, obligations).[6] It must be remembered that many features of Inca society were much older than the Inca realm, having emerged among the communities that preceded it.

The *curacas* or chiefs (hereditary nobles from among whom the person best suited to the task was chosen) headed the *ayllu* or the larger ethnic community. They had their own land tended by members of the *ayllu* apart from the land belonging to the kinship community. The *curacas* were expected to show their generosity, although complete reciprocity between them and the community functioned only at the level of ideology, but not in practice. An imbalance remained with regard to the community. Nonetheless, the chief would distribute everything that he did not need. Many *curacas* died in poverty, as was also required by the *cargo* system. The higher the position, the more gifts were due to the subordinates (Moseley 2001, pp. 69–70; Ramírez 1996, pp. 12–26). There were no full rights of ownership in the European sense; there were only usufruct rights that could also be shared among several parties. For the natives, the "ownership" of crude or unworked land, in particular, did not make sense, and no one could have control of it. Only human labor applied to the land provided a yield. Power was based on steering and controlling the work of people. The Indians thus made a distinction between the crude and unworked on the one hand and the processed and worked on the other. Only the latter was of value and people could have control of it (Ramírez 1996, pp. 42–61).

The community of family and kin produced more resources than it needed for its own subsistence and reproduction. The surplus was appropriated by the state, which constructed its own model of redistribution imitating the reciprocity of the lower levels and implying that this was the same thing (Métraux 1983, pp. 88–89). In the Inca empire, kinship communities were taxed in the form of labor obligations. There were no other taxes, as observed by the Spanish administrative official Juan Polo de Ondegardo in the sixteenth century: "All that they gave the king were personal services ... [N]o one contributed from his own things, nor from what he harvested – only the work of his own person." (Murra 1980, p. 95). The rotating *mit'a* obligation to provide labor service[7] applied to married males aged 25–50 and indirectly to their households. It was performed by farming the lands of the state, cults or elites, in military service, and in building roads, bridges or public buildings, the high standard of which amazed the Spanish, or by working in mines. Women took part in farm work and would sometimes accompany their men on military expeditions and to the mines. The members of the *ayllu* worked for local and state-wide cults, the ruler (i.e. the state) and their own chiefs. The Inca state stockpiled foodstuffs and clothing in large storehouses. They were needed for the maintenance of soldiers and men engaged in labor service. Reciprocity was also realized in this way. The *mit'a* obligation was assigned to kin communities in quotas, whereby a given number of men would serve in rotating order. The *curaca* would make sure that the local labor obligation was carried out. Those who remained at home carried out the work of those who were away, receiving in due time service of equal value from the latter. The weaving of textiles and clothing from raw materials provided by the state, above all women's work, was an important part of the labor service. Social status and ethnic identity were indicated with the colors and decoration of textiles. Valuable textiles were used by rules as gifts and means of diplomacy.

The Inca rulers regarded the ending of wars and land disputes and the arbitration of disagreements as their merits, and they were among their most important duties. The king would symbolically launch the agricultural work that was due to be carried out, such as the planting of maize. At the celebration held for the occasion, he would display his generosity by sponsoring a feast for the participants. One of the titles of the king was "he who loved (cared for) the weak" (Murra 1980, p. 121). At the same time, high state officials and *curacas* carried out similar ceremonies in other localities. The state fed the people in labor service and the soldiers who served it. This was no longer symbolic but reciprocity in quite real terms.

On the other hand, the state and the nobles in their symbiosis with it could have considered themselves entitled to much greater benefits than their subjects had they calculated matters in ways contrary to official thinking. Like many other Spaniards, the Jesuit chronicler Bernabé Cobo, who was active in Peru in the seventeenth century, sought to reinforce the image of the Incas as tyrants: "To tame the people ... they arranged that their subjects be poor and constantly busy with excessive duties ... and thus lack aspiration to rebel" (Murra 1980, p. 113). The rulers had private farmed holdings set apart from the lands of the state, which passed on after their death to their descendant clan, the royal kinship community. "Private" land holding and inequality were increasing under the last Inca rulers.

The *curacas* and the members of the royal families were exempt from labor service, as also the retainers (*yanacona*) who served on a full-time basis and for their whole lives on the private farmed holdings outside the kinship communities and who did not belong to any *ayllu*.

Precolonial African societies practiced reciprocity following rules highly similar to those of the Inca realm both among individuals and families and between the community and its chief. The sponsoring of feasts by the recipient of the labor services was an important aspect of the ritualized procedure that aimed at bolstering solidarity within the community.[8] The spread of European-style land ownership among the Kikuyu in early twentieth-century Kenya ended former land-use partly based on a moral economy and placed strain on solidarity within the community.[9]

While there was inequality within the Andean community, the management of class contradictions, to use a European term, was easier than handling ethnic issues. The Inca realm was a patchwork of different ethnic groups held together by Inca domination. Therefore, conflicts within the empire were mostly ethnic, either between various groups or involving relations between the ruling ethnic group and subject peoples.

After 1100 CE, the climate of Peru and Bolivia became drier, and higher mountain slopes than previously began to be terraced for cultivation, because sufficient rainfall for farming was more certain there than at lower altitudes. Terracing increased the area of cultivated land and helped to prevent erosion. More favorable climatic conditions after the middle of the fifteenth century again permitted cultivation on the lower slopes of mountains (Moseley 2001, pp. 72–74). The Inca rulers took credit for taking new land under cultivation and for irrigation systems. It is a fact that in many areas of the Andes, the area of cultivated land under the Incas was 25–95% larger than at present, implying that the supply of foodstuffs for the population was also at a higher level than at present. The present populations of Peru and Bolivia are 30 and 10 million respectively, but the much larger Inca realm had a population of only 4–15 million (Klarén 2000, p. 49). Pandemics introduced by the Spanish led to an immense reduction of population, with the terraced fields left untilled and allowed to deteriorate. The European population despised the Indians and their culture and were not interested in the traditional methods of agriculture. Despite its new plants, animals and machinery, European farming led to poorer results than pre-conquest agriculture, resulting in land erosion, among other effects (Moseley 2001, pp. 245–258, 276–278; Kolata 1993, pp. 190–198; Rostworowski 1999, pp. 193–194, 196).

In the late sixteenth and early seventeenth century, El Inca Garcilaso de la Vega, a descendant of Inca kings on his mother's side and the son of a Spanish soldier on his father's side[10] created the image of the Inca realm as a welfare state. John V. Murra regards this as an embellishment of the facts. Garcilaso also implied that human sacrifices were not practiced in the Inca realm. The apologist of Incas had to sweep them under the carpet, because they were unacceptable to Christian Europeans. Murra maintains that it was primarily the *ayllu* that maintained welfare-type services for its members. The state did not assist the ill, elderly or others in distress. Murra suggests that the Inca state opened its large stores of goods to the general population only in times of exceptionally severe crop failure. The prime consideration for the state was to prevent the loss of the labor that it needed. This was the aim of most rulers of the past. The Old Kingdom pharaohs of Egypt also provided emergency assistance from royal granaries when famine was imminent (Wilkinson 2011, pp. 60, 142).

The Incas had large stores of gold and silver, which the Spanish coveted more than anything on earth, but precious metals were not means of exchange. For the Incas, gold was the sweat of the Sun God and silver the tears of the Moon Goddess. Although no money was used, administration functioned well. Records of people and resources were kept with the various knots and colors of bunches of knotted strings, or knot documents (*khipus*). According to Polo de Ondegardo, the Incas "kept such a record of everything delivered that they do not lose count of a single hen or load of firewood ..." (Murra 1980, p. 110). It should be remembered that in post-Columbian exchange, hens, cattle, horses, pigs, sheep, wheat, rice and coffee, among others, as well as diseases such as smallpox, were brought from the Old to the New World, while maize, potato, tomato and cocoa passed in the opposite direction. The main domesticated animals of the Americas before 1492 were llama, alpaca, dog, guinea pig and turkey (Bakewell and Holler 2010, pp. 27–28, 233, 239–241).

Barter was practiced, but there is no definite information about its actual extent. Moreover, it may have served to reinforce the power of chiefs instead of aiming at profits. In any case, the coastal fishing and farming communities were more advanced than the mountain regions in barter and specialized crafts. In the Andes, the exchanges of produce such as maize or fruit for potatoes or the meat or wool of tylopoda were partly based on the internal reciprocity of a community utilizing partly different ecological zones.

Since there are no written sources from the Incas themselves, our image of the Inca realm and Inca society has to be based on the accounts of the Spanish and of partly Hispanicized Christians of Inca origin. These sources suffer from the interruption of information caused by the sudden destruction of the Inca realm and the inability of Europeans or Europeanized people to interpret correctly the principles whereby this society and culture alien to them operated.

In any case, it is obvious that reciprocity, the institution of the gift and the principle of redistribution had a strong presence in the Inca realm. Relations between rulers and subjects show that they were described in reciprocal terms even in situations of redistributing resources for the benefit of the elites involving the lower level of society in the guise of genuine reciprocity. Human reciprocity should not be imagined to be a paradise on earth. Instead, it has usually operated within broader social relations, i.e. subject to hierarchy and inequality. Anthropologist Marshall Sahlins underlines that even the parties of gift exchange are not usually equals (Sahlins 2004, pp. 127, 190). This supports the view that the difference between reciprocity and redistribution is highly imprecise.

"One Must Have Lost All Fear of God to Commit Such Iniquities"[11]

The Spanish crown ordered adult native males of the Inca realm, which it had conquered in the 1530s, to pay a separate tribute, the proceeds of which were divided among crown administration, local elites, parish clergy and the *curacas*. The crown aimed at having the tribute paid mostly in cash. The purpose was thus to make Indian labor benefit the towns, textile workshops, mines and haciendas. It was not, however, capitalistic wage labor but for the most part a system based on coercion and insufficient wages (Klarén 2000, pp. 44–48, 61–64; Stern 1993, pp. 81–89, 140–146 and *passim*).

In the early 1570s, Francisco de Toledo, the Viceroy of Peru, decreed that the Indian communities of Peru and Upper Peru (Bolivia) were required to send part of their male population according to a roster to labor for set periods in mines or public works chosen by the crown, textile workshops or haciendas. This requirement, in other words forced labor, was called *mita* in the Inca fashion. The workers under the *mita* system in the Spanish mines, however, received wages which were insufficient to meet the cost of living, while the Incas provided the full upkeep of labor service workers. Over half of the workers of the Potosí mine, however, were paid wages and did not belong to the *mita* system. Their standard of earnings was improved by the prevailing shortage of labor.[12]

The profitability of the Potosí mines was based on the use of underpaid forced labor. Restrictions on working hours and other matters instituted for the protection of the Indians were circumvented as much as possible. The best way to force the natives to work long hours and consecutive shifts was to lay down quotas for quarrying and similar work with pay docked if these figures were not met (Tandeter 1997, pp. 131–169). Mercury, which was life-threatening for those who handled it, began to be used in process of refining silver. The mercury came from the Huancavelica mine, monopolized by the Spanish crown. The Potosí silver mines were privately owned, but the crown levied the so-called "royal fifth" (*quinto real*) on the silver that was produced. This was a source of income of vital importance for the Spanish Empire. By linking these two mines, Viceroy Toledo said that he had arranged "the most important marriage in the world" (Mann 2011, p. 141). Considering the location of the Potosí mine at an elevation of over four kilometers and the unhealthy and life-threatening nature of mining, a funeral is the church service to which he should have referred.

The new political and economic system instituted by the Spanish crown, the forced removal of population and appropriation of land gradually eroded the indigenous communities. The Indians, however, stubbornly demanded reciprocity from the authorities, their masters and the *curacas*. Steve J. Stern has shown how skillfully Peruvian Indians utilized Spanish administration and laws, largely negating the *mita* system created by Toledo.[13] The purpose of administration and law was not just to give the elites the opportunity to exploit the indigenous population but also to protect the latter. For the elites, the *mita* functioned poorly and unreliably, but nothing saved the natives from having to work outside their communities in the private sector and ending in a situation of economic dependence on the haciendas, workshops and those who sold them overpriced European goods. The focus of political and economic control shifted from the institutions of the state to subjugation of a more private nature (Stern 1993, *passim*).

Despite their suppressed status, the indigenous population was able to adapt to the requirements of a cash and market economy. Adaptation aimed at preserving the reciprocity of the community but also at private gain. Depending on the situation, the Indians either engaged in market trade or priced their goods and services according to the principle of reciprocity. This custom has survived to the present day (Stern 1995, pp. 73–92; Harris 1995, pp. 297–322).

Some of the Spanish already noticed in the sixteenth century that the easiest way to benefit from the Indians was to follow pre-conquest practices. The community preferred to work 15 days for their guardian rather than pay a few potatoes in taxes. The Indians were happy to weave woolen clothes for a master who had the sense to supply them with wool as the Incas had done. In most cases, however, the Indians discovered to their disappointment that the masters cared only for their own interests instead of the principles of reciprocity (Stern 1993, pp. 31, 33, 38, 40–42 and *passim*; Wachtel 2008, pp. 160–161, 177–178).

Túpac Amaru, the leader of the Great Rebellion that broke out in the Andes in the 1780s distributed part of his booty to his followers with a view to continuing the struggle. In this respect, he distinguished himself from Spanish administration and imitated the Inca kings, whose heir he considered himself to be (Campbell 1987, p. 125; Serulnikov 2013, p. 44; Walker 2014, pp. 43–44, 47–48). The creoles of European origin ensured that the suppression of indigenous people continued and deepened as Peru and Bolivia gained independence in the early nineteenth century. By the early twentieth century the indigenous communities had lost most of their land (Klarén 2000, pp. 122–136, 208–209; Klein 2011, pp. 89–107, 147). Towards the end of the nineteenth century, Latin America—with Peru as an example—was less equal in the distribution of income than the countries of East Asia, which presumably led to permanently impaired economic growth in the Spanish-speaking countries of the Americas (Vries 2013, pp. 264–267, 312). In 1877, 77% of the Mexican population were illiterate. The proportion of illiterates among the free population of Portuguese-speaking Brazil was 85% in the late nineteenth century. Around the middle of the century, only one Bolivian out of five spoke Spanish; most of the population spoke Quechua or Aymara and only 7% were literate (Hamnett 2006, p. 173; Burns 1993, pp. 206–207; Klein 2011, pp. 120–121).

Old notions lingered and it was, for example, still true in Bolivia in the early nineteenth century that without the "chicha, food, and coca provided by the *recaudador* (moiety tax collector – AK and MD) and the ayllu chiefs [*principales*], there is no human power that can wrench from them (the indigenous community – AK and MD) a single half-real of contribution" (Platt 1987, p. 290). The representatives of the Bolivian Congress of Indigenous People in 1945 imagined that Major Gualberto Villarroel, head of a ruling military junta, had made an agreement on reciprocity and mutual aid with them when he had shared the cup of brotherhood with an Indian leader in the required manner of ritual drinking feasts. Villarroel's promises to the Indians of doing away with the obligation to provide domestic services at the house of the hacienda owner and of opportunities for education proved, of course, to be false.[14]

It is obvious that the long-term suppression of the indigenous population is one of the reasons why Peru and Bolivia are still relatively poor and underdeveloped countries.

MAYA RECIPROCITY

The Maya of Southern Mexico and Guatemala provide the best example of the survival of reciprocity to the present day. Despite strong pressure from outside, many Maya communities have managed to protect their own culture, although the institutions, customs and religion of the Spanish have naturally added their own elements to it. Maya culture and beliefs include many pre-conquest features mixed with Christianity that are not in accordance with the official teachings of the Catholic Church. Nonetheless, the local church has to accept the fact that the Maya practice their pre-Christian rites and shamanism even in churches.

In the 1950s and 1960s, researchers of Harvard University (Evon Z. Vogt et al.) investigated the life of the Tzotzil Maya community of Zinacantán near the city of San Cristóbal de las Casas in the state of Chiapas in Mexico. The institute of *cargo* (burden or position) thrived fifty years ago, just as it does today, for it defines the boundaries of the community, i.e. membership. The married adult males who refuse to participate in *cargo*, are excluded from the community, leaving them in principle with no other alternative than to blend into the *ladino*, or mestizo, community. Some choose this path voluntarily, knowing that there is no return.

Cargo maintains and reinforces the values specific to the community, preventing and restraining internal conflicts and supporting traditional models of kinship. In the *cargo* system, a member of the community progresses from lower to higher duties. With some exceptions, each position is held for one year. The higher the position in the hierarchy that is achieved by a member of the community, the more he will be expected to offer his property by hosting feasts for holders of other positions, his own assistants and other members of the community. The objective is for the communities' most highly considered members, who have afforded to hold the highest positions, to "retire" from them highly respected but also as having spent their funds and property for the good of other members. The members of the community thus take turns in serving each other. *Cargo* maintains economic and social equality among the members of the community, preventing the rich from rising above others and the envy and discord that would result from it. Those who are regarded as having enriched themselves unfairly at the cost of others can be suspected and accused of witchcraft.

Cargo is used to celebrate the main holidays of the Christian church year, but the pre-Columbian Maya culture and its cyclical concept of time, which includes occasional destruction, are its background factors. For the world to remain in order, the gods take their turn in bearing the burden of time and the holders of *cargo* positions do the same in their own communities. This social institution has non-Christian religious roots.

In Zinacantán, *cargo* mostly concerns only the religious hierarchy, i.e. activities related to performing ecclesiastical and religious offices and rituals. The only exceptions are the duties of the lowest grade, such as serving as policemen or messengers. The largest amounts of money and property apparently need to be spent already at the lower levels of the hierarchy. At the top, the duties and obligations are slightly lighter. Authority to make decisions is naturally at this level.

Few people manage to perform their obligations solely with their own funds. Assistance (loans and volunteer labor) is sought from relatives and godparents. In the Spanish system of co-godparenthood (*compadrazgo*), the role of the godparent involves obligations especially in relations between godparents and the parents of the godchild. The Maya adopted this system from the Spanish. Those who want to advance in the hierarchy of the community will maintain relations with family and kin and acquire many godparents for themselves in order to meet the obligations of *cargo*. The system effectively maintains coherence within the community and the obligations of assistance to neighbors. Even a wealthy man will fall into debt when performing the costliest duties. He will have to pause to be able to pay his debts and become rich in order to hold a position once again. Celebrations, rituals and the mutual sponsorship of feasts within *cargo* are subject to strict rules. It should be noted that reciprocity, i.e. gifts and return gifts, play an important role in the lives of the Tzotzil Maya, not only within the *cargo* institution (reciprocity involving gifts is based on equality while that of *cargo* is based on inequality, being in other words redistribution as defined by Polanyi) (Vogt 1969, pp. 25–26, 120–124, 140–144, 195–217, 224–271, 297–567, 596–605; Coe 2005, pp. 221–223, 239, 244–249). The system resembles Inca reciprocity to such a degree that there must be some shared roots in the distant past. An explanation of why *cargo* acquired its present radically redistributive nature is also to be found in South America.

Thierry Saignes maintains that in the indigenous communities of the Andes the obligation of sponsoring feasts originally applied to chiefs.

Under colonial rule, *cargo* became ritual theft or ritual impoverishment providing its participants with full membership in the community and maintaining mutual solidarity. As the hereditary chiefs lost their former status in the seventeenth century, and even more in the following century (no longer having religious authority), local political and ritual leadership passed on to new temporary holders of positions. Both the municipal administration of communities and the lay religious fraternities (*cofradías*) active within them followed the principles of *cargo*. The merging of the *ayllus*, the regionalized kinship communities, with the religious fraternities and their activities in accordance with *cargo* also promoted the integration of immigrants from "outside" into their new community (Saignes 1999, pp. 84, 104–106).

NOTES

1. According to the official position of the state, the Inca ruler had granted to communities and elites the rights of tenure to their lands. The description of the social structure of the Inca realm in this chapter is based on pioneering research by John V. Murra (1980, *passim*). Other accounts of Inca society include: Métraux (1983, pp. 52–105), Rostworowski (1999, pp. 38–47, 137–219), D'Altroy (2003, pp. 86–310), and Kolata (2013, pp. 49–239).

2. On the concept of hegemony and its various forms (the relationship of coercion and consensus), see Kolata (2013, pp. 1–27). According to Kolata, the power of the Inca ruler was based on reciprocity, the system of marriage among Inca nobles, cosmology, the record-keeping and sound logistics of resources, and of course coercion.

3. Some scholars have regarded the term "Indian" as coined by outsiders (Europeans) and unsuitable in other ways as well, but only artificial and confusing replacements for it have been found. Indians themselves have not been bothered by this generic term. Of course, when referring to a specific ethnic group it is possible and recommendable to use their own name. See Mann (2006, pp. XI, 339–341), Andrien (2001, pp. XI–XII).

4. The Aymara word *ayni* means service associated with the expectation of a mandatory and similar service. In the Quechua language, *mit'a*, in turn, refers to a work shift and the exchange of labor services of the same value Moseley (2001, p. 55). See also D'Altroy (2003, p. 200), Kolata (1993, pp. 26–27), Spalding (1984, pp. 56–60), Sallnow (1993, p. 210), Stanish (1992, pp. 24–26).

5. On the *ayllu* and reciprocity within it see, in addition to Murra, Moseley (2001, pp. 53–66).

6. For more on these, see Moseley (2001, pp. 53–55, 66–67). Regarding *cargo*, see Spalding (1984, pp. 249, 264), Saignes (1999, pp. 84, 104–106), Klein (2011, pp. 42–43).
7. Moseley (pp. 71–72) and Kolata (1993, pp. 209–211) distinguish the *mit'a* from a separate agricultural labor tax. According to Murra (pp. 31, 90), Rostworowski (p. 184) and D'Altroy (pp. 265–266), the *mit'a* also comprised the obligation to provide farm labor. Rostworowski maintains that the requirement of reciprocity concerning the state forced it to expand its area and increase its sources of income (pp. 46, 222).
8. Randles (1974, pp. 1320–1326), Chrétien (1974, pp. 1327–1337), Koponen (1988, pp. 273–275, 278). The pre-colonial chiefs of Bantu-speaking peoples in southern Africa were under the obligation to help members of the own people in distress Iliffe (1987, pp. 70–71) (on assistance to the poor in Africa, *passim*).
9. In some localities, land-holding Kikuyu would deny their landless tenants' former contractual moral right to the land that they farmed, which led to reprisals during the Mau Mau uprising of the 1950s. Under colonial rule, traditional hereditary and inalienable right-holding, based on the original claiming and taking into use of the land by an extended family or clan became land ownership, leaving those without the former traditional rights in a weaker position. In the traditional communities, a woman and her children would be included via marriage in her husband's extended family. Families maintained mutual reciprocity through marriages. Before the coming of the Europeans, a Kikuyu man without land could simple take into use uncultivated land that was sufficiently available. The Kikuyu maintained that a man without land was not an eligible adult male, but a mere boy regardless of his physical age. Without land, he could not pay bridewealth to the family of his intended bride. After European immigrants had seized the best land, the Kikuyus suffered from a shortage of land, which was the ultimate reason for the Mau Mau rebellion Anderson (2005, pp. 9–13, 23–32, 122–142, 147–151 and *passim*), Elkins (2014, pp. 9–18), Berman and Lonsdale (1992, Chapters 11–12).
10. On Garcilaso de la Vega, see Bernand (2006).
11. Jorge Juan and Antonio de Ulloa on the forced sale of mules to Indians in the Viceroyalty of Peru in 1742, Lavallé (2011, p. 52).
12. Klarén (2000, pp. 62, 66–68), Hemming (1993, pp. 355–359, 388–394), Bakewell and Holler (2010, pp. 245–247, 308), Vries (2013, pp. 38–39, 42–43), Arroyo Abad et al. (2012, pp. 149–160, pp. 156, 159) (the high real wages raised by the labor shortage as mentioned here concerned the wage laborers of Potosí, not the *mita* laborers, whose wages were less than the subsistence minimum and it is no wonder then that they stayed on to work at Potosí after the *mita*). The decrease of the indigenous

population from pandemics introduced by the Europeans led to a long-term shortage of labor in Latin America.

13. Indigenous resistance partly led to a shortage of labor and raised the wages of hired labor in the mines of Potosí.

14. Dandler and Torrico (1987, pp. 351–358). Villarroel flirted with reformist-socialist and fascist ideology and liquidated the leaders of various political parties in Bolivia. In July 1946, a mob dragged him out of presidential palace in La Paz and hanged him from the nearest lamp post (Klein 2011, pp. 201–203). There is now a statue at the site where this mendacious friend of the people died.

REFERENCES

Anderson, David. 2005. *Histories of the Hanged: The Dirty War in Kenya and the End of Empire.* New York and London: W.W. Norton.

Andrien, Kenneth J. 2001. *Andean Worlds: Indigenous History, Culture and Consciousness Under Spanish Rule, 1532–1825.* Albuquerque: University of New Mexico Press.

Arroyo Abad, Leticia, Elwyn Davies, and Jan Luiten van Zanden. 2012. Between Conquest and Independence: Real Wages and Demographic Change in Spanish Latin America, 1530–1820. *Explorations in Economic History* 29 (2): 149–166.

Bakewell, Peter, and Jacqueline Holler. 2010. *A History of Latin America to 1825.* Malden and Oxford: Wiley.

Berman, Bruce, and John Lonsdale. 1992. *Unhappy Valley: Conflict in Kenya & Africa: Violence and Ethnicity,* Vol. 2. London: James Currey.

Bernand, Carmen. 2006. *Un Inca platonicien: Garcilaso de la Vega 1539–1616.* Paris: Fayard.

Burns, E. Bradford. 1993. *A History of Brazil.* New York: Columbia University Press.

Campbell, Leon G. 1987. Ideology and Factionalism During the Great Rebellion, 1780–1782. In *Resistance, Rebellion and Consciousness in the Andean Peasant World, 18th to 20th Centuries,* ed. Steve J. Stern, 110–139. Madison: The University of Wisconsin Press.

Chrétien, Jean-Pierre. 1974. Échanges et hiérarchies dans les royaumes des Grands Lacs de l'Est africain. *Annales ESC* 29 (6): 1327–1337.

Coe, Michael D. 2005. *The Maya.* New York: Thames & Hudson.

Dandler, Jorge, and Torrico A. Juan. 1987. From the National Indigenous Congress to the Ayopaya Rebellion: Bolivia, 1945–1947. In *Resistance, Rebellion and Consciousness in the Andean Peasant World, 18th to 20th Centuries,* ed. Steve J. Stern, 334–378. Madison: The University of Wisconsin Press.

D'Altroy, Terence N. 2003. *The Incas*. Malden: Blackwell.
Elkins, Caroline. 2014. *Britain's Gulag: The Brutal End of Empire in Kenya*. London: The Bodley Head.
Hamnett, Brian R. 2006. *A Concise History of Mexico*. Cambridge: Cambridge University Press.
Harris, Olivia. 1995. The Sources and Meanings of Money: Beyond the Market Paradigm in an *Ayllu* of Northern Potosí. In *Ethnicity, Markets, and Migration in the Andes: At the Crossroads of History and Anthropology*, ed. Brooke Larson and Olivia Harris, 297–328. Durham and London: Duke University Press.
Hemming, John. 1993. *The Conquest of the Incas*. London: Macmillan.
Iliffe, John. 1987. *The African Poor: A History*. Cambridge: Cambridge University Press.
Klarén, Peter Flindell. 2000. *Peru: Society and Nationhood in the Andes*. New York and London: Oxford University Press.
Klein, Herbert S. 2011. *A Concise History of Bolivia*. New York: Cambridge University Press.
Kolata, Alan L. 1993. *The Tiwanaku: Portrait of an Andean Civilization*. Cambridge, MA and Oxford: Blackwell.
Kolata, Alan L. 2013. *Ancient Inca*. New York: Cambridge University Press.
Koponen, Juhani. 1988. *People and Production in Late Precolonial Tanzania: History and Structures*. Helsinki: Finnish Historical Society.
Lavallé, Bernard. 2011. *L'Amérique espagnole de Colomb à Bolivar*. Paris: Belin.
Mann, Charles C. 2006. *1491: New Revelations of the Americas before Columbus*. New York: Alfred A. Knopf.
Mann, Charles C. 2011. *1493: Uncovering the New World Columbus Created*. New York: Alfred A. Knopf.
Métraux, Alfred. 1983. *Les Incas*. Paris: Éditions du Seuil.
Moseley, Michael E. 2001. *The Incas and Their Ancestors: The Archaeology of Peru*. London: Thames & Hudson.
Murra, John Victor. 1980. *The Economic Organization of the Inca State*. Research in Economic Anthropology. Supplement 1. Greenwich: JAI Press.
Pärssinen, Martti. 1992. *Tawantinsuyu: The Inca State and Its Political Organization*. Studia Historica, vol. 43. Helsinki: SHS.
Platt, Tristan. 1987. The Andean Experience of Bolivian Liberalism, 1825–1900: Roots of Rebellion in 19th-Century Chayanta (Potosí). In *Resistance, Rebellion and Consciousness in the Andean Peasant World, 18th to 20th Centuries*, ed. Steve J. Stern, 280–323. Madison: The University of Wisconsin Press.
Ramírez, Susan Elizabeth. 1996. *The World Upside Down: Cross-Cultural Contact and Conflict in Sixteenth-Century Peru*. Stanford: Stanford University Press.

Randles, W.G.L. 1974. La réciprocité en Afrique bantu. *Annales ESC* 29 (6): 1320–1326.

Rostworowski de Diez Canseco, María. 1999. *History of the Inca Realm*, trans. Harry B. Iceland. Cambridge: Cambridge University Press.

Sahlins, Marshall. 2004. *Stone Age Economics*. London and New York: Routledge.

Saignes, Thierry. 1999. The Colonial Condition in the Quechua-Aymara Heartland (1570–1780). In *The Cambridge History of the Native Peoples of the Americas. South America*, Vol. III. Part II, ed. Frank Salomon and Stuart B. Schwartz, 59–137. Cambridge: Cambridge University Press.

Sallnow, M.J. 1993. Precious Metals in the Andean Moral Economy. In *Money and the Morality of Exchange*, ed. J. Parry and M. Bloch, 209–231. Cambridge: Cambridge University Press.

Serulnikov, Sergio. 2013. *Revolution in the Andes: The Age of Túpac Amaru*, trans. David Frye. Durham and London: Duke University Press.

Spalding, Karen. 1984. *Huarochirí: An Andean Society Under Inca and Spanish Rule*. Stanford: Stanford University Press.

Stanish, Charles. 1992. *Ancient Andean Political Economy*. Austin: University of Texas Press.

Stern, Steve J. 1993. *Peru's Indian Peoples and the Challenge of Spanish Conquest: Huamanga to 1640*. Madison: The University of Wisconsin Press.

Stern, Steve J. 1995. The Variety and Ambiguity of Native Andean Intervention in European Colonial Markets. In *Ethnicity, Markets, and Migration in the Andes: At the Crossroads of History and Anthropology*, ed. Brooke Larson and Olivia Harris, 72–100. Durham and London: Duke University Press.

Tandeter, Enrique. 1997. Forced and Free Labor in Late Colonial Potosí. In *Mines of Silver and Gold in the Americas*, ed. Peter Bakewell, 131–169. An Expanding World, The European Impact on World History, vol. 19. Aldershot: Variorum/Ashgate.

Vogt, Evon Z. 1969. *Zinacantan: A Maya Community in the Highlands of Chiapas*. Cambridge, MA: The Belknap Press of Harvard University Press.

Vries, Peer. 2013. *Ursprünge des modernen Wirtschaftswachstums: England, China und die Welt in der Frühen Neuzeit*, trans. Felix Kurz. Schriftenreihe der FRIAS School of History Bd. 8. Göttingen: Vandenhoeck & Ruprecht.

Wachtel, Nathan. 2008. *La vision des vaincus: Les Indiens du Pérou devant la Conquête espagnole 1530–1570*. folio histoire, vol. 47. Paris: Gallimard.

Walker, Charles F. 2014. *The Tupac Amaru Rebellion*. Cambridge, MA and London: The Belknap Press of Harvard University Press.

Wilkinson, Toby. 2011. *The Rise and Fall of Ancient Egypt: The History of a Civilisation from 3000 BC to Cleopatra*. London: Bloomsbury.

CHAPTER 3

The Indian Gift and Village Servants

In the ancient Hindu tradition, society was divided into four *varnas*, or social groups or ritual statuses, i.e. the brahmans (priests and scholars were the purest and thus highest group in the hierarchy), rulers and warriors (*kshatriya*), merchants and farmers (*vaishya*) and *shudras*, whose duty it was to serve the former. A hymn of the late *Vedas* dating from the early first millennium BCE describes how the four varnas came about as the parts of the body of a mythical primal being: "The brahman was his mouth, of his arms were made the warrior. His thighs became the *vaishya*, of his feet the *shudra* was born."

Outside or beneath the *varna* system were the untouchables (the touch of whom would defile; the currently used term is *dalit*, meaning "the oppressed"), who would carry out tasks such as the collection of latrine waste and the handling of dead animals and cremation remains, which were regarded as impure or polluting. In many cases, the untouchables were originally forest tribes living in the outskirts of Indo-Aryan communities, who spoke a different language and subsisted on hunting and gathering. According to the Hindu view, the untouchables were the result of an unholy union between the brahmans and the *shudras*.

The actual castes and sub-castes (*jati*; the word "caste" is a loan from Portuguese) also began to emerge at a very early stage. The caste system is based on the Hindu religion, and each caste belongs to one of the above-mentioned *varnas*. The castes were not originally defined as strictly or with as rigid boundaries as they were later, from the nineteenth

© The Author(s) 2019   39
A. Kujala and M. Danielsbacka, *Reciprocity in Human Societies*,
https://doi.org/10.1007/978-3-319-96056-2_3

century onwards, nor did even the highest-ranking groups follow the requirements of purity as strictly as required by religion and the rules of ritual. The system of hundreds of different castes (and even more sub-castes) evolved as new occupations, tribes and immigrant groups were added to it. In principle, there is no personal conversion to Hinduism. Instead, one is born into it, as into one's caste, which cannot be changed. Therefore, people adopted Hinduism according to occupation, tribe (the forest tribes were traditionally outside the caste system) or immigrant group.

People professing other religions are outside the caste system as virtual castes of a kind, and they, too, have had to adapt their ways of life in varying degrees to the requirements of the Hindu caste system.

Membership in a caste is hereditary. The castes and sub-castes are endogamous, i.e. people of the same caste intermarry, though avoiding close relatives and people regarded as such. The castes are loosely based on an occupation (occupational monopoly), but the same caste can include representatives of several occupations and in addition the members of many castes engage in agriculture. Because of the many languages spoken in India and the variations of the caste system on the subcontinent, the names and occupations of castes vary regionally. The corresponding castes of different regions are independent of each other. The castes have local influence, with the hierarchy of the area dictating locally the relations between them and their members. A village will usually have a leading caste whose power is based on possession of the land, political authority and often its large numbers. The position of a leading local caste within the overall caste system could, however, be quite lower. The caste hierarchy is based on the Hindu tradition and notions of the relative degree of purity of the various castes. The preservation of purity is important, because more permanent impurity can lead to lower caste status. The caste hierarchy dictates with whom one may eat and from whom one can receive food made in certain ways. In principle, only the members of mutually equal castes may eat together, and a person of higher status may not receive food from someone of lower standing, because that would be defiling. In practice, however, the system pertaining to food is more complex than described above. A caste can try to improve its relative standing only with collective effort. The hereditary low castes were a permanent source of cheap labor for the elites.[1]

Recent theoretical studies have structured Hinduism with reference to three elements or spiritual ideals (and their relationships), serving as the path to virtue and the sources of harmony and justice: (1) a brahman officiating as a priest, (2) the ascetic renouncing the world and (3) the exercise of power by kings. According to Susan Bayly, who has written of the history of the caste system, the immense diversity of India and its historical dynamism make it impossible to understand caste with reference to a single model (Bayly 2001, pp. 11–26; Burghart 1978, pp. 519–536; Raheja 1988a, pp. 497–522).

Nicholas Dirks points out that in pre-colonial India social identity was not based solely on castes but also on regional communities, lineage segments, family units, trading associations, sectarian communities etc. The castes did not gain their leading role in structuring society until colonial rule (Dirks 2001, p. 13).

According to Hinduism, the reincarnation of the individual soul is defined by his or her actions (*karma*). While highest ideal is *moksha*, liberation from the cycle of reincarnation, most people only seek to improve their worldly status in their next incarnation. This is done by following their caste-defined obligations (*dharma*). Neglecting duty and immoral behavior will lead to reincarnation at a lower level. According to the prevailing way of thinking, it is better to follow the obligations of one's own caste even imperfectly than the *dharma* of a different caste with near perfection. The latter is regarded as outright dangerous (Kolenda 1981, pp. 106–107; Thapar 2002, pp. 130–131, 278; Burghart 1978, pp. 521–522).

The so-called Indian gift perplexed Marcel Mauss. Although fascinated by it, he misunderstood its essence. According to him, the universal obligations of giving and receiving gifts also applied to the Indian gift: "Food given away means that food will return to the donor in this world; it also means food for him in the other world and in his series of reincarnations" (Mauss 1954, p. 55). The brahmans required other social groups to provide them with gifts when they performed sacrifices and rituals. The brahmans lived from these gifts and traditionally did not practice other occupations as was often the case in later periods. On the other hand, they imposed strict terms on the gifts that they would accept—for example the gift had to be completely spontaneous. This group that raised itself above others was wary of receiving gifts, because it involved dependence (Mauss 1954, pp. 53–59, 122–126).

Anthropologists have elaborated on the concept of the Indian gift institution on the basis of Mauss's ideas, ancient written sources, observation and interviews. The recipient of an Indian ritual gift was the brahman, a representative of the highest caste. Irrespective of whether the donor was the ruler or a Hindu from the street, the ritual gift (whether cash or commodities) embodied the sins of the donor[2] (in the ruler's case also those of the realm) and involved no expectation whatsoever of its being returned or repaid. The brahman had to digest the evil or transfer it further. Otherwise he or his descendants would suffer misfortune. The brahman was required to receive the gift, but it would never be returned, continuing instead on its eternal cycle. A gift is voluntarily donated to a recipient who, in principle, is unwilling to receive it. All ties between the donor and the gift are severed.

Jonathan Parry maintains that a gift of this kind resembles the "altruistic" gifts between members of contemporary society which maintain relationships between individuals without an economic dimension to them. Parry sees a connection between gifts of this kind, major religions of salvation and market exchange based on voluntary agreement. Unlike in archaic societies, when the owner of a commodity changes in market exchange all connections with its former owner are severed. In archaic societies, the exchange of gifts created inter-group reciprocity and a social contract, and the religions of these societies decreed immediate concrete punishment for breaches of the related norms just as for transgressing reciprocity. In ethical religions of salvation, the consequences of people's acts pass on to the afterlife. Unselfish acts and suffering will ensure salvation. In contemporary society, the reciprocity (social contract) of archaic societies as based on gift exchange has become a bond of obligations between the state and citizens, social security. This is Parry's view of Mauss's notion of the gift, which he develops further with emphasis on the institution of the contract.

According to Parry's interpretation, the ethical background of the Indian gift is the repudiation of the idea that "atonement for sin can be simply purchased." The brahmans are supposed to be an ascetic world-renouncer, but, in practice, they not only accept gifts without transferring them further, but also pester their clients for worldly rewards. Generally speaking, it is ethically dubious to atone for sins with money or solely by ritual. This kind of behavior violates the moral norm of reciprocity and the social order based on it.[3]

Parry's and Gloria Godwin Raheja's concept of the Indian gift is largely based on their anthropological research conducted in present-day India. Maria Heim has investigated the institution of the gift with reference to medieval Hindu, Buddhist and Jain texts. It did not involve reciprocity or the obligation to receive a gift or repay it. The direction of the gift was from lower to higher rank. The donor had to hold the recipient in esteem. The merit accorded by the gift to its donor depended on the recipient's high moral caliber, being thus unconnected to the donor's intentions. When giving a gift to a brahman or ascetic monk, the donor should not, however, pay much attention to the recipient's personal qualities, because brahmans and monks included individuals of dubious morals.[4] The gift expressed the esteem felt for the religious community, thus seeking to prevent preference for some brahmans or monks as opposed to others. Receiving a gift would dignify its recipient. According to medieval views, the gift itself did not bear evil or sin. Giving assistance to the poor out of compassion was generally regarded as activity of lesser value.

One of the forms of the medieval gift was poor relief provided by the king, the construction of irrigation pools and refraining from violence against subjects. This was a gift and not just an expression of compassion (Heim 2004, pp. 33–82, 99–102, 111–127).

THE INDIAN VILLAGE SERVANTS

According to the Sultan of Delhi,[5] Ala-ud-din Khalji (reigned 1296–1316) "[t]he Hindus will never be submissive and obedient unless they are pressed down to poverty." That is why they should not be left more than just enough to survive. Half of the harvest ought to be taken in tribute by the state (Kulke and Rothermund 2006, pp. 222–223). Nevertheless, the rulers of Indian states usually provided relief by remission of land revenue and loans during famines (Chandra 1982, p. 463). Their attitude resembled that of the Inca kings.

A different kind of reciprocity, between people of more equal status, was also found in some parts of India. The Japanese historian Fukazawa Hiroshi's articles dealing with the social system of the Deccan from the sixteenth to the eighteenth century were posthumously published in an English-language book in 1991. In the eighteenth century, many villages collectively maintained so-called village servants (a blacksmith, carpenter, potter, leather-worker, rope-maker, washerman, astrologer, Hindu shrine-keeper or *Mahar*, an untouchable menial worker). One representative of each group or caste held his sphere of service as a hereditary and alienable patrimony (*vatan*). The *vatan* could be shared by more than one person, but they also had to share the emoluments due from the *vatan*. All the other village servants representing the same crafts worked there only on a temporary basis. The village servants were paid for their services by the village as a whole in kind or in cash annually at harvest time. Each peasant had to contribute to the remuneration of the village servants regardless of whether he had used their services or not. The village servants also enjoyed various perquisites, and, moreover, *vatan*-holders could hold tax-free land allocated to them by extra-village authorities. The remuneration of the village servants involved a lot of haggling between them and the villagers, which was typical of the economic but not the religious system. Elsewhere in India the village servants were sometimes employed and maintained by dominant peasant patrons or private landlords. The authorities or overlords (and subsequently the British) demanded unpaid labor services from the village servants (or from all the villagers) in the name of customary dues.

In Sumit Guha's opinion, the *baluta* (village servant) system flourished in commercialized areas of Maharashtra. *"[T]he cash economy and competition made hereditary office a desirable acquisition, and its creation and adjudication a source of profit to the state and its ever-hungry local functionaries"* (italics by Guha). In Western Maharashtra, saleable hereditary office was institutionalized by the sixteenth century. For Guha, the *baluta* system was exclusively an economic institution with no cultural background. This is how Guha appraises Louis Dumont's well-known theory of a unique Indian culture as a manifestation of a fundamentally inegalitarian spiritual or religious principle, encompassing (subordinating) "shamefaced" economic and political spheres: "Economic success being permanently reserved for the West, something else had to be found for India; and what better candidate than Hinduism, broadly construed?"

The relations between the peasants and the village servants were asymmetrical or inegalitarian to the disadvantage of the latter (this applies especially to the untouchables),[6] but these relations also provided protection during the recurrent famines. According to Tapan Raychaudhuri, "those who, like the weavers in the Surat area during the 1630s famine, left the relative secure shelter of the rural community to produce more gainfully for the market, were among the first to die of starvation whenever food became scarce" (Raychaudhuri 1982, p. 280).

The system in which the village as a whole paid the land tax and regulated the services of the village servants broke up in the course of the nineteenth century. Colonial rule broke down the old sense of community. A new economic practice emerged towards the end of the century. In it two or more *individual families of different castes* (usually representing farmers, artisans and untouchables) exchanged customary payments (often in kind) against occupational services and servitude. Outside these customary and hereditary relations, the artisans also produced for the market, expecting payment in cash in return for their work. The notion of an ancient religious or religious-economic *jajmani* system, which replaced the older theory of the village servants and prevailed in sociology and social anthropology until the 1980s, has now been refuted and rejected (although some scholars still advocate *jajmani* in a more restricted form or another).[7]

THE DISMANTLING OF RECIPROCITY

The caste classification drawn up by the British reinforced the caste system with the boundaries of castes becoming stricter during colonial rule. This course of development was also influenced by the Indian castes that benefited from it (Bayly 2001, *passim*). The British maintained that the Indian caste system was an expression of backwardness in comparison with European civil society. The Indians were not capable of governing themselves and needed their colonial masters for the purpose. Knowledge of the Indian heritage was a mean of colonialist control (Dirks 2001, pp. 6–18, 40–41 and *passim*).

In the late eighteenth century, the British East India Company organized land ownership and taxation in Bengal so that local leaders who collected and forwarded tax revenue from peasants to the Mughal administration[8] were given the status of landholder-lord, in keeping with British ideals of the period. The landholder-lord would be responsible for the revenue with his own property as security and the peasants became his tenants. The tax was a fixed sum and was not adjusted even in years of crop failure, unlike under Mughal rule. The set arrangement obviated negotiation, which had been part of Indian political culture. Because taxation was at first raised considerably in comparison with the pre-colonial level, the system, contrary to expectations, did not produce a stable landholder class, and instead it was common for members of the elite to be replaced owing to tax arrears. Men now became landholders, who unlike the former leaders, had no qualms about collecting their rent from the farmers with accumulated interest. The collection of arrears and usury were more important for them than the development of agriculture. Owing to support from the British, the landholder-lords no longer needed to negotiate with their tenants or the community. Internal solidarity disappeared.

At the turn of the eighteenth and nineteenth centuries, the British instituted in part of Southern and Western India a system, which unlike the oligarchic Bengali system, did not require local leaders, and instead individual peasant-landholders were personally responsible for paying their taxes. It was now believed that India consisted of autonomous villages, which strong leaders had arbitrarily taken under their control. Wars had eradicated many of these leaders. The British believed that their new system would be an efficient way to get rid of the intervening middleman class, which was of course an illusion (Wilson 2016, pp. 143–149, 167–170; Dirks 2001, pp. 111–115; *Histoire de l'Inde moderne [1480–1950]* 1994, pp. 357–364).

Between 12 and 30 million people died of hunger and famine-related diseases in the great Indian famines of 1876–1878, 1896–1897 and 1900–1901, and in smaller crises in the intervening years. The famines were due to crop failure caused by drought, taxes, rises in the price of foodstuffs and the loss of grain from local markets via the railways. It was profitable for the British managing agencies and local magnates to sell their wheat and rice on the world market. Previously, the latter would have had to consider the needs of the peasants, but now the British colonial army ensured stability in society. Emergency aid from the Raj was insufficient. Many people were put to useless relief work. The British were afraid that the recipients of aid would become dependent on it and began to regard themselves as entitled to it. Combating freeloaders was more important than combating death from famine (Wilson 2016, pp. 318–331, 343–348; Davis 2002, pp. 25–59, 141–175, 311–340; Kulke and Rothermund 2006, pp. 333–338).

Colonial rule also destroyed intra-community reciprocity in Algeria, East Africa and Vietnam. During the great Algerian famine of 1867–1869 the traditional stores of grain no longer existed, from which emergency relief could have been provided (Ageron 1991, pp. 35, 44; Chrétien 1974, pp. 1136–1137; Kiernan 2017, p. 326).

NOTES

1. Dumont (1980, *passim*), Kolenda (1981, pp. 68–70 and *passim*), Kulke and Rothermund (2006, pp. 55–59), Thapar (2002, pp. 62–68, 122–126 [quote p. 125], 135–136, 150–154, 190–193, 208, 251–252, 260–261, 275, 389–390, 439, 462–466), Bayly (2001, pp. 1–32).

2. A problematic situation for the donor of the gift would be a priest unfit to receive it who would use the gift for dissolute purposes. In that case, the donor's sins would not be exonerated. Parry (1994, pp. 122–125, 135).

3. Parry (1986, pp. 453–473; 1993, pp. 64–93 [quote p. 75]; 1994, pp. 119–148, 269). On the Indian ritual gift, see also Raheja (1988a, pp. 503–504, 510–517; 1988b, pp. 31–36, 248–254; 1989, pp. 82–99). Romila Thapar discusses gift-giving and the ritual of sacrifice in early Indian history, noting features in them that are similar to *potlatch* (2002, p. 116, 119–130). Moses I. Finley, a scholar of ancient history, points out that in the Ancient Greek Homeric poems and the hero poetry of the South Indian Tamils gift-giving was completely in accordance with Mauss's theory of the gift. Finley (1978, pp. 145–146 [61–62, 64–67, 88–90, 95–98, 120–123, 137]). See also Morris (1986, pp. 1–17) (gift exchange coexisting with the market in Ancient Greece).

4. This reflects an idea slightly similar to the evolutionary psychological observation that in everyday life people have to accept mediocre achievements from each other.

5. The Islamic sultanate of Delhi was founded in 1206.

6. The village servant system and its relationship to *jajmani* have been studied by: Fukazawa (1991, pp. 199–244), Guha (2004, pp. 79–101, quotes pp. 80 and 100), Fuller (1993, pp. 36–41, 51–53, 58), Mayer (1993, pp. 357–395), Stein (1980, pp. 171, 177, 424–425), Davis (2002, p. 313). Cf. Dumont (1980). Karl Marx and Max Weber also discussed the Indian village servants. Marx (1972, pp. 378–379), Weber (2011, pp. 115–117, 189–190, 196). For critiques of Marx's notion of the unchanging traditional Indian village and society, see Fuller (above); Anderson (1977, pp. 462–495, 516–520, 548). The Indian village has been a veritable killing field of social theories. See also note 7.

7. Dumont (1980, pp. 97–108, 175–176) (religiously determined *jajmani*), Kolenda (1981, pp. 10–77, 89–95) (also presents the views of other researchers concerning *jajmani*), Neale (1957, pp. 218–236) (advocates the myth of the grain heap), Dube (1967, pp. 57–79) (a good description of how exchange worked in practice in the early 1950s), Fuller (1993, pp. 33–63), Mayer (1993, pp. 357–395), Lerche (1993, pp. 237–266), Guha (2004, pp. 79–101), Raheja (1988a, pp. 497–522), Bayly (2001, pp. 190–196, 206, 222–223, 226).

8. The Mughal rulers, who were Muslims, gained control of large areas of Northern India in the sixteenth century. The Mughal empire began to disintegrate in the eighteenth century.

REFERENCES

Ageron, Charles-Robert. 1991. *Modern Algeria: A History from 1830 to the Present*, trans. and ed. Michael Brett. London: Hurst & Company.

Anderson, Perry. 1977. *Lineages of the Absolutist State*. London: NLB.

Bayly, Susan. 2001. *Caste, Society and Politics in India from the Eighteenth Century to the Modern Age*. The New Cambridge History of India, Vol. IV: 3. Cambridge: Cambridge University Press.

Burghart, Richard. 1978. Hierarchical Models of the Hindu Social System. *Man* 13 (4): 519–536.

Chandra, Satish. 1982. Standard of Living: Mughal India. In *The Cambridge Economic History of India, Vol. 1, c. 1200–c. 1750*, ed. Tapan Raychaudhuri and Irfan Habib, 458–471. Cambridge: Cambridge University Press.

Chrétien, Jean-Pierre. 1974. Échanges et hiérarchies dans les royaumes des Grands Lacs de l'Est africain. *Annales ESC* 29 (6): 1327–1337.

Davis, Mike. 2002. *Late Victorian Holocausts: El Niño Famines and the Making of the Third World*. London and New York: Verso.

Dirks, Nicholas B. 2001. *Castes of Mind: Colonialism and the Making of Modern India*. Princeton and Oxford: Princeton University Press.

Dube, S.C. 1967. *Indian Village*. New York and Evanston: Harper & Row.

Dumont, Louis. 1980. *Homo Hierarchicus: The Caste System and Its Implications* (Complete Revised English Edition), trans. Mark Sainsbury et al. Chicago and London: The University of Chicago Press.

Finley, M.I. 1978. *The World of Odysseus*. New York: The Viking Press.

Fukazawa Hiroshi. 1991. *The Medieval Deccan: Peasants, Social Systems and States, Sixteenth to Eighteenth Century*. Delhi: Oxford University Press.

Fuller, C.J. 1993. Misconceiving the Grain Heap: A Critique of the Concept of the Indian Jajmani System. In *Money and the Morality of Exchange*, ed. J. Parry and M. Bloch, 33–63. Cambridge: Cambridge University Press.

Guha, Sumit. 2004. Civilisations, Markets and Services: Village Servants in India from the Seventeenth to the Twentieth Centuries. *The Indian Economic and Social History Review* 41 (1): 79–101.

Heim, Maria. 2004. *Theories of the Gift in South Asia: Hindu, Buddhist, and Jain Reflections on Dāna*. New York and London: Routledge.

Histoire de l'Inde moderne (1480–1950). 1994. Ed. Claude Markovits. Paris: Fayard.

Kiernan, Ben. 2017. *Viet Nam: A History from Earliest Times to the Present*. New York: Oxford University Press.

Kolenda, Pauline. 1981. *Caste, Cult and Hierarchy: Essays on the Culture of India*. Kirpa Dai Series in Folklore and Anthropology 3. Meerut: Folklore Institute.

Kulke, Hermann, and Dietmar Rothermund. 2006. *Geschichte Indiens: Von der Induskultur bis heute*. Munich: Verlag C.H. Beck.

Lerche, Jens. 1993. Dominant Castes, Rajas, Brahmins and Inter-caste Exchange Relations in Coastal Orissa: Behind the Facade of the '*Jajmani*' System. *Contributions to Indian Sociology* 27 (2): 237–266.

Marx, Karl. 1972. *Das Kapital: Kritik der politischen Ökonomie.* Bd. 1, ed. Erster Band, Karl Marx, and Friedrich Engels. *Werke.* Bd. 23. Berlin: Dietz Verlag.

Mauss, Marcel. 1954. *The Gift: Forms and Functions of Exchange in Archaic Societies,* trans. Ian Cunnison. Glencoe: The Free Press.

Mayer, Peter. 1993. Inventing Village Tradition: The Late 19th-Century Origins of the North Indian 'Jajmani System'. *Modern Asian Studies* 27 (2): 357–395.

Morris, Ian. 1986. Gift and Commodity in Archaic Greece. *Man* 21 (1): 1–17.

Neale, Walter C. 1957. Reciprocity and Redistribution in the Indian Village: Sequel to Some Notable Discussions. In *Trade and Market in the Early Empires: Economies in History and Theory,* ed. Karl Polanyi, Conrad M. Arensberg, and Harry W. Pearson, 218–236. Glencoe: The Free Press.

Parry, Jonathan. 1986. The Gift, the Indian Gift and the 'Indian Gift'. *Man* 21 (3): 453–473.

Parry, Jonathan. 1993. On the Moral Perils of Exchange. In *Money and the Morality of Exchange,* ed. J. Parry and M. Bloch, 64–93. Cambridge: Cambridge University Press.

Parry, Jonathan P. 1994. *Death in Banares.* Cambridge: Cambridge University Press.

Raheja, Gloria Goodwin. 1988a. India: Caste, Kingship, and Dominance Reconsidered. *Annual Review of Anthropology* 17: 497–522.

Raheja, Gloria Godwin. 1988b. *The Poison in the Gift: Ritual, Prestation, and the Dominant Class in a North Indian Village.* Chicago and London: The University of Chicago Press.

Raheja, Gloria Goodwin. 1989. Centrality, Mutuality and Hierarchy: Shifting Aspects of Inter-caste Relationships in North India. *Contributions to Indian Sociology* 23 (1): 79–101.

Raychaudhuri, Tapan. 1982. Non-agricultural Production: Mughal India. In *The Cambridge Economic History of India, c. 1200 –c. 1750,* ed. Tapan Raychaudhuri and Irfan Habib, Vol. 1, 261–307. Cambridge: Cambridge University Press.

Stein, Burton. 1980. *Peasant State and Society in Medieval South India.* Delhi: Oxford University Press.

Thapar, Romila. 2002. *Early India from the Origins to AD 1300.* London: Allen Lane/Penguin.

Weber, Max. 2011. *Abriß der universalen Sozial- und Wirtschaftsgeschichte. Mit- und Nachschriften 1919/20.* Max Weber. *Gesamtausgabe.* Abt. III. Bd. 6. Tübingen: J.C.B. Mohr (Paul Siebeck).

Wilson, Jon. 2016. *India Conquered: Britain's Raj and the Chaos of Empire.* London: Simon & Schuster.

CHAPTER 4

Moral Obligations in Early Modern Japan

In 1944, during the War in the Pacific, the American anthropologist Ruth Benedict was commissioned to write a book on the patterns of Japanese culture. *The Chrysanthemum and the Sword* (1946) provided the American authorities in charge of the occupation of Japan with necessary background information on the patterns and structures of Japanese behavior. The Americans understood that, in order to maintain social tranquility, it was advisable to leave the Emperor system in place, though dismantled from its semi-divine character and its links with militarism. Emperor Hirohito was not to be indicted for war crimes.

Benedict emphasized the hierarchy inherent in Japanese society. Everybody must take their proper station. *On* (generosity) is an obligation received passively from the Emperor or one's own parents or lord or teacher. The limitless repayment of indebtedness is called *gimu*. *Chū* (loyalty) is the duty to the Emperor, the law and Japan, *kō* (filial piety) the duty to the parents (covering also the descendants). These are two forms of *gimu*. Even the fullest repayment of these obligations cannot be more than partial. "One never repays one ten-thousandth of (this) *on*" (Benedict 1989, pp. 115–116 and *passim*). Originally *on* meant land enfeoffed by a lord to his vassal. In the years of the Tokugawa Shogunate (Edo period 1603–1867) people were expected to have a limitless obligation to the shogun (generalissimo). After the Meiji Restoration, this obligation was transformed into concern for the Emperor.

According to Japanese views, the *on* obligation is also generated when people are in contact with each other and receive services from one

© The Author(s) 2019
A. Kujala and M. Danielsbacka, *Reciprocity in Human Societies*,
https://doi.org/10.1007/978-3-319-96056-2_4

51

another. Therefore, the Japanese words for "thank you" also mean apology or other regrets for a situation that has aroused. The person who thanks regrets that he or she is unable to completely compensate for the service or favor that has been received. People prefer to avoid creating an *on* obligation.

Giri is a debt and a relationship between two persons who are more equal to each other than in the case discussed above. *Giri* must be repaid with mathematical equivalence. It applies to relatives other than those whom *on* concerns, and to all the gifts and favors received from non-related persons. This is reciprocity *par excellence*. The repayable *giri* debt also applied to one's liege lord. During the Edo period a samurai often based his acts on the allegiance (*giri*) to his own overlord, which was more compelling to him than the loyalty (*on*) he was supposed to repay to the shogun. That is why the Meiji reformers attempted to minimize *giri* and underline *gimu* (or *chū* to the Emperor and *kō* to one's parents). The consequences of *gimu* in terms of human sacrifice during the Pacific War are well-known.

Benedict also pointed to the fact that religion does not play a major role in Japanese life, with Buddhist priests and monks as exceptions. The problem of evil is not important. Japanese culture is one of shame, not guilt like, for example, civilizations with a Christian basis. In this respect, Benedict concurred with the views of British historian George Sansom (Benedict 1989, pp. 190, 197–198 and *passim*; Sansom 1990, pp. 80–81). Japanese-American researcher Takie Sugiyama Lebra notes that the Japanese also feel guilt. Her book complements and updates Benedict's depiction of Japanese patterns of behavior.[1]

Benedict argued that the Chinese ethical postulate of benevolence (in Japanese *jin*) was never adopted in Japan except in a perverted form.[2] She was mistaken, as will be demonstrated below. The Shogunate never elaborated an ideology of its own. Japanese scholars created rival ideologies in order to curry favor with the *bakufu* (military government). The ingredients were, as a rule, taken from Neo-Confucianism and Shinto. Confucianism underscores obedience towards patriarchal authority, thus representing conservatism. The basic relationships of society are derived from familial relationships.

Central concepts pertaining to social relations in Tokugawa Ieyasu's alleged Testament were punishment by Heaven (inflicted on unjust regimes), Heaven's Mandate, the principle of Heaven and Earth, loyalty (*chūshin*) towards superiors, and benevolence (*jihi*—a Buddhist term instead of the *jinsei*, the Confucian benevolent government). Ieyasu, who established the Tokugawa shogunate in 1603, had obtained his mandate to rule from Heaven. The shogun had to observe benevolence vis-à-vis his subjects and love them as parents love their children (and receive their love and submission). The issue of the delegation of authority from the Emperor to the shogun was bypassed in the Testament. Ieyasu's grandson Tokugawa Iemitsu maintained that the Emperor owed *on* to the shogun, not vice versa (Ooms 1989, pp. 66–72, 160–161, 170, 193, 287–298). His grandfather, the above-mentioned Ieyasu had humiliated members of the imperial court by drawing up a set of regulations for them that was of a condescending tone. One of the instructions read "no pissing but in the pissoir" (Ooms 1989, p. 51).

The Regulations for the Villages of All Provinces (1649) stipulated that "[o]ne should obey the shogunal law, respect district officials and intendants, and consider headmen and goningumi (five-household group) heads as one's real parents" (Ooms 1996, p. 364).

Although the mainstream of Japanese scholars adhered to Neo-Confucianism supplemented with Shinto, the Buddhist ideas of Suzuki Shōzan (1579–1655) would have served the purposes of the Shogunate ideally, because he dealt with social questions and the relationship between those in power and the subjects in an exceptionally concrete manner. People received generosity (*on*) from Heaven and Earth, their teachers, the lord of the land and their parents. One owed indebtedness to the lord as the provider of peace and good government. Shōzan stressed the point that the generosity (*on*) of the superior became part of the body and personality of the recipient. "Your body is your lord's" (Ooms 1989, pp. 122–151, quote p. 130). Benedict also paid attention to the same feature of *on*. It resembles the Maori gift, which retained a bond between the donor and the recipient (Benedict 1989, p. 109; Mauss 1954, pp. 8–10). According to Shōzan each class or group of society must provide service in keeping with its occupation. *On* bound all the groups of society into mutual dependence (Ooms 1989, pp. 130–132).

Yamazaki Ansai (1619–1682) maintained that there were kings and vassals, i.e. a hierarchy, even among ants and bees. The true cosmic path consisted of five relationships: parent–child, lord–minister, husband–wife, elder–junior, and friend (teacher)–friend (pupil). The relationship was hierarchic, but it also placed obligations on the higher-ranking party. This was neo-Confucianism, with which Ansai combined Shintoism in his later years. He felt that obligation (*giri*) alone was not enough, a sincere heart and empathy were also needed (Ooms 1989, pp. 194–232, especially 200, 248; *Sources of Japanese Tradition* 1964, pp. 354–362).

The Tokugawa state never acknowledged any popular rights for its subjects. In practice, however, the system was based on mutually acknowledged obligations, or a moral economy, between the people and those in power. The subjects had to pay their taxes and carry out their other duties. The government was committed to ruling in a benign manner and would alleviate the burden of the people in times of distress and when poor peasants risked losing their land. This meant tax relief or loans or emergency aid in the cities. The shogunate also felt it was its obligation to prevent officials or *daimyos* (regional magnates) from oppressing their subjects with unduly severe taxes. Roughly 15% of the country's productive capacity was under the direct control of the shogunate and paid taxes to it. The rest belonged to the *daimyo* families, whose relations with the shogunate varied from kinship to antagonism. The shogunate's attitude to the moral economy was highly similar to many European states of Early Modern Times. Between 25 and 35% of the yield of the land went into taxes, possibly more in the early stages of the Tokugawa period. According to Honda Masanobu, a *daimyo* closely allied to Ieyasu, "[t]he proper way to govern is to ensure that peasants don't accumulate wealth yet don't starve either." The land tax should absorb every surplus grain of rice. Honda's view keeping the people in place through poverty was similar to that of Ala-ud-din, the sultan of Delhi. Peasant families were in control of their own land, while the village was collectively responsible for the taxes of its farmers. Increases in taxation were restrained by the petitions and protests of peasants.

The shogunate followed the position that no one had the right to questions its laws and ordinances. Defying them could be punishable by death, without any restrictions. On the other hand, it was prepared to give redress to its own subjects and those of the *daimyos* in response to petitions that it regarded as justified when such petitions were passed on to it. The shogunate specifically wanted to prevent arbitrary action by *daimyos* and officials and increases in their power. Open defiance, conspiracy and bearing tools interpreted as weapons were definitely banned. When conflicts arose, they were allowed to die down of their own according, and then only the worst troublemakers were punished as a warning to others.[3] In the meantime, the dispute could have led to results that were favorable for the peasants.

The shogunate thus could not keep to its requirement of a debt of honor and obedience applying to its subjects, and it followed its own guideline of benevolent governance more for reasons of expedience caused by the situation at hand than in compliance to any official ideology. Benevolence and reciprocity were suited above all to be the tools of the common people, as noted by James W. White, the author of a work of synthesis on social conflicts in Japan in Early Modern Times. On the other hand, the common people were usually aware of the risks of excessively challenging authority and were careful not to go too far. There were also violent movements, but none of the protest movements threatened the Tokugawa system (White 1995, pp. 27–61, 75–77, 83–312; Furushima 1991, pp. 478–518, quote p. 494; Vlastos 1990, pp. 1–79; Totman 2010, pp. 228, 278–284).

The Japanese peasants believed that they had an inherent right to a materially secure life. "That proposition sprang directly from Confucian doctrine (the principle of benevolent rule – AK and MD) that the regime had embraced, and it encouraged villagers to present petitions to the rulers with the presumption that legitimate grievances would be heard and meliorative action taken" (Totman 2010, p. 278 quote; Vlastos 1990, pp. 15–17). It included both material relief (alleviation of taxes or bestowal of loans during famines) and political redress. Innumerable popular petitions, acts of relief and formal channels of appeal prove that those in power and their subjects recognized the validity of an informal social contract (White 1995, p. 36, 109 and *passim*).

Stephen Vlastos has underscored the point that it was in the interests of the lord to grant tax relief, because a single-minded pursuit of maximal tax revenue drove more and more peasants to insolvency, resulting in the shrinking of tax revenue, and rebellion (Vlastos 1990, pp. 39–41).

Notes

1. Lebra (1976, pp. 12–13, 90–109, 158). Also (Befu 1986, pp. 158–170) (gift-giving in Japan). Yan (1996) discusses gift-giving in the People's Republic of China (pp. 167, 246—shared cultural roots with Japanese gift-giving). In the People's Republic there was also a prevailing practice of negative reciprocity whereby "when the social superior's power is based on a monopoly of resources, the subordinates' gifts become obligatory dues, with unilateral gift giving serving to express subordination." The cadres of the Communist Party were under no obligation to provide a return gift.

When asked what he had given in return for gifts received, a local party secretary replied: "For those sycophants, I gave them shit!" Yan (1996, pp. 154, 168 [151–169]).

2. Benedict (1989, pp. 117–119). C. Douglas Lummis legitimately criticized Benedict for bypassing terms such as benevolence and mutual aid as if they were not part of Japanese culture. Lummis maintained that Benedict presented the Meiji period and the militaristic ideology of the early twentieth century as the culture of the whole nation. He also pointed to the fact that Benedict's study was largely based on information from only one person, although it must be said that this person's knowledge was mostly of an excellent standard. According to Maurice Godelier, the debt of humans to the gods (and of the Ancient Egyptians to their divine pharaoh) is so absolute and irreplaceable and their mutual relationship so asymmetrical that we cannot speak of any reciprocity between humans and the gods. Godelier (2008, pp. 44–47, 257–275). A debt of this kind resembles the Japanese *on* obligation, which for Godelier is seemingly not within the sphere of reciprocity.

3. Also in Russia—and many other countries in the Early Modern Period—only the leaders of protests were punished while necessary relief was granted for the problems of peasants who repented their actions. This maintained an illusory notion of harmony between benevolent masters and faithful subordinates that had been temporary disturbed by a few rabble-rousers. The peasants had thus achieved some of their aims with only the instigators being punished. Moon (1999, pp. 268–269).

REFERENCES

Befu Harumi. 1986. Gift-Giving in a Modernizing Japan. In *Japanese Culture and Behavior: Selected Readings*, ed. Takie Sugiyama Lebra and William P. Lebra, 158–170. Honolulu: University of Hawaii Press.

Benedict, Ruth. 1989. *The Chrysanthemum and the Sword: Patterns of Japanese Culture*. Tokyo: Tuttle.

Furushima Toshio. 1991. The Village and Agriculture During the Edo Period. In *The Cambridge History of Japan Early Modern Japan*. ed. John Whitney Hall, Vol. 4, 478–518. Cambridge: Cambridge University Press.

Godelier, Maurice. 2008. *L'énigme du don*. Paris: Flammarion.

Lebra, Takie Sugiyama. 1976. *Japanese Patterns of Behavior*. Honolulu: University of Hawaii Press. http://www.japanfocus.org/-C_Douglas-Lummis/2474. Accessed 5 Mar 2014.

Mauss, Marcel. 1954. *The Gift: Forms and Functions of Exchange in Archaic Societies*, trans. Ian Cunnison. Glencoe: The Free Press.

Moon, David. 1999. *The Russian Peasantry 1600–1930: The World the Peasants Made*. London and New York: Longman.

Ooms, Herman. 1989. *Tokugawa Ideology: Early Constructs, 1570–1680*. Princeton: Princeton University Press.

Ooms, Herman. 1996. *Tokugawa Village Practice: Class, Status, Power, Law*. Berkeley: University of California Press.

Sansom, George. 1990. *A History of Japan: To 1334*. Tokyo: Tuttle.

Sources of Japanese Tradition. 1964. ed. Ryusaku Tsunoda, Wm. Theodore de Bary, and Donald Keene, Vol. 1. New York: Columbia University Press.

Totman, Conrad. 2010. *A History of Japan*. Malden: Blackwell.

Vlastos, Stephen. 1990. *Peasant Protests and Uprisings in Tokugawa Japan*. Berkeley: University of California Press.

White, James W. 1995. *Ikki: Social Conflict and Political Protest in Early Modern Japan*. Ithaca and London: Cornell University Press.

Yan Yunxiang. 1996. *The Flow of Gifts: Reciprocity and Social Networks in a Chinese Village*. Stanford: Stanford University Press.

CHAPTER 5

Gift Exchange and Reciprocity in the Nordic Countries

According to Finnish anthropologist Martti Haavio, the ancient Finnish rites following the successful hunting of a bear (*karhunpeijaiset*) were meant to lead the killed bear on its way back to its original home, from where it would return to the hunting grounds like its ancient bear mother had done. The bear is killed and returned home in an endless cycle. Haavio points out that bear hunters must take care of sending the killed animal back home in order to preserve the bear family, i.e. the species.

The bear-kill rites were for the purpose of appeasing the "bear tribe" to prevent these predators from killing cattle or causing other misfortune. A folk incantation states the request: "My bear, my sweet bird, my fairest, dearest one, give peace to the cattle, atonement to the ones with dung on their legs." The bones of the bear were buried to await reincarnation and the skull was attached to a pine looking eastward toward sunrise, to the lands where the bears were originally born. According to folk poetry, the skull of the ancestral mother of the bear family had once been put in a similar fashion on a bear-kill pine and permission had to be requested from her for a new bear hunt. Many hunter-gatherer cultures of Northern Eurasia and North America have similar bear-kill rites and beliefs (Haavio 1967, pp. 15–41, quotes pp. 17, 37). Part of the original population of Finland and even the initial forms of the Finno-Ugrian languages originated in Siberia or in the borderlands of Europe and Siberia. These rites and beliefs resemble the Maori custom of giving gifts to forests where birds were hunted to maintain their yield. This was

© The Author(s) 2019
A. Kujala and M. Danielsbacka, *Reciprocity in Human Societies*,
https://doi.org/10.1007/978-3-319-96056-2_5

done by priests who ate some of the hunted birds that were cooked over a holy fire. For the Maori, the yield of the bird-hunting forest was part of a gift that had to be returned (Sahlins 2004, pp. 149–168). By the same token, the bear-kill feast can be considered a religious-mythical gift exchange with the family of the bear as the other party.

The Russian researcher of medieval and early Nordic history, Aron Gurevich has demonstrated that the institution of the gift and the return gift as outlined by Mauss still thrived in Viking Age and early medieval Scandinavian societies. Even enemies could maintain civil relations through the gifts. On the other hand, there was the generally held notion that the recipient of a gift would fall under the power of the giver. The ancient Scandinavians were often as averse to remaining in a debt of gratitude as the Japanese were to *on* debt. Feasts, hospitality and generosity were part of the Viking Age communities. Feasts and drinking bouts were associated with non-Christian religious ceremonies in both Scandinavia and Finland. The Finnish idea of the feast for obtaining rain that was held in honor of the god Ukko held that "[t]he more people were drunk, the better the grain crop." The Norwegian Gulating provincial law, which is known in its thirteenth-century form, decreed the following about dividing inheritance: "If a man gives more to one son than to another, he (the latter) shall, when they are dividing the inheritance after the father, take as much out of the undivided property as was given to the other one who got more, and thereafter they shall divide equally between themselves what remains. Therefore, a gift is better than a compensation, that everyone has his gift unrequited; no gift is requited unless a return gift of equal value has been made." Laurence Larson and Gurevich interpret this obscure sentence in a way that appears to be credible on the basis of what immediately follows ("no gift is requited …"): "Everyone has a right to recall a gift unless it has been requited with a better one."

While the section of law primarily refers to the division of inheritance, it also laid down the fundamental principle of gift exchange. According to Gurevich, the Langobards regarded this matter in precisely the same terms. An edict issued by Langobard King Liutbard (reigned 712–744) who ruled over large areas of Italy stated that a gift was not legally valid if it had not been confirmed with a return gift or in a court of law.[1]

A culture of the gift that is also highly similar in other respects can be seen in early medieval Europe. Rulers and warlords were expected to share their booty and the subjects were expected to reward their masters with gifts. Gifts from the king were believed to bring luck. Even ordinary tax contributions were masked in rhetoric as gifts. Gifts maintained friendly state and social relations and were forms of assistance to the poor, and ritual drinking bouts reinforced social cohesion. The church acquired its vast property through gifts (Duby 1992, pp. 45–57, 66–69, 165, 232–234; Gurevich 1995, pp. 34–35).

The system of taxation in Västergötland in Sweden (the province east of present-day Gothenburg) had different roots than in the areas of Sweden bordering on the Baltic Sea. In Västergötland, the rulers based taxation on the obligation of the people to provide hospitality. Also in Continental Europe, medieval kings continuously toured from one royal manor or castle to another, where the common people provided the food and drink required by the ruler and his armed retinue and attended to their sustenance during the journeys. This procedure was well suited to undeveloped agrarian societies with poor communications. Royal power thus exploited folk hospitality, which it converted to channeling resources for its own use. The common people of Uppland, on the other hand, were on the losing side in the Battle of Sparrsätra fought in 1247 between the parties of so-called leading men (aristocracy). The obligation of the peasants to provide ships and crewmen (*ledung*) for warring expeditions in the Baltic and to provision them was converted to taxes. The example of Denmark was followed here. The ruler, in turn, had the obligation of protecting his subjects.[2]

The oldest taxation in the North-eastern Baltic area (Livonia and Estonia) was carried out by the Germans on the basis of folk hospitality. The Russians organized local administration and taxation in Karelia through *pogosts* and their sub-units *pereva(a)ra*. The names of these administrative areas derive from the Russian *pogostit'* (to visit, to be a guest or to be entertained) and *perevarit'* (to brew beer) (Korhonen 1923, pp. 206–210 and *passim*; Kuujo 1959, pp. 11–19).

It is thus no surprise that part of medieval and Early Modern Period taxes in Finland belonging to the Swedish realm were in the guise of hospitality and gifts, even though it is obvious that people never paid taxes willingly or completely voluntarily.[3] Besides, it was common for officials of the crown to demand from the common people "voluntary gifts" and hospitality during their travels, even though this was illegal (Kujala 2010, pp. 308, 334).

As can be seen, Nordic kings organized taxation on the basis of previously established social relations. In precisely the same manner, the Inca rulers made mutual assistance between families in the kinship communities of the Andes the basis of the labor obligations that they decreed.

Barter related to the gift institution was still practiced in Finland in the nineteenth century as a relic of a probably ancient practice. Both clergymen (who did not usually fish) and quite ordinary people would offer drinks of spirits to seine fishermen for fish, to haymakers for hay, or for other harvested produce. Before the spread of distilled spirits in the seventeenth and eighteenth centuries, beer was part of bartering. People who owned sought-after products would understand even without being told what was expected of them in return for drinks. On the other hand, when spirits were offered to obtain scarce produce outside its season, the party offering drinks had to express in some way what his household was lacking. In the Åland Islands it was believed that those who were stingy when giving fish would lose their own fishing luck. A proverb gave the advice: "God gives to him who gives, and the giver shares equally." Fishermen in the archipelago of the Gulf of Finland would traditionally barter fish for grain with farmers in Estonia. The relationship of exchange was established and did not correspond to prevailing commercial prices (Andersson 1953, pp. 1–96; Vilkuna 1964, pp. 117–149, quote p. 148; Raussi 1966, pp. 113–123; Peltonen 1988, pp. 37–54).

THE SWEDISH SOCIAL CONTRACT

Just as in India, also in medieval Europe and in Sweden in Early Modern Times, apologists of social hierarchy compared society to the human body. The sought to describe it as a harmonic entity in which the lower orders had to obey and serve those who were above them (Duby 1982, pp. 254–255, 264–266; Englund 1994, pp. 25–48). A more factual picture of society, however, is gained by analyzing the mutual rights and obligations of the people and those in authority. The Austrian social historian Otto Brunner has demonstrated that medieval European society was based on such a system, the relationship of dominion between the lord (knight) and vassal or serf sealed with a pledge of allegiance. The peasant had to pay his rent and when necessary to assist his lord with extra taxes and to serve him. The lord had to protect his vassals. If he failed to meet this obligation, the vassal's obligations toward him ceased and the vassal could seek a new lord or even rebel (Brunner 1990, pp. 254–303, 343–348; Bloch 1961, pp. 219–230).

Peter Reinholdsson has applied Brunner's main ideas to the Late Middle Ages in Sweden. The lending of seed grain and lowering of rent in times of crop failure were part of the protection accorded by the landlord to his peasants. The relationship of dependence was marked by a strong ethical obligation. Both parties were expected to serve the common good instead of pursuing only their own interests. When protection functioned satisfactorily for the peasants, it ensured the legitimacy of the relationship of dependence; otherwise the lord could expect considerable problems (Reinholdsson 1998, pp. 146–219).

During the first half of the seventeenth century, the Swedish rulers and regency regimes donated large numbers of peasant holdings or, more precisely, their crown taxes to the nobility. In 1680, Charles XI began a restitution in which the vast majority of the taxes donated to the nobles were restored to being collected by the crown. The peasants' expectations of protection, emergency assistance and foreseeable obligations applied to the crown and noble lords alike.

Peter Englund has described the attitude of seventeenth-century Swedish nobility to their peasants as paternalism. The relationship of mutual obligations between nobles and peasants, their "love" was embodied in the noble giving orders and the peasant obeying them. Englund maintains that such "love" was based on a pure relationship of subjugation. The intimacy and personal nature of the relationship were the theater of power; the daily role game was meant to keep everything unchanged. The nobles, however, had the ideal of treating their peasants well, and it was often followed in practice. The peasants could also benefit from the rules of the game of power. One of the most efficient means to do so was to appeal to the benevolence of those in authority. Moreover, many nobles knew that it was politically short-sighted to oppress the peasants too much. This would jeopardize the legitimacy of power and could even lead to rebellion (Englund 1994, pp. 25–48, 90–102, 194–204).

My (AK) research on a number of Finnish noble properties of the seventeenth century showed that the relationship between nobles and peasants was often arranged on the basis of this kind of interaction, in which both parties avoided leading matters to breaking point. The nobles tested if the peasants' rent or day-labor obligations could be raised. If this led to major resistance, the nobles would then take on the role of a benevolent master and cancel raises in rent.

In principle, the nobility levied from their peasants on donated land everything that the crown had previously demanded according to the crown cadaster, i.e. all the taxes and labor service which the crown had relinquished now came to benefit the recipient of the donation. The peasants who had preserved their hereditary rights (tax peasants) paid their cadaster-listed taxes to their nobleman landlord. In 1651–1652 their day-labor services were given a maximum definition (18 auxiliary labor days per year for a whole farm unless the landlord and the peasants had agreed otherwise by mutual contract).

Unpaid taxes for a period of three years would make the peasant lose his hereditary rights to his holding. The size and nature of the rent were defined by the landlord, at least in theory in agreement with the tenant, and were not bound by the payments of tax entered into the crown cadaster. In practice, however, it was often impossible to raise the taxes from their previous level, because the tenant would have been unable to pay,[4] but the composition of the tax paid by peasants without hereditary rights could be changed by altering the proportion of day labor. It was possible to demand more day-labor services from a peasant without hereditary rights than was decreed by the *riksdag* for tax peasants. As a result, the tax burden would be reduced nominally but not in real terms—day labor was a considerable encumbrance for the peasant's management of his own farm, auxiliary means of livelihood and his freedom.[5]

Count Karl Gustav Wrangel[6] and the tenants of Bjärnå manor in Southwestern Finland thus sought to benefit at the cost of others, the manor by seeking higher rent and more day labor and the peasants through complaints and other forms of pressure (by demonstrating their unwillingness). The complaints of the latter were often noted to be contrary to the truth or at least exaggerated, but it was also the underlying logic of the complaints and appeals to exaggerate in order to draw attention to real problems. The peasants regarded the bailiff or lessee of the manor, not the count, as the source of their problems. In part, they may have actually thought in these terms, and partly not. Both parties played the role game of a just landlord and his faithful tenants. But even for the nobles the model of the just landlord was not necessarily a charade, but an obligation which one took to heart—as Wrangel certainly did—or not. On the other hand, he or those who administered his property liked to test whether the peasants would accept raises in rent and encumbrances. Economic benefits would easily relegate high moral principles to second place. It is no less insufficient to explain the actions of peasants or their aristocratic landlords solely in terms of rational calculations of profit or ideology; both aspects played a part.

Regardless of whether the complaints of the peasants were resolved by the count himself or his administrators, it must be acknowledged that complaints accompanied by pressure were anything but useless activity for the peasants. There are thus grounds to speak of interaction between completely unequal parties. Wrangel had to follow the same policy as the crown, i.e. to recognize the social contract formed by the encumbrances marked in the cadaster for each holding (Kujala 2003, pp. 69–77).

Kumogård manor in Southwestern Finland provides on the other hand an example of the cold-hearted and conflict-oriented economic management pursued by some members of the nobility. In the severe winter of famine and mortality of 1695–1696 Count Axel Julius De la Gardie and Countess Sofia Juliana Forbus blankly refused to listen to or believe their bailiff's report that hardly anything could be expected from the peasants because they were dying of hunger. In an unsigned draft letter to the bailiff written by the count or countess in Stockholm on May 12, 1696, at a time of famine and high mortality which could not have passed unnoticed even in the capital, the bailiff is criticized for not following the agreement drawn up in 1694 between the tenant farmers of Kumogård and the provincial governor requiring the former to supply 100 barrels of grain per annum regardless of crop failure. In closing, the author of the letter sarcastically asks the bailiff whether the crop failure also applied to butter, frieze and slaughter animals, which the peasants were contractually obliged to send to their masters in Sweden.

The relations between Kumogård manor and its peasants were quite strained. But this was at most a question of insubordination; to speak of rebellion and insurgency would be an exaggeration. The conflict was due to the landlords' repeated attempts to raise rent and day-labor obligations in various ways. It was largely the personal choice of the noble landlord whether to seize all benefits that could be obtained from the peasants or whether to avoid problems and keep to the role of the fair landlord. Where relations between the manor and its peasants had become inflamed, the conflicts tended to go on indefinitely and would flare up from time to time, as at Kumogård. The policy of appropriation led to passive resistance among the peasants and was probably no more profitable for the master than compromise would have been.[7]

Day labor became the symbol of noble authority, and especially the peasants who had lost their hereditary rights to their farm were powerless in this respect. On the other hand, the nobles could not do very much about the inability—or unwillingness—of the peasants to pay rent. In times of shortages of labor it was impossible to evict all those who had accumulated arrears. The nobles largely had to accept whatever rent could be obtained from the peasants.[8]

It was characteristic of the political culture of seventeenth-century Sweden that the crown had exceptionally good ability to harness the limited resources of a society that was poor by European standards. Sweden's role as a leading power was based on this, and the weakness of neighboring Denmark, Poland and Russia. The strong position of the crown compensated for the weakness of the Swedish nobility. On the other hand, the ruling elites were unified in the seventeenth century, which prevented any major revolts. The upper and lower estates (nobility, clergy, burghers and peasants) participated on a broad basis in local administration and the activities of the *riksdag*. The representation of the peasants in the *riksdag* was exceptional in comparison with the rest of Europe. For the peasants, the *riksdag* was an opportunity for presenting petitions to the ruler in seeking improvements to shortcomings and grievances (Villstrand 2005, pp. 17–101; Katajala 2002, pp. 283–312).

Approximately 20 years ago research generally underlined the view that the Swedish crown had forcibly acquired the soldiers and tax revenue needed for its war, but recent Nordic studies have shifted focus to the interaction of the crown and its subjects, while not ignoring the earlier perspective of the powerful or militarized state. The perspective of unilateral downward authority has been replaced by mutual interaction (Villstrand 2005, pp. 17–101; 2017; Kujala 2003, pp. 15–33).

Following the example given by Barrington Moore, taxation in Sweden has been considered as a kind of unofficial social contract (Frohnert 1993, pp. 16–17, 282). The division of income between the crown and its subjects was based on a contract of this kind expressed in the fixed annual taxes for each farm as laid down in the cadaster and the obligation of the people to provide the crown with soldiers in accordance with specific ratified agreements. This suited the crown, as it was able to acquire increased resources by obtaining the approval of the people for additional taxes. The principle was that the encumbrances of no estate could be increased without consulting it. In practice, the crown could usually make the *riksdag* follow its will, with persuasion, and where necessary with ruthless coercion. In addition, King Charles XI (reigned 1672–1697) established autocracy toward the end of the seventeenth century, giving the sovereign the right to lay down and amend laws and to decide on extraordinary taxes and military call-ups without consulting the *riksdag*. Nonetheless, the principle of entering in the cadaster the fixed tax contributions of each holding, which was in the interests of the peasants, remained in force.[9]

If a peasant was unable to pay taxes because of age, illness or crop failure, the crown could grant his holding tax exemption or a reduction of taxes for a set period. During the seventeenth century, with its cold climate, a large portion of the peasants were exempted from taxes or accumulated tax arrears for their farms. The system was a major concession from the crown, albeit without alternatives as it was wiser to reduce taxes than to make taxpayers insolvent with inflexible tax collection and thus jeopardize the taxational basis of the crown economy. In practice, the system of tax reductions was anything but optimal. Sometimes it was stated outright in the lists of arrears that unduly high taxes had ruined the farm in question. Aged, blind, disease-ridden peasants and their widows could not manage their farms and tax payments and had to beg for their sustenance as their arrears to the crown continued to grow (Kujala 2003, pp. 115, 143–151).

Although the perspective of interaction is better suited to a description of seventeenth-century Swedish society than approaches underlining coercion, there is no reason to idealize the society of the period or to regard it as a prototype of twentieth-century Nordic democracy and the welfare state. According to taxation instructions issued by the Swedish crown in the 1690s, half of the yield of a farm belonged to the crown in taxes and half to the peasant after deductions for sowing and tithes.[10] Oriental rulers, generally—and mistakenly—regarded as despots by Europeans, usually left a greater proportion of the crop to the farmer. Only Ala-ud-din, the sultan of Delhi (r. 1296–1316), was as merciless in matters of taxation as the Swedish crown of the seventeenth century. For the Mughal ruler Akbar of India (r. 1556–1605), the normal proportion of tax was one third. Japanese peasants of the Edo period paid from 25 to 35% of the yield of the land in taxes.[11]

When appointing Baron Gabriel Bengtsson (Oxenstierna) as governor-general of Finland in 1631, King Gustav II Adolf[12] (Gustavus Adolphus, r. 1611–1632) ordered him to end the country's numerous unnecessary tax commissioner positions, which had been more of a hindrance than a benefit to the crown. The king urged the governor-general to collect tax arrears with due consideration and moderation to prevent the common people from becoming unable to pay taxes and to protect them from ruin. Gustav II Adolf raised his subjects' taxes more than any other Swedish ruler and levied for his foreign wars the maximum number of soldiers, i.e. labor, that the tax-paying agricultural economy could withstand. Nonetheless, he was completely aware of the ruler's obligation to protect his subjects, which was the grounds for his specific right to demand taxes and soldiers from them.

While fighting in Germany with his troops in the war that would ultimately last 30 years (1618–1648), Gustav II Adolf could not rid himself of the thought that his officials and military commanders of the high nobility were misusing their authority while the king was away. In November 1631, he ordered Marshal Herman Wrangel inspecting the Finnish troops, to administer the death penalty to deserters only to a limited extent and not as widely as had been done previously. Deserters who repented their actions and returned to the levy meetings were to be treated leniently. "For we would almost prefer to see that the infantry soldiers would go their own way rather than a completely innocent person would have to suffer from this or the land already beleaguered enough by such (levy) commissions would be ruined even more" (National Archives, Helsinki, Gustav II Adolf's *registratur* [copy], 1631, pp. 347–348 [February 25] and pp. 384–386 [November 2]). This king who burdened the people with taxes and levies of troops probably more than any other Swedish monarch considered ethical and political issues of this kind. This, however, did not alleviate his strict policies to any degree.

If a peasant was unable to pay taxes because of crop failure or risked being taken into military service, it was common for him to react by fleeing and starting a new life in a region where the authorities did not think of looking for him. The slash-and-burn peasants of East Finland practiced cultivation by burn-clearing plots (swiddens) in forests. They were not bound to permanent arable land like the farmers of Sweden and West Finland; all they needed to take with them were their families and cattle. Large numbers of East Finnish peasants fled to Estonia or Kexholm Province and Ingria conquered from Russia in 1617, where troops were not levied. On the other hand, most of the Orthodox population of the conquered areas in the east moved to Russia by 1658 because of economic distress and some degree of religious discrimination. The Orthodox peasants did not rebel before the Swedish-Russian War of 1656–1658 (Kujala 2016, pp. 545–574). Fleeing was an alternative to revolt by which the peasants could try to escape their distressed situation. There were few peasant revolts in India, where the same means were actively pursued (Thapar 2002b, pp. 191, 208, 373, 444). Where unoccupied land was extensively available it was worthwhile for peasants to try to flee their problems by leaving their former localities.

An example of mobility at the lower level of society and the continuous changing of landholding peasants even in the core areas of the Swedish realm is the parish of Ramkvilla in South Sweden, where in the seventeenth and eighteenth centuries and the early nineteenth century, the same peasant would keep his holding for only an average of 12–13 years, i.e. a considerably shorter period than a generation (Perlestam 1998).

RELIEF AID IN FINLAND DURING THE FAMINE OF 1696–1697

Harvests were exceptionally meager in Finland, Northern Sweden and Ingria in 1695 and the following year. Cold weather and rain caused almost total crop failure during two consecutive years and led to a famine and the spread of contagious epidemics. During the great famine of 1696–1697, 22% of Finland's population perished. In Ingria and Kexholm Province, famine and infectious diseases took at least an equally high toll of human life. The famine of 1696–1697 was the worst disaster in the history of Finland in terms of loss of population (Muroma 1991).

Eino Jutikkala, the grand old man of Finnish historical research, regarded the relief measures of the Swedish government as entirely insufficient. Moreover, "the guiding principle of the government was to save the crown from forfeiting a single penny or distributing for free a single bushel of grain to stricken Finland." The grain supplies were sold or loaned against security. When a normal harvest could again be reaped in 1698, "bailiffs were sent to every farm to collect debts for His Majesty" (Jutikkala and Pirinen 1984, pp. 113–114).

The picture conveyed by Jutikkala, however, did not correspond to the actual situation, and it has been rectified in current research. The grain delivered to Finland was indeed not distributed for free, but I (AK) have estimated that the major part of the crown's relief aid was never recovered, or at least not returned to Stockholm. The reason for this was the outbreak of the Great Northern War in 1700. The flow of resources from Finland to Stockholm prevailing in 1698–1699 was again reversed in the opposite direction.

According to the present view, the crown assisted the people to the best of its abilities, but the related logistics and other difficulties proved to be insurmountable. Looking back on the seventeenth century nothing approaching the massive relief efforts of the crown in 1696–1697 can be discerned (Mäntylä 1988; Kujala 2010, pp. 436–447; Lappalainen 2012).

The Swedish crown was guided by principles similar to the *bakufu* in its relief measures. Lutheran charity played a certain role, but if it had been the only criterion, one could have expected aid to have been loaned to all who suffered from hunger. This was, however, not the case. The crown withheld its aid from the peasants subordinated to the nobility. They were to be supported by their masters. In practice, quite a large number of them must have starved to death, because the noblemen did not have the necessary resources or logistics (and often neither the will) to assist their peasants. The crown also refused to help the landless population. Unlike the landholding peasants they did not pay the land rent (tax). The crown paid no attention to their distress. Protecting the basis of the tax revenue in the long run mattered to the crown. By providing relief to the tax-paying peasants, the crown fulfilled its obligations to them (Kujala 2010, pp. 441–442).

Perhaps we should not, however, excuse the Swedish crown this easily. Famines are usually not just about the lack of food but also involve a combination of poor harvests, the high cost of grain, disturbances caused by the markets and insufficient action by the authorities (Davis 2001, pp. 19–21). Jutikkala points out that in the severe famine years of 1696–1697 grain was exported from South Sweden. During the years of poor crops in the 1610s and 1620s, Gustav II Adolf had banned grain exports. At the time, he did not think only of the common people but also of his troops. The regency which was instituted in 1632 because of the minority age of Princess Christina, the heir to the throne, no longer banned the export of grain, and neither did the crown do so in 1696–1697 (Kujala 2010, pp. 246, 317).

The crown's obligations to the people concerned not only emergency relief but also protection against aggression by an enemy from outside. A Russian army of massive numerical superiority invaded Southern Finland in May 1713. When the peasants realized that the king's army in Finland only retreated before the Russians and was not going to protect them, they refused to supply it with food and stopped paying their taxes. Beginning in the summer of 1713, the army had to collect a newly imposed auxiliary advance tax with coercive measures. The moral economy collapsed in the same way as the defense of the realm. Finland remained under severe Russian occupation for eight years (Sweden's period of dominion ended with the Great Northern War of 1700–1721 and Russia became the leading power in Northern Europe). Although the military outcome in 1713 was mainly due to the strength of the invader and not the ending of support from the subjects, it became nonetheless obvious how dangerous neglecting obligations could be for those in authority (Kujala 2001a, pp. 307–318; Kujala 2000, pp. 82–85).

The relationship between the crown, the nobility and their peasants corresponded to the general European pattern of the time. There were very few traits, if any, in Finnish society that could not be found elsewhere in Europe, especially in the north.[13]

POOR RELIEF IN EUROPE AND CHINA

In Early Modern Times many governments maintained granaries from which their subjects could receive relief in times of crop failure. In eighteenth-century Prussia and Russia, the granaries also supplied the armies and maintained balance in the economy. Peer Vries has shown that the role of grain stores in eighteenth-century China in ensuring the subsistence of the population has been exaggerated. In relation to gross national product, English and Dutch investments in poor relief were clearly greater than in China. Unlike in Scotland and France, there were no longer famines in these economically developed countries. In the Protestant countries of Western and Central Europe, towns and cities were responsible for the care of the poor. In the Catholic countries, religious communities and hospitals attended to these tasks. In England, the government passed legislation laying down the forms, duties and taxational basis of care for the indigent at the local level. The costs of the system were paid by the more affluent population. It was common for governments to interfere with market mechanisms and restrain the raising of prices in times of scarcity.

West European and Swedish poor relief cannot be considered solely as reciprocity. It also had the aim of controlling the poor and improving their habits. A distinction was made between the "deserving" ("worthy") and "undeserving" ("unworthy") poor. The former had arrived in their predicament for no reason of their own and needed assistance. Hardened beggars and vagabonds, on the other hand were a threat to morals and social stability alike and had to be disciplined. The English workhouses were a way of moving the poor out of sight and an effort to force them to mend their ways.[14] According to Arthur Young, the English writer on agriculture, "[e]veryone but an idiot knows that the lower class must be kept poor or they will never be industrious." Roy Porter regards eighteenth-century poor relief as fruitless as it addressed only the symptoms and not the root causes of poverty (Porter 1990, pp. 130, 132–133).

NOTES

1. Gurevitj (1979, pp. 74–94 [p. 81]), Gurevich (1972, pp. 195–217), *Norges Gamle Love indtil 1387* (1846, p. 54 [Cap. 129]), Larson (1935, p. 118), Meißner (1935, p. 94), Grønbech (1912, pp. 4–14, 60–88), Vilkuna (1954, pp. 58–61, quote p. 60). Mauss (1954, pp. xiv–1, 47, 59–62) appears to regard the pledge of Germanic contracts as the bridge leading toward modern contractual society. A borrower or buyer would give the opposite party a pledge, security, that would be forfeited along with the borrowed sum or traded article, if the obligation of payment could not be kept. According to Mauss, the pledge evolved from the gift and it originally included archaic properties obliging and restricting the giver and the recipient of the pledge similar to those of the gift.
2. Harrison (2002, pp. 147–153), Skovgaard-Petersen et al. (1978, pp. 391–392), Voionmaa (1912, pp. 15–17, 247–252). King Magnus Ladulås (1275–1290) decreed that the common people must offer travelers hospitality (sustenance) against payment. *Svenska landskapslagar tolkade och förklarade för nutidens svenskar* (1933, pp. 153–155). In Norway, the oldest taxes came about from converting the peasants' *leidang* obligation and the hospitality obligation of the people to the king and aristocracy into taxes (in the latter case also into payments of tax or rent to the royal officials). Gurevitsj (1977, pp. 36–37), Gurevitj (1979, p. 90), Helle (1995, pp. 62–64, 84, 479).
3. Voionmaa (1912, pp. 252–295). Cf. Finley (1978, pp. 66, 96).
4. Nobles had free rein to evict a peasant who lost hereditary rights from his holding but during shortages of labor only those who had neglected their obligations the most could be evicted.
5. Kujala (2003, pp. 39–41). I refer in the following to my own book in English on this topic with sources and research literature given in its notes. For a comparison of taxes and encumbrances imposed by the crown and the nobility on their peasants, see Ågren (1964). A major study on seventeenth-century Swedish society: Nilsson (1990).

6. Military commander of the Thirty Years' War and the wars of Charles X Gustav (1654–1660), privy councillor, governor-general of Pomerania.
7. Kujala (2003, pp. 85–94, 113). James S. Scott's study (1985) of domination and forms of everyday resistance applies well to the social relations of noble properties of the seventeenth century in the Nordic countries. There were also occasional peasant revolts and serious incidents of unrest in the Nordic countries. See *Northern Revolts* (2004).
8. Kujala (2003, pp. 78–85 [County of Björneborg], 112). Other examples of the social relation of the noble properties of the seventeenth century: pp. 94–114; Katajala (2004, pp. 167–181). Also the Russian nobility often had to accept the rent that the peasants agreed and managed to pay, with part of the payments remaining in arrears. Moon (1999, pp. 76–77, 94).
9. Kujala (2001a, pp. 86, 134, 335–343), Kujala (2001b, pp. 78–89). On the emergence of Absolutism in Sweden, see Upton (1998).
10. Kujala (2003, p. 38). The real proportion of taxes decreased in years of good harvests, but in years of crop failure, which were highly numerous during the cold seventeenth century, farm yields were not sufficient for taxes and basic subsistence. Tax arrears would then accumulate.
11. Kulke and Rothermund (2006, p. 223), Thapar (2002a, p. 66), Chandra (1982, p. 459), Totman (2010, p. 228), White (1995, p. 76). See however *Histoire de l'Inde moderne (1480–1950)* (1994, p. 355) (extremely high taxation in some areas of India in the eighteenth century due to the wars that weakened Mughal rule in which Europeans were also involved).
12. Biographies of Gustav II Adolf: Ahnlund (1940), Roberts (1992), Oredsson (2007).
13. It should be mentioned that from the eighteenth century onwards more homicides per 100,000 people were committed in Finland than in the western half of the Swedish Kingdom, i.e. present-day Sweden. A relatively high incidence of violence linked Finland to Eastern Europe. This pattern has persisted to the present day. See Ylikangas (1999, p. 168).
14. Vries (2015, pp. 190–204, 421–426), Wong (2000, pp. 24–27, 97–99, 113–120, 134, 209–227) (China), Clark (2007, pp. 92–93) (Prussia), Moon (1999, pp. 94–95) (Russia), Porter (1990, pp. 127–133) (England), Jütte (2001, pp. 100–142) (the organization of poor relief in Europe), Alaja (2013), Pulma (1985), Teerijoki (1993) (Sweden and Finland).

REFERENCES

Ågren, Knut. 1964. *Adelns bönder och kronans: Skatter och besvär i Uppland 1650–1680.* Studia Historica Upsalensia 11. Stockholm: Svenska bokförlaget/ Norstedts.

Ahnlund, Nils. 1940. *Gustav Adolf the Great*, trans. Michael Roberts. Princeton: Princeton University Press.

Alaja, Paavo. 2013. *Suomen maalaisseurakuntien köyhäinhoito luterilaisen ortodoksian aikana (1571–1686).* Suomen kirkkohistoriallisen seuran toimituksia 225. Helsinki: Suomen kirkkohistoriallinen seura.

Andersson, Sven. 1953. Primitiv byteshandel på forna fisklägen. *Budkavlen* 32: 1–96.

Bloch, Marc. 1961. *Feudal Society*, trans. L.A. Manyon, Vols. 1–2. Chicago: The University of Chicago Press.

Brunner, Otto. 1990. *Land und Herrschaft: Grundfragen der territorialen Verfassungsgeschichte Österreichs im Mittelalter.* Darmstadt: Wissenschaftliche Buchgesellschaft.

Chandra, Satish. 1982. Standard of Living: Mughal India. In *The Cambridge Economic History of India: C. 1200–c. 1750*, ed. Tapan Raychaudhuri and Irfan Habib, Vol. 1, 458–471. Cambridge: Cambridge University Press.

Clark, Christopher. 2007. *Iron Kingdom: The Rise and Downfall of Prussia, 1600–1947.* London: Penguin.

Davis, Mike. 2001. *Late Victorian Holocausts: El Niño Famines and the Making of the Third World.* London and New York: Verso.

Duby, Georges. 1982. *The Three Orders: Feudal Society Imagined*, trans. Arthur Goldhammer. Chicago and London: The University of Chicago Press.

Duby, Georges. 1992. *The Early Growth of the European Economy: Warriors and Peasants from the Seventh to the Twelfth Century*, trans. Howard B. Clarke. Ithaca: Cornell University Press.

Englund, Peter. 1989. *Det hotade huset: Adliga föreställningar om samhället under stormaktstiden.* Stockholm: Atlantis.

Finley, M.I. 1978. *The World of Odysseus.* New York: The Viking Press.

Frohnert, Pär. 1993. *Kronans skatter och bondens bröd: Den lokala förvaltningen och bönderna i Sverige 1719–1775.* Rättshistoriskt bibliotek XLVIII. Lund: Institutet för rättshistorisk forskning.

Grønbech, Vilh. 1912. *Vor folkeæt i oldtiden: Hellighed og helligdom*, Vol. III. Copenhagen: V. Pios boghandel.

Gurevich, A. Ia. 1972. *Kategorii srednevekovoi kul'tury.* Moscow: Iskusstvo.

Gurevich, Aaron. 1995. *The Origins of European Individualism*, trans. Katharine Judelson. Oxford and Cambridge, MA: Blackwell.

Gurevitj, Aron J. 1979. *Feodalismens uppkomst i Västeuropa*, trans. Marie-Anne Sahlin. Stockholm: Tidens förlag.

Gurevitsj, A. Ja. 1977. De frie bønder i det føydale Norge. In *Frihet og føydalisme: Fra sovjetisk forskning i norsk middelalderhistorie*, ed. Steinar Supphellen, 15–144. Oslo: Universitetsforlaget.

Haavio, Martti. 1967. *Suomalainen mytologia*. Porvoo and Helsinki: WSOY.

Harrison, Dick. 2002. *Jarlens sekel: En berättelse om 1200-talets Sverige*. Stockholm: Ordfront.

Helle, Knut. 1995. Down to 1536. In *Norway: A History from the Vikings to Our Own Times*, ed. Rolf Danielsen, Ståle Dyrvik, Tore Grønlie, Knut Helle, and Edgar Hovland, trans. Michael Drake, 1–119. Oslo: Scandinavian University Press.

Holmbäck, Åke, and Elias Wessén (eds.). 1933. *Svenska landskapslagar tolkade och förklarade för nutidens svenskar* (Första serien). *Östgöta- och Upplandslagen*. Stockholm: Hugo Gebers förlag.

Jutikkala, Eino with Kauko Pirinen. 1984. *A History of Finland*, trans. Paul Sjöblom. Espoo: Weilin + Göös.

Jütte, Robert. 2001. *Poverty and Deviance in Early Modern Europe*. Cambridge: Cambridge University Press.

Katajala, Kimmo. 2002. *Suomalainen kapina: Talonpoikaislevottomuudet ja poliittisen kulttuurin muutos Suomessa Ruotsin ajalla n. 1150–1800*. Historiallisia Tutkimuksia 212. Helsinki: SKS.

Katajala, Kimmo. 2004. The Changing Face of Peasant Unrest in Early Modern Finland. In *Northern Revolts: Medieval and Early Modern Peasant Unrest in the Nordic Countries*, ed. Kimmo Katajala. Studia Fennica Historica 8. Helsinki: Finnish Literature Society, 149–187.

Keyser, R., and P. A. Munch (eds.). 1846. *Norges Gamle Love indtil 1387* (Bind 1). *Norges Love ældre end Kong Magnus Haakonssöns Regjerings-Tiltrædelse i 1263*. Christiania: Chr. Gröndahl.

Korhonen, Arvi. 1923. *Vakkalaitos: Yhteiskuntahistoriallinen tutkimus*. Historiallisia Tutkimuksia 6. Helsinki: SHS.

Kujala, Antti. 2000. The Breakdown of a Society: Finland in the Great Northern War. *Scandinavian Journal of History* 25 (1–2): 69–86.

Kujala, Antti. 2001a. *Miekka ei laske leikkiä: Suomi suuressa pohjan sodassa 1700–1714*. Historiallisia Tutkimuksia 211. Helsinki: SKS.

Kujala, Antti. 2001b. Why Did Finland's War Economy Collapse During the Great Northern War? *Scandinavian Economic History Review* 49 (2): 78–89.

Kujala, Antti. 2003. *The Crown, the Nobility and the Peasants 1630–1713: Tax, Rent and Relations of Power*, trans. Jüri Kokkonen. Studia Historica 69. Helsinki: Finnish Literature Society.

Kujala, Antti. 2010. Viipurin Karjala, Käkisalmen lääni ja Inkerinmaa Ruotsin suurvaltakaudella 1617–1710. In *Viipurin läänin historia, Suomenlahdelta Laatokalle*, Vol. III, 239–461. Lappeenranta: Karjalan kirjapaino.

Kujala, Antti. 2016. Sweden's Russian Lands, Ingria and Kexholm Province, 1617–ca. 1670: The Interaction of the Crown with Its New Subjects. *Jahrbücher für Geschichte Osteuropas* 64 (4): 545–574.

Kulke, Hermann, and Dietmar Rothermund. 2006. *Geschichte Indiens: Von der Induskultur bis heute.* Munich: Verlag C. H. Beck.

Kuujo, Erkki. 1959. *Taka-Karjalan verotus v:een 1710.* Historiallisia Tutkimuksia 52. Helsinki: SHS.

Lappalainen, Mirkka. 2012. *Jumalan vihan ruoska: Suuri nälänhätä Suomessa 1695–1697.* Helsinki: Siltala.

Larson, Laurence Marcellus. 1935. *The Earliest Norwegian Laws: Being the Gulathing Law and the Frostathing Law.* New York: Columbia University Press.

Mäntylä, Ilkka. 1988. *Kruunu ja alamaisten hätä: 1690-luvun katovuosien verotulojen vähennys Pohjanmaalla ja esivallan vastatoimenpiteet.* Acta Societatis Historicae Ouluensis XIII. Oulu: Societas Historica Ouluensis.

Markovits, Claude (ed.). 1994. *Histoire de l'Inde moderne (1480–1950).* Paris: Fayard.

Mauss, Marcel. 1954. *The Gift: Forms and Functions of Exchange in Archaic Societies,* trans. Ian Cunnison. Glencoe: The Free Press.

Meißner, Rudolf. 1935. *Norwegisches Recht: Das Rechtsbuch des Gulathings,* trans. Rudolf Meißner. Germanenrechte. Texte und Übersetzungen Bd. 6. Weimar: Verlag Herm. Böhlaus Nachf.

Moon, David. 1999. *The Russian Peasantry 1600–1930: The World the Peasants Made.* London and New York: Longman.

Muroma, Seppo. 1991. *Suurten kuolovuosien (1696–1697) väestönmenetys Suomessa.* Historiallisia Tutkimuksia 161. Helsinki: SHS.

National Archives (Kansallisarkisto). 1631. Helsinki, Gustav II Adolf's registratur (copy).

Nilsson, Sven A. 1990. *De stora krigens tid: Om Sverige som militärstat och bondesamhälle.* Studia Historica Upsalensia 161. Stockholm: Almqvist & Wiksell International.

Oredsson, Sverker. 2007. *Gustav II Adolf.* Stockholm: Atlantis.

Peltonen, Matti. 1988. *Viinapäästä kolerakauhuun: Kirjoituksia sosiaalihistoriasta.* Helsinki: Hanki ja jää.

Perlestam, Magnus. 1998. *Den rotfaste bonden—myt eller verklighet: Brukaransvar i Ramkvilla socken 1620–1820.* Malmö: Team Offset & Media.

Porter, Roy. 1990. *English Society in the Eighteenth Century.* London: Penguin.

Pulma, Panu. 1985. *Fattigvård i frihetstidens Finland: En undersökning om förhållandet mellan centralmakt och lokalsamhälle,* trans. Jan-Ivar Lindén. Historiallisia Tutkimuksia 129. Helsinki: SHS.

Raussi, Eljas. 1966. *Virolahden kansanelämää 1840-luvulla.* Suomalaisen Kirjallisuuden Seuran Toimituksia 280. Helsinki: SKS.

Reinholdsson, Peter. 1998. *Uppror eller resningar?: Samhällsorganisation och konflikt i senmedeltidens Sverige.* Studia Historica Upsalensia 186. Uppsala: Uppsala universitet.

Roberts, Michael. 1992. *Gustavus Adolphus.* London and New York: Longman.

Sahlins, Marshall. 2004. *Stone Age Economics.* London and New York: Routledge.

Scott, James C. 1985. *Weapons of the Weak: Everyday Forms of Peasant Resistance.* New Haven and London: Yale University Press.

Skovgaard-Petersen, Inge, Aksel E. Christensen, and Helge Paludan. 1978. *Danmarks historie, Tiden indtil 1340,* Vol. I. Copenhagen: Gyldendal.

Teerijoki, Ilkka. 1993. *Nälkävuosien turva?: Pitäjänmakasiinit Suomessa 1700-luvulla.* Historiallisia Tutkimuksia 175. Helsinki: SHS.

Thapar, Romila. 2002a. *Aśoka and the Decline of the Mauryas.* New Delhi: Oxford University Press.

Thapar, Romila. 2002b. *Early India from the Origins to AD 1300.* London: Allen Lane/Penguin.

Totman, Conrad. 2010. *A History of Japan.* Malden: Blackwell.

Upton, Anthony F. 1998. *Charles XI and Swedish Absolutism.* Cambridge: Cambridge University Press.

Vilkuna, Kustaa. 1954. Olut muinaissuomalaisessa yhteiskunnassa. *Alkoholipolitiikka* 19 (2): 57–61.

Vilkuna, Kustaa. 1964. Suikiminen ja saaliin vaihtokauppa. *Kalevalaseuran vuosikirja,* vol. 44, 117–149. WSOY: Porvoo and Helsinki.

Villstrand, Nils Erik. 2005. Stormaktstidens politiska kultur. In *Stormaktstiden, Signums svenska kulturhistoria,* ed. Jakob Christernsson, 17–101. Lund: Bokförlaget Signum.

Villstrand, Nils Erik. 2017. Monolog eller dialog?: Den tidigmoderna svenska staten i möte med sina undersåtar. *Historisk Tidskrift för Finland* 102 (3): 458–479.

Voionmaa, Väinö. 1912. *Suomalaisia keskiajan tutkimuksia: Veroja, laitoksia, virkamiehiä.* Porvoo: WSOY.

Vries, Peer. 2015. *State, Economy and the Great Divergence: Great Britain and China, 1680s–1850s.* London: Bloomsbury.

White, James W. 1995. *Ikki: Social Conflict and Political Protest in Early Modern Japan.* Ithaca and London: Cornell University Press.

Wong, R. Bin. 2000. *China Transformed: Historical Change and the Limits of European Experience.* Ithaca and London: Cornell University Press.

Ylikangas, Heikki. 1999. Reasons for the Reduction of Violence in Finland in the 17th Century. In *Crime and Control in Europe from the Past to the Present,* ed. Mirkka Lappalainen and Pekka Hirvonen, 165–173. Helsinki: Hakapaino.

CHAPTER 6

Reciprocity in the French Army in the First World War and in the Finnish Army in 1941–1944

Armies are among the most hierarchical of human communities. The authority of officers and NCOs over their subordinates is, at least apparently, absolute. But not all subordinates accept it, as in the case of the Finnish man quoted below, who was sentenced in 1941 for desertion from the front, refusing to follow the orders of a superior officer, and complaining openly about the hardships of military service: "The Finnish army is the lousiest fucking institution in the whole world. I'd rather be in prison than here."[1]

Throughout history, soldiers in the lower ranks of armies have resorted to forms of everyday clandestine opposition when trying to stay alive in the field of battle. They usually do not rebel openly against authority, but will instead drag their feet, feign ignorance, run off, pretend to obey and mock their superiors behind their backs. Masked everyday resistance does not require organized cooperation. It will avoid direct conflict with authority and often disguise itself as acts that are trivial or seemingly only for purposes of individual gain. But even this opposition challenges the hegemony of authority and can therefore even seriously undermine it (Scott 1985, pp. XV–XVI, 29, 30, 36, 289–350). While "the weapons of the weak" and their use serve the universal human aim of survival, they also reflect a sense of reciprocity deeply ingrained in human nature.

There has almost always been everyday resistance among soldiers in armies (Scott 1985, *passim*), but it was not until the conscript armies created through the evolution of nation-states that its potential risks

© The Author(s) 2019
A. Kujala and M. Danielsbacka, *Reciprocity in Human Societies*,
https://doi.org/10.1007/978-3-319-96056-2_6

increased. During the nineteenth century, most European countries adopted conscription based on the civil rights and civic duty (Keegan 1993, pp. 221–234; Overmans 2005). Conscription as the basis of recruiting soldiers changed the character of armies as it linked the obligation of participating in national defense with civil rights (Mälkki 2008, pp. 12–15, 21, 51–127). Conscription based on the civic duty, in turn, created a new kind of "citizen-soldier" who could expect, because of his civil rights, reciprocity from both his superiors in the army and his own country. Armies of conscripts were thus a double-edged sword for the government. While increasing the military potential of states, they also made all men soldiers, thus exposing authority to the power of the masses and expectations of reciprocity and justice.[2]

These expectations became evident during the major wars of the twentieth century when soldiers of democracies such as France and Finland created their own systems of norms that applied alongside the official hierarchies of army command. Soldiers expected the war to be waged in a way that, in principle, would make survival possible despite the risks involved. They were not ready for sacrifices required by the aims of war and orders that they found to be senseless. Soldiers did not accept the disproportionate use of troops in the front line without protest. They also expected officers to keep their promises of providing rest. While armies did not recognize the soldiers' own unofficial system of norms, officers had to adapt their actions to provoke the least amount of difficulties when carrying out their duties of leading troops.

THE REVOLT OF FRENCH CITIZEN-SOLDIERS IN THE FIRST WORLD WAR

The bloody reality of the First World War (1914–1918) and the destructive power of new weapons were a shock for Europeans who had enjoyed a long period of peace. The military enthusiasm of 1914 soon gave way to the misery of life at the front and offensives that proved to be pointless and did not change the front but instead caused greater losses. On the Western Front between Germany and the Western Allies, in particular, the war remained at a standstill in the trenches for several years. The conditions led to an extreme strain on the physical and mental endurance of the troops. By early 1917, after two and a half years of war, almost a million soldiers had been killed in France (Ferguson 1999, pp. 174–211,

339–366; Smith et al. 2003, pp. 68–75, 77, 86, 89–90, 96). By the spring of 1917, the soldiers of the French army were fed up with the hopeless situation.

The events in question began with the Chemin des Dames offensive. In late 1916, General Robert Nivelle replaced Joseph Joffre as the commander-in-chief of the French army. Nivelle planned the major offense against Chemin des Dames (the Second Battle of the Aisne), which was meant to crush all German defense of the Western Front with only minor losses on one's own side. British troops took part in the operation with the task of supporting the French by carrying out an attack further north at Arras. Nivelle promised his troops that the German front would be completely overwhelmed in 48 hours. His predecessor Joffre had been severely criticized for conducting trench warfare where breakthroughs had proven to be impossible, resulting only in the senseless slaughter of troops. Nivelle duly promised to interrupt the offensive if the German lines could not be broken. The French offensive began on April 16, 1917, but as had been the case many times earlier, advancing further became immediately impossible. Nivelle was removed his post a month later (May 15), and General Philippe Pétain was now appointed commander-in-chief.

Even the change of command did not help, for the whole French army had fallen into a deep "crisis of discipline" in May–June 1917 (Loez 2010, pp. 540–541). Desertion had increased at a regular pace since the end of April among the troops that took part in the Chemin des Dames offensive. By the end of May, it had turned into widespread mutinying. Soldiers left the front in large numbers and withdrew further away to the rear.

There were mutinies in approximately half of all the divisions in the French army. This mostly concerned infantry troops, who had suffered the most from the slaughterous trench warfare. Between 25,000 and 35,000 French soldiers are estimated to have mutinied, not a very large proportion of an army of over eight million soldiers. Nonetheless, the officers regarded protests that had spread into so many divisions as dangerous. At the very least, the war would not be won with troops that refused to attack. The number of soldiers taking part in actual protests can be regarded as only the tip of the iceberg, since protesters would efficiently incapacitate the operations of their whole unit. As pointed out by Leonard V. Smith, Stéphane Audoin-Rouzeau and Annette Becker (2003, pp. 96, 122–123), the mutinies were a crisis for the whole French army. Rebellion was expressed in most cases by units that had been sent to rest by their simple refusal to return to the front. The military leadership tried to placate the soldiers by promising them leave, rest and better provisioning. In addition, Nivelle's ill-fated attempt at an offensive was halted.

Protests among the troops and the attempts of officers to resolve the situation took a course in which commanding officers still dismissed 26 incidents of mutiny during the first months after the Chemin des Dames offensive as mainly troublesome and did not consider them to be any direct threat to the command structure. The initial mutinies involved a relatively small number of troops and they were concentrated only in combat units. In May, rebellion spread to comprise some 46 incidents, now including whole divisions, not all of which had even participated in the Chemin des Dames offensive. Representatives of the mutinying regiments conferred with each other at meetings resembling the soldiers' soviets or councils of revolutionary Russia. The mutinying troops began to speak openly of ending the war by marching on Paris. In early June, there was the risk of the mutinies taking a violent turn in some of the military units. At the end of the month, commanding officers finally began to regain control, but despite this, isolated collective protests continued to break out until January 1918. Since it would have been impossible to punish all the soldiers who mutinied, the military leadership sought to bring the "leading figures" to justice by letting officers choose the worst "ringleaders" from their units. Death sentences were given to over 600 soldiers in mass courts-martial, but only around one-tenth of the sentences were carried out. Almost 3,000 soldiers were sentenced to forced labor. Some of the officers, especially NCOs, were sympathetic to the mutinying soldiers and tried to restore order verbally (Smith 1994, pp. 181–182, 199–206; see also Bach 2013; Pedroncini 1967).

In terms of its timeline, the revolt in the French army can be regarded as a more traditional case of unrest due to combat fatigue than the protests of Finnish soldiers during the Second World War. In France, collective insubordination did not begin until the war had lasted several years, while the Finnish army suffered from the collective protests of its soldiers in the early stage of the Finnish-Soviet Continuation War of 1941–1944. The French soldiers, however, did not protest against miserable conditions or the hard fighting during the first years of the war, although conditions were at least as bad and losses even greater than in 1917. The soldiers were not properly "politicized" until they felt that their commanders had betrayed them in them in the spring of 1917 by having promised them a different kind of warfare and rest (Smith 1994, p. 117). Prior to this, in 1914–1917, approximately 15,000–16,000 French soldiers per year had been recorded as absent without leave, and even of them the majority had, at the most, returned late from leave. In other words, before the events of spring 1917, the troops had followed their duty and stayed at the front despite the horrific conditions.

On the Eastern Front, Russian soldiers had been deserting from the Tsar's army in large numbers throughout the war, but it was not until the end of 1917, the year of revolution, that desertion grew to hundreds of thousands—even millions—and the Russian army was in a state of disintegration. In the summer of 1917, there were also minor mutinies in units of the German army on the Western Front. The working-class soldiers of the British army resorted to strikes and protests following the pattern of peacetime civilian life, including collective demands for improved accommodation and higher pay, but there were no major mutinies or large-scale incidents of desertion (Ferguson 1999, pp. 344–346; Smith et al. 2003, p. 100). As war historian Niall Ferguson (1999, p. 343) points out: "Given the awfulness of the conditions soldiers had to endure, the most surprising thing of all about the war, perhaps, is that military discipline did not break down much more often, or earlier, than it did [until in 1917]."

Researchers have suggested various reasons for mutinying in the French army. On the home front in France, pacifists calling for an end to the war had become increasingly vociferous in 1917, and soldiers at the front also demanded peace. Some researchers have therefore regarded mutiny as political and revolutionary activity in the traditional sense, with the aim of ending the war. In addition, knowledge of the February Revolution of 1917 in Russia, an ally of France, and the chaotic state of the Russian army also influenced the behavior of French troops. There was not, however, any direct contact between the revolutionary pacifists of the home front in France and the mutinying soldiers.

The mutinies of the French troops have also been interpreted as protests against the destructive conduct of the war. The soldiers were fed up with the endless waste of human life in attempted attacks that were carried out incompetently. Collective insubordination was ultimately based on the requirement of being able to wage war so that, in principle, survival could be possible rather than on any demands to end the whole war (Loez 2010, p. 545). The "crisis of discipline" in the French army no doubt concerned both aims. The troops were tired of both the war and its methods and wanted to have their voices heard. In civilian life in their democratic country, they had become accustomed to a political and trade-union tradition of mass demonstrations and action.

In France, conscription already had old traditions from before the First World War, dating from the revolution of 1789, and it was expanded even further before the war. The obligation to take up arms for the republic, however, was an expression of French citizenship rather than its consequence already before the First World War. For young men, national service was a rite of beginning manhood along with making them full-fledged citizens (Smith et al. 2003, pp. 18–19). In the United States, for example, the post-Civil War veterans' pension was awarded to those who had proven their loyalty to the Union. In France, citizenship was defined as "l'impôt du sang – the blood tax of military service" (Mann 2012, p. 501). Emphasis on civil rights was part of French culture. The French had been educated in schools of a republican spirit that they are born as citizens with rights for which they were in no debt to anyone (Smith 1991). It was thus no wonder that they included the notion of the rights of citizenship as part of the identity of the citizen-soldier.[3] There was thus a basis in mentality for collective rebellion.

The mutinies of French troops have also been interpreted as manifestations of "direct democracy," to which the French have often resorted after the revolution of 1789. Direct democracy meant that citizens could take matters into their own hands and express their collective demands in public, as was done by French soldiers in the spring of 1917. The mutinying soldiers also called for an end to the war, but not at any price (Smith 1994, pp. 189, 195). They did not want to France lose the war. A soldier who had participated in the mutinies wrote home: "We refused to march not to bring about a revolution, rather to attract the attention of the government in making them understand that we are men, and not beasts to be led to the *abattoir* to be slaughtered, that we want is what is due to us and that we demand peace" (Smith et al. 2003, pp. 125–126). The same soldier, however, also mentioned in his letter that the troops would finally agree to attack again, for otherwise France would be forced to agree to shameful terms of peace that would only lead to more misery (Smith et al. 2003, pp. 125–131).

The revolts were very similar to workers' strikes in civilian life, which also shows how much they were associated with civil rights and the exercise of these rights. Contemporaries even referred to the mutinying soldiers as "being on strike." The soldiers also expressed their demands directly to members of the French parliament, indicating that they were thus acting not only as soldiers but also as citizens. The Russian soldiers rebelling in 1917 wanted to overthrow the whole tsarist regime and subsequently the Provisional Government for not bringing the war to an end. The insubordinate French soldiers, on the other hand, considered themselves to be part of the nation-state. The European socialist revolution sought by Lenin, with the aim of changing the social order of states, did not find any broad support among the French either at the front or on the home front. As citizens of the republic, French soldiers felt they were serving only themselves and their compatriots. The soldiers of imperial Russia, on the other hand, had little identity as citizens in national or political terms. It was partly for this reason that Aleksandr Kerensky's attempt to turn Russian soldiers into the citizen-soldiers of a revolutionary Russia failed completely. It was only the Bolsheviks who understood that Russian soldiers of peasant birth wanted above all land and peace and took declared this to be their main political demands (Smith 1994, pp. 184, 193–195, 247–258).

THE FINNISH CITIZEN-SOLDIERS OF THE CONTINUATION WAR OF 1941–1944

This is truly frustrating. Our company has been in the front line for days on end, but the ones higher up still call for more. I am annoyed, really annoyed! I'm starting to lose my fighting spirit. So far, I've still been active, even quite foolhardy, but before long I'll stop and quit. There has been no news about leave at least here, and if we don't soon get any, there won't be many to send on leave. Even my platoon, despite reinforcements, is quite small. This unit of ours is needed almost everywhere, or so it seems.[4]

The above is an excerpt from a letter home sent by a soldier of Infantry Regiment (IR) 60 in the late fall of 1941. It reflects well the frustration felt by men who set out on a brief summer war as the offensive with its continuous losses continued into a gloomy fall and an early winter in the wilderness of East Karelia, a region that had never been part of Finland. The writer's negative mood may have been only an isolated complaint, but it is also possible that he was one of the thousands of soldiers in the Finnish army who decided to desert from the front.

Finland was involved in the Second World War through the Finnish-Soviet Winter War of 1939–1940, the Continuation War of 1941–1944 against the Soviet Union, and finally the brief Lapland War of 1944–1945, which was fought against the Germans. In the Continuation War, Finland in fact entered the war as an ally of Germany within the Axis camp. The Continuation War was in many ways different from the preceding Winter War, in which Finland defended herself alone against an overpowering aggressor, which at the time had a nonaggression pact with Nazi Germany. In the Continuation War, Finland was an ally of Germany and an active invading party (Jokipii 1987, pp. 603–628; Jokisipilä 2004, p. 32; see also Kujala 2009; Vehviläinen 2002).

The Finnish government presented the Continuation War as a defensive or retributive war for the purpose regaining the areas ceded to the Soviet Union in the Winter War, and the majority of Finns regarded it to be justified in this sense (Manninen 1980, p. 312). There was obvious enthusiasm for the war both among troops at the front and on the home front. Compared with the Winter War, however, the legitimacy of the Continuation War was weaker among citizens from its very beginning (Salminen 1976, pp. 63–66). There were hardly any deserters when the Winter War broke out, and very few during it. As many as 1,500 men, however, chose to go into hiding when the Continuation War began and a few hundred refused to leave for the front. Mobilization was mostly avoided for political reasons. There were desertions predominantly in localities where the far-left Society for Peace and Friendship between Finland and the Soviet Union, a banned Communist organization during the Continuation War, was strongest (Kulomaa 1995, pp. 42–49, 95–119, 363; Muttilainen 1984, pp. 25–31, 37–39; Rentola 1994, pp. 340–348).

In the so-called offensive stage of the Continuation War in the summer and fall of 1941, the Finnish army first advanced quickly to the pre-1940 Finnish-Soviet border and a long distance past it in the regions north of Lake Ladoga. At the same time, troops at the front began to display causes of concern for commanding officers. Some of the soldiers did not want to cross the old border, and the further the army advanced into the wilderness of East Karelia, the more there were instances of individuals refusing to serve, extensive strikes halting combat and desertion.

Military historian Harri Heinilä (1997, pp. 86–87, 91–98, 100, 108, 122–124; Heinilä 2006) who has studied cases of insubordination at the former Finnish-Soviet border came to the conclusion that there were negative attitudes of various kinds to crossing the old border in at least 22 regiments out of 45. This phenomenon included a large number of troops although ultimately there were fewer than 2,000 soldiers who actually refused to cross the border. Negative attitudes were expressed in the form of mass insubordination, written petitions and at their mildest as talk of a negative tone. The largest number of actual refusals, i.e. soldiers stating that they would not continue across the old border were among the soldiers and NCOs of reservist regiments on the Karelian Isthmus, where the old Finnish-Soviet border was crossed in August–September 1941, approximately a month later than by the troops that proceeded to East or Soviet Karelia. The Finnish troops on the Karelian Isthmus, however, did not attack Leningrad and instead participated passively in the blockade of the city—the conquest of Leningrad was gladly left to the Germans. The soldiers who refused to cross the old border consisted mostly of smallholders and workers and surprisingly included members of the Civil Guards. The Civil Guards were a volunteer nonsocialist national organization in Finland that operated from 1918 until 1944. Its members could be assumed to have had a positive attitude to the national defense. In many cases, soldiers who refused to continue past the border cited their military oath as requiring them to defend only Finnish territory. Others argued for their refusal by claiming that they had understood that the fighting would end at the border, having been promised this by their officers. Some referred to the heavy losses suffered by their units. The majority of the soldiers who had initially refused ultimately agreed to continue across the border. In most cases, the situation was resolved by officers addressing the soldiers and only a small number of cases went as far as court-martial. The court-martial cases indicate that men refusing to cross the old border were typically from East or Central Finland, smallholders or workers and aged between 30 and 39.

There were also incidents of refusing to continue after crossing the old border particularly in units advancing into East Karelia. These incidents concentrated in the years 1941 and 1942, occurring mainly in the offensive stage in 1941. Most of them were of a collective nature. Since these situations were usually resolved by officers directly addressing the troops, only a fraction of these crimes of insubordination ever led to a court-martial (Muttilainen 1984, pp. 58–65, 67–68, 80). Most likely, higher officers, not to mention military headquarters, were never informed of the majority of the minor infractions. The backgrounds of the soldiers who refused to continue in East Karelia were similar to those who refused at the old border: reservists who were older than conscripts, workers in civilian life and originating from the rural areas of Central and Western Finland.

Along with incidents of insubordination, at least 31,000–35,000 men eluded service in the Continuation War in various ways (Kulomaa 1995, pp. 25, 44, 363). The number of men avoiding service was only around 5% of all 650,000 men in military service. Over half of them were classifiable as deserters, i.e. having deserted as defined in the Military Penal Code (SRL 76 §) or were guilty of cowardice (SRL 70, 71 §). The remainder were men who had avoided mobilization, and cases of absent without leave or not returning in time to their units from leave. The most serious incidents of avoiding service, i.e. acts sentenced as desertion or cowardice, accumulated during the offensive stage of the Continuation War in 1941 and the defensive combat stage in the summer of 1944.

As there was hardly any instances of insubordination or desertion during the Winter War, the military leadership and commanding officers were not prepared for them in the ensuing war, at least to such extent. Responses to the now surprising problems in the army were the possibility to postpone indictments for deserters and the founding of a special disciplinary or penal battalion. The military command argued for both measures with practical military concerns, i.e. keeping as many men as possible at the front. Changes to punitive measures aimed at controlling desertion. It was not attempted to end evasion of service with force alone, and there were instead negotiations with men avoiding military service (Kulomaa 1995, pp. 177–182; Danielsbacka 2007, pp. 59–60).

The postponement procedure meant that a deserter who had been caught was given the opportunity to return to his unit without further sanctions. He could also choose a court-martial and be sentenced to a penitentiary or prison. There was also a penal battalion known as the Pärmi Battalion after its commander Lieutenant-Colonel Nikke Pärmi, an original figure. It consisted of convicted servicemen who were sent to the front, and even that was voluntary for ordinary convicted soldiers. On the other hand, political prisoners who had been imprisoned for opposing the war were sent forcibly to the front. When the Continuation War broke out, the transfer of pro-Soviet left-wing extremists to the front failed badly, as a large number of them escaped while in transit to the Pärmi Battalion or defected to the Soviet side when they were near the front line.

Both penal battalions and indictment postponements of various kinds were also used by other armies in twentieth-century wars. During the Second World War, the Germans and the Soviets punished soldiers convicted of military crimes by sending them to the most dangerous places on the front, and a similar policy was followed in the French army during First World War. In these armies, service in penal military units was not a matter of choice. In addition, both Germany and the Soviet Union had even stricter measures to stop desertion. The Red Army had special units that would shoot soldiers leaving the front line. The choice was between possible death coming from in front of the soldier, or certain death from behind. The German army, in turn, executed between 15,000 and 20,000 of its own soldiers on suspicion of desertion, the majority of them in the final stages of the war on the Eastern Front where the Germans were overrun by the Soviet army (Bellamy 2007, pp. 203, 260, 271; Ferguson 2004; Nuorteva 1987, p. 133; Smith 1991, pp. 64–65).

The Finnish Military Penal Code also allowed the death sentence for crimes of insubordination. In 1941, seven men were sentenced to death for refusing an order from a superior officer, but only two of them were ultimately executed. By the final stage of the Continuation War and the panicked retreat caused by the overwhelming Soviet offensive, amendments to legislation had made it easier to pass the death sentence. During the summer of 1944, 76 Finnish soldiers were sentenced to death for cowardice or desertion and 46 of them were shot. In addition, one man was sentenced to death and shot for a crime of insubordination in 1944. During the summer of 1944, a total of 12 deserters or soldiers refusing to fight were shot by officers on the basis of a superior officer's right to use firearms against his own troops in combat or in other compelling situations. This particular figure and the number of soldiers shot by the Finnish army in general in the summer of 1944 have been disputed, and much larger figures have been suggested, although conclusive evidence can be found only concerning the twelve cases mentioned above (Lindstedt 1999, pp. 196–203, 560–561; Ylikangas 2007).

An estimated 100,000 soldiers deserted from the British army during the Second World War, roughly 1.7% of all 5,896,000 mobilized troops. None were executed. British commanding officers followed the policy that every man has his breaking point and that anyone could suffer from shell shock and nervous collapse. This was largely due to the experiences of the First World War. Attitudes to deserters and "cowards" during the Second World War were more understanding than in the First World War.

British deserters from the front were classed, in theory, into three categories. The first category was mentally unstable who would not have withstood war conditions and should not have been recruited to the front in the first place. In practice, however, many of these cases slipped through the military assessment system, as the psychological evaluation of all recruits did not become standard procedure until mid-1942. Owing to the large numbers of replacements required by losses, unfit men were posted to the front line even toward the end of the war. The same happened in Finland during the Continuation War.

The second category in the British classification was for men who broke down from continuous psychological and physical combat stress. They were to be treated, at least in theory, as wounded. Occasionally, however, these soldiers, too, were given courts-martial. The third category contained the actual deserters, soldiers of "normal" mental stability who left the front line without due cause, i.e. their only goal being to leave the front, as was claimed by many higher officers. During the Second World War, British officers wanted to reinstate the death penalty for these soldiers. This was attempted several times during the war, but unsuccessfully. While the death penalty was argued for with the need to prevent the collapse of discipline, British combat operations were never jeopardized by any considerable degree of desertion. Another reason for avoiding the death penalty was that there was no sure way to distinguish shell-shock patients from deliberate deserters. Men who had suffered nervous breakdowns were already regarded as wounded and there was no desire to punish them anymore. Third, the death sentence would have been very difficult to implement politically. In order to have grounds for it, a truly large number of deserters would have been required and the public would, of course, have had to be told about it. Such information, however, could not have been released without risking a collapse of public war morale.

The British army ultimately chose a similar postponement procedure as was followed in Finland, where deserters were first sentenced to three to five years in a penitentiary, but the sentences were reassessed at three-month intervals, whereby the convicted soldier could return to his unit and restore his reputation. The aim here was to avoid wasting manpower with prison sentences or "rewarding" soldiers with them. Deserters were given an opportunity to regain their personal honor. The main reason for leniency toward deserters, however, was the need to maintain troop numbers. A comparison between procedures of the First and Second

World War shows that the death penalty was not even a very efficient deterrent to desertion (French 1998).

Just as in Britain, there was a discussion in Finland about expanding the death penalty during the Second World War. Already in the offensive stage of the Continuation War in 1941, Major-Generals Paavo Talvela and Antero Svensson supported giving the death penalty for desertion and refusal to serve more often than previously. The seven death sentences given in this stage of the war were, in fact, in the Sixth Army Corps commanded by Talvela, but of these only two, in its Seventh Division, were carried out upon the decision of a quickly assembled court-martial. In most cases, military headquarters supported a more lenient view and instructed that the postponement procedure should be followed. In other words, the primary course of action would be to return caught deserters to their units upon the decision of the unit commander. The expansion of applying the death penalty was not chosen until the military authorities were frightened by mass desertion in the summer of 1944. Amendments to legislation at the time allowed the death penalty also for repeated desertion alone (Lindstedt 1999, pp. 138–145, 480–482; Ylikangas 2007, p. 206; see also Talvela 1977, pp. 68–70, 107–108).

Not all Finnish military judges took a completely condemning view of deserters, although there were also strict judges. In his diary, Paavo Alkio (2003, pp. 64–65, 112, 140–141, 162), who served as the military judge of the 11th Division of the Finnish army, observes in several connections that desertion or refusal to attack by men who had suffered nervous breakdowns after heavy fighting was understandable. On the other hand, even he did not regard fear as a mitigating factor, although the sentenced soldiers often cited it. In interrogations, fear was often given as a mitigating factor in quite direct terms. In one case, a soldier stated "that his nervous system was completely wrecked so that could not endure being at the front, and he maintained that he had not been guilty of a crime when he had refused to take part in attack."[5] Another soldier, in turn, claimed in a written appeal to the armed forces' Supreme Court-Martial that he had deserted because of a nervous disorder, which he claimed was both a hereditary condition and brought on by a head wound that he had suffered in the Winter War, stating in closing that he was therefore in no way responsible for his actions.[6]

These were precisely the arguments with which military psychiatrists explained the psychological disturbances of men unfit for front line duty (Donner 1942). To cite fear could thus be a completely explicit way of reducing one's own responsibility for the acts concerned and to explain them to oneself and more broadly to others. This was also done in an uncalculating way to arouse human feelings of compassion among interrogators and judges. Moreover, the explanation was no doubt true for many soldiers. They left the front line of their own accord because they were overcome with the fear of death or being wounded.

Psychological trauma and desertion often went hand in hand among soldiers. The observations of the British army also applied in Finland. Ville Kivimäki (2013) has studied psychologically damaged Finnish soldiers in the Second World War, some 15,700 of whom required psychiatric treatment during the Continuation War. The numbers of soldiers admitted to psychiatric care followed almost identically the chronological distribution of losses in battle and conformed to a great degree to the accumulation of cases of desertion.

As mentioned above, Finnish deserters mostly cited fear and nervous breakdowns as reasons for their acts, which suggested that exceeding the limits of mental endurance could truly be a background factor for desertion. Fear and nervous collapse were also the "most acceptable" reasons among one's peer group for letting down others. The men appear to have felt that some could endure the front while others just couldn't and could not be condemned too strictly for that. This was also evident in the weakening of overall morale in the ranks caused by the executions of deserters and soldiers refusing to fight, which had a negative effect on achieving the goals of the military leadership (Lindstedt 1999, pp. 492–500; Pipping 1978, pp. 162–164; Santa 1997, p. 97). Soldiers serving at the front had no doubt often seen mental disturbances caused by shell shock and warfare in general and thus they had no cause to find such things odd or to condemn them. In January 1942, a report issued by the surveillance section of the Finnish Military Headquarters duly noted: "… it has no longer been a shameful matter for a man to confess fear. It was not regarded as shameful by individual interrogated soldiers or groups considering to refuse to fight in a more dangerous section of the front."[7]

Loss of life and battle stress that had already been experienced and were to be expected were a major—but not the only—reason for the mental collapse, refusal to serve or desertion. Nonetheless, soldiers refusing orders to fight, and deserters cannot be directly compared to those who lost their mental stability. Psychological symptoms namely cannot be considered a premeditated group action such as going on strike and refusing to fight. Moreover, the Finnish army suffered its clearly worst losses of the summer and fall offensive of 1941 in August, but incidents of desertion and refusal to fight did not peak until October–November, when the troops proceeded from Petrozavodsk. The peak of psychiatrist treatment figures, on the other hand, coincided with the largest loss of life in August 1941. The Soviet offensive in the summer of 1944 led to a highly similar peak in losses, desertion and cases of psychiatric treatment. Desertion and refusal to fight in the fall of 1941 thus appear to have been a highly different phenomenon than the incidents in the summer of 1944. This impression is confirmed by information that the deserters in 1944 were clearly younger than those of 1941.

The mass nature of desertion and refusal to fight in the fall of 1941 and the age of the men involved playing a key role in understanding these phenomena. Comparing the desertion and refusal incidents of 1941 with cases of men requiring psychiatric treatment, we see not only a chronological connection but also the fact that men committed to psychiatric treatment were soldiers older than average and with families. Young unmarried men had a much greater ability to deceive themselves that they would not be hit by the enemy's bullets in battle than older men with families. If a soldier does not have unswerving faith in his own ability to survive, his mental balance may be undermined, or a dangerous situation may become a temptation for him to shirk duty. This is why young men, in particular, have been put in the most dangerous places in wars throughout history.[8]

The mass nature of incidents of desertion and refusal to fight, on the other hand, is converse proof of what kept men at the front: a feeling of solidarity with fellow platoon members and a strong conviction that you must look after your mate or pal. When this norm was broken or, more precisely, when it turned against itself, the possibility of "war cowardice" emerged. When sufficient numbers of older men saw that they agreed about the senselessness of war or felt they had been deceived into risking their lives, the former sound team spirit would disintegrate, luring men to desert.

Finnish researchers have suggested that one of the main reasons for refusal to serve and desertion in the fall of 1941 was the poor motivation of the lowest social groups to engage in offensive warfare (Heinilä 1997; Kulomaa 1995, pp. 60–63, 363–365; Muttilainen 1984, pp. 81–82; Salminen 1976, pp. 100–102). According to the researchers, poor motivation, however, was not completely due to political views (many members of the nonsocialist Civil Guards also refused to proceed beyond the old border), unlike the clearly political avoidance of mobilization slightly earlier. The above researchers attribute refusal and desertion to the soldiers in question having looser ties to existing society than those who remained in their units and followed discipline. The explanations given by the deserters and refusing soldiers themselves, however, actually reflect the indignation that followed when the promises of rest and demobilization that were first given were broken by officers in the fall of 1941. These soldiers of the ranks felt that their expectations of reciprocity and justice had been betrayed and they demanded that the promises be kept. Contrary to earlier interpretations of matters, the protests in the fall of 1941 did not come from among those who had weak ties with society, but from those who felt they were part of society—citizens— with certain rights alongside duties (Danielsbacka 2007, pp. 71–77).

The interrogation records of men court-martialed for various infractions of discipline express in surprisingly distinct terms the strongly held views of the men concerning their own rights and the reciprocity that they expected from their superior officers:

> The interrogated soldier promised in turn to go to the front if he is given the two weeks' leave that he was promised.[9]

> Even a crude notion of justice maintains that a promise must definitely be kept, especially one for which the other party has been required to make sacrifices.[10]

The demand for reciprocity began to be heard with growing clarity after the conquest of Petrozavodsk, because this city had been the goal of the army's advance in the minds of many soldiers in the ranks. Finnish troops occupied Petrozavodsk in early October 1941. However, since the so-called White Sea Isthmus between Lake Onega and the White Sea still remained to be taken, as one of the original aims of the war, the offensive was resumed north toward the Maaselkä watershed area. Medvezh'egorsk (Karhumäki), the main center of the area, was occupied on December 6, 1941. Finnish troops did not continue their advance to the White Sea, and the front line of the "three isthmuses" was marked, along with the old border on the Karelian Isthmus and the Svir' River between Lake Onega and Lake Ladoga, by the isthmus separating Lake Onega and Lake Segozero (Seesjärvi), which was originally an interim objective (Juutilainen 2006; Kulomaa 1995, p. 96).

Reservist Infantry Regiment 60 arrived in Petrozavodsk along with the first Finnish troops at the very beginning of October 1941. Like many others, the soldiers of the regiment had got the idea that the war was now over for them or that they could at least remain for a longer period in the city to rest. The order to leave, however, was already given on the morning of the 4th of October.[11]

Finnish soldiers in Petrozavodsk had found a Russian vodka factory, where one of the containers had remained intact. With no concern for the danger of being poisoned, they immediately drank this booty of war while some of it was stored away for later use. Officers did not react in time to the situation. The men of IR 60 took part in the public revelry like all the other soldiers, but their drinking did not turn to disorder until the order to leave had already been given. Drunken soldiers of the regiment's Third Battalion fired into the air and threw hand grenades and their departure was delayed until the evening. The worst shooters were relieved of their firearms and fifteen men remained in Petrozavodsk, being too drunk to accompany the others. In one case, drunken soldiers had informed their company commander "that they had been told that Petrozavodsk was the objective and they could rest here, which is why they will not go anywhere."[12] According to commanding officers, the reason for the protests were rumors of the demobilization of the oldest soldiers and the ending of the war, the great losses of men in the home localities of the soldiers and a shortage of labor at home. The events in Petrozavodsk were symptomatic and even though the men ultimately moved on, the numbers of deserters grew sharply over the following weeks. There was also widespread refusal to take part in an attack among men of the Seventh Company of the regiment, which led to sentences for several men (Danielsbacka 2007, pp. 62–66).

Desertion in the Finnish army as a whole clearly increased after the conquest of Petrozavodsk, which suggests that soldiers in other units had also thought that the taking of the city would mark an end to the war for them. Protests were particularly aroused by the continued advance of the army rather than new severe battles, since the combat losses of October–November were smaller than in the fighting in August.

Minor losses, however, may have been partly due to the soldiers' own system of norms. It is namely possible that they sought to reduce losses simply being more careful and less enthusiastic in attacks than previously (Smith 1994, pp. 14, 45, 64, 66–73). This procedure may already have been followed since the beginning of the war. A good example of it was events in the light infantry platoon of the Seventh Company of IR 60 in November 1941.

The platoon had been ordered on November 22 to carry out recon-naissance behind enemy lines, where they immediately encountered strong resistance and retreated. The battalion commander ordered the platoon to carry out the assignment again, and he was duly obeyed. The result, however, was the same. After encountering resistance, the men returned to their tents without a specific order from their platoon com-mander, "… for they had been outnumbered by the enemy and every-one knew from their own experience that it would have been impossible to proceed there."[13] The battalion commander arrived at the platoon's accommodation area on the following day and disbanded the platoon, sending the men to other platoons. This was not readily accepted by the soldiers. One of the soldiers later explained the disbanding of the platoon as follows: "These measures had been caused by the fact that the bat-talion commander had heard that the men had refused to carry out the above-mentioned patrol assignment. The interrogated soldier had not refused to proceed, and neither had any of the men in the platoon, but there had been talk in the platoon that the objective of the patrol duty would have been tantamount to death for each man."[14]

On the same day that the battalion commander disbanded the platoon, at least eight of its men, i.e. roughly one-third, deserted (Danielsbacka 2007, pp. 94–95). The men were caught later either in the front zone or in their own localities and were court-martialed. One of the interrogated men said that they had operated in the reconnais-sance patrol assignment prior to the disbanding just as they had done many times previously—i.e. retreating of their own accord from a situ-ation that they regarded to be impossible. (In principle, this was quite sensible if there was truly a great risk to life. Wars are not won by getting men killed unnecessarily.) The soldiers had chosen to go absent without leave because the commander had unjustly punished the platoon by dis-banding it.[15]

The above case is an extreme example, because some of the men deserted and were ultimately court-martialed. The war diaries of this regiment alone reveal, however, several less serious and probably much more common instances of men leaving an assigned task of their own accord or refusing to move on when ordered to, but not being punished in any way for this.[16]

Knut Pipping's study *Komppania pienoisyhteiskuntana* (An Army Company as Society in Miniature, 1978) is, without doubt, a classic of Finnish sociology. Based on his own war-time observations and earlier research, Pipping identified two important features that also applied to the Finnish military community. One was the importance of small groups for battle motivation among soldiers and the other one was the simultaneous influence of two different systems of norms at the front: the official system according to military regulations and the unofficial system of norms that evolved within the social groups of the troops (Pipping 1978, pp. 160–212; see also Harinen 1993, pp. 92–124, 141–143; cf. Kivimäki 2013). The behavior of the men of IR 60 in battle situations that seemed hopeless manifests the unofficial system of norms that emerged among the social groups of the troops. A typical form of activity within the unofficial system of norms was also the custom among the men of IR 60 to set out on their return trip to their unit on the very last day of leave, which meant that arrival on time was completely impossible (Danielsbacka 2007, pp. 100–107).

When the fighting in the Continuation War paused in December 1941 and the oldest men at the front were allowed to visit their homes, incidents of desertion and serious refusals to fight ceased almost completely. They were replaced by disorderly conduct (mainly drunkenness) and overstays of leave. Expectations of demobilization in the spring of 1942, however, once again highlighted the requirements of reciprocity and justice.

In early 1942, the morale reports of the military headquarters' surveillance section pointed to the dejected moods and depression of the "old men" (i.e. born in 1912 or over 30-year-olds) expecting demobilization when these expectations were not fulfilled. Their unwillingness to carry out tasks of any kind increased, and various instances of mass behavior regarded as negative by commanding offices and petitions began to appear. Censors intercepted many letters home which contained "... criticism of commanding officers because demobilization had been promised and promised, but always postponed." In many units, a particular cause of bitterness was the fact that at other sectors of the front and even in neighboring regiments or other sections of the same regiment men of the same age and even younger ones had already been allowed to return home.[17] In the late spring of 1942, there even began to appear serious incidents of refusing to fight. The reasons for this were both a counteroffensive by Soviet troops in the region of the River Svir' and the expectations of demobilization among the older servicemen. Men refused to fight because they learned that the demobilizations had ended. Not all the incidents could be resolved by officers addressing their troops, and some went all the way to court-martial (Kulomaa 1995, pp. 195–197; Muttilainen 1984, pp. 85–88; see also Salminen 1976, pp. 108–110). Desertion, however, grew to be just as, and even more, common than in the fall of 1941, not to be matched until the major Soviet offensive in the summer of 1944. On the latter occasion, it was mostly a question of the last attempts of panicking men to stay alive in a desperate situation.

Insubordination among the ranks in the Finnish army during the Continuation War, both desertion and personal refusal to follow orders to fight, often involved "everyday resistance" for the simple purpose of trying to stay alive. Turning points, such as crossing the old Finnish-Soviet border, having to leave Petrozavodsk and the postponement of demobilization, also revealed, however, a strongly held view of justice and reciprocity. The soldiers in the ranks expected and demanded a response to this from their superiors. Finnish soldiers actually maintained the idea of a kind of contractual relationship at the least between officers and subordinates, but apparently also between the state and its citizens. A process of negotiating the rights and obligations of soldiers was continuously underway in the units of the Finnish army serving at the front in the Continuation War.

Attitudes of protest remained under the control of commanding officers in the Finnish army during the Continuation War and there was no widespread mutinying. Although the notion of implemented reciprocity held by the lower ranks was tested especially in the offensive stage of the Continuation War, it was not completely negated. The situation was worse in the French army in 1917.

Mutinies and breaches of discipline among soldiers in the conscript armies of Finland in the Continuation War and France during the First World War are good examples of how the innate human notion of reciprocity in social relations is expressed in the hierarchical relationship between military officers and the lower ranks. Soldiers expected and demanded reciprocity from their officers and the leaders of their country, because the status of citizen and conscription had introduced a system of rights and obligations into armies which could not be completely disregarded by commanding officers. During the war, the requirement of reciprocity affected the way in which the lower ranks agreed to wage war. In addition, the world wars of the twentieth century led to the idea that citizens who had fought for their country at the front or had made sacrifices on the home front were entitled to expect something in return from the state. After the Second World War, the guaranteed right to social security for all citizens began to be regarded as the obligation of the state to a completely different extent.

NOTES

1. Kuulustelupöytäkirja, Tjokkilassa 14.8.41, 1.D:n Keo, asiakirjavihko 15.8.41, §1, T–18899, NA (Interrogation records, Tjokkila August 14, 1941, Court Martial of the First Division of the Finnish Army). 1.D:n Keo, luettelot ja pöytäkirjat 15.8.41, §1, T–18899, NA (Records of the court martial of the First Division of the Finnish Army, August 15, 1941). The sentence was four years and 10 days in a penitentiary.

2. This chapter and in particular the original sources quoted in the text are mainly based on two earlier studies: Danielsbacka (2007), Danielsbacka (2008). In the present connection, original sources are referred to only in the case of direct quotes.

3. The labor movement of the early twentieth-century in Sweden and Finland regarded universal suffrage, social reforms and equality as preconditions for efficient national defense. In order to achieve this, those in power in society needed to carry out these reforms instead of accusing social democrats and workers without rights of being unpatriotic. This notion was related to the citizen identity of French soldiers with its stress on reciprocity. *Redogörelse öfver Sveriges Socialdemokratiska Arbetarepartis Femte Kongress i Malmö* (1900, pp. 59–62), Kujala (1995, pp. 128–130, 278–281, 314 and *passim*).

4. JR 60:n esikunta, 25.1.42, Liite Kar.AE:n kirj. N:o 112/Ttus.2/L, Mielialaa ilmaisevia lausumia, T–1716, NA (Statements reflecting morale among troops, Headquarters, Infantry Regiment 60, 25 January 1942).

5. 1.D:n Keo, pöytäkirja 20.10.41 §2, stm. Kingelin, T–18899, NA (Minutes of the court martial of the First Division August 20, 1941, concerning Private Kingelin).

6. Karanneen sotamiehen valitus sotaylioikeudelle, folio 3, SYO asiakirjavihko n:o 185/1942, T–18825, NA (Appeal addressed to the Supreme Court Martial by a deserter).

7. Päämajan valvontaosaston kuukausikatsaus tammikuulta 1942, T–8362/9, NA (Monthly report of the surveillance section of the Finnish Military Headquarters, January 1942).

8. On self-deception and its manifestations in warfare, see e.g. Danielsbacka (2013, pp. 22–25). Having a family could of course have the effect on men that they felt they had something to defend, not just needing to survive. See Smith et al. (2003, p. 109). On soldiers placed in psychiatric care: Kivimäki (2013).

9. Kuulustelupöytäkirja, Rauman maalaiskunnan sk-talolla Ottilassa, 16.10.41, Vakka-Suomen skp:n Keo, asiakirjavihko 20.12.41, §4, T–18981, NA (Interrogation minutes, Ottila, Rauma, October 16, 1941, court martial of the Vakka-Suomi region civil guards district.).

10. Sotamiehen valitus sotaylioikeudelle, folio 5, SYO, asiakirjavihko n:o 819 ja 823/1941, T–18823, NA (Appeal addressed to the Supreme Court Martial by a soldier).

11. II/JR 60:n spk 13503, 4.10.41; III/JR 60:n spk 13514, 4.10.41; kol./ JR 60:n spk 13476, 1.10.41, 2.10.41, 5.10.41; II/JR 60:n spk 13503, 4.10.41, NA (War diaries of the Second and Third Battalions of Infantry Regiment 60).

12. III/JR 60:n esikunta, n:o 656/I, Koskee: pataljoonassa 4.10.41 tapahtunutta juopottelua ja ammuskelemistapausta, 6.10.41, T–1716, NA (Records concerning drinking and unauthorized shooting in the Third Battalion of Infantry Regiment 60 on October 4, 1941).

13. Kuulustelupöytäkirja, 9.SPol.K:n majoituspaikassa Jessoilassa, 27.11.41, 1.D:n Keo asiakirjavihko 9.12.41, §4, T–18899, NA (Interrogation minutes, November 27, 1941, First Division Court Martial documents December 9, 1941).

14. Kuulustelupöytäkirja, 9.SPol.K:ssa Jessoilassa, 26.11.41, 1.D:n Keo asiakirjavihko 9.12.41, §7 (Vuoristo), T–18899, NA (Interrogation minutes, November 26, 1941, First Division Court Martial documents, December 9, 1941).

15. 1.D:n Keo asiakirjavihkot 9.12.41, §4 ja §7, T–18899, NA (First Division Court Martial documents, December 9, 1941).

16. E.g., 9./JR 60:n spk 13489, 26.11.41, 7.12.41; 12./JR 60:n spk 13493, 5.12.41, NA (War diaries of the 9th and 12th Companies of Infantry Regiment 60).

17. The petition schemes usually involved soldiers of lower ranks, in most cases of a company or battalion, signing a petition that they had drawn up demanding demobilization or an explanation why it had been delayed. The petitions were usually addressed to the commander of their battalion, regiment or division. Päämajan valvontaosaston katsaus tammikuulta 1942, T–8362/9; Päämajan valvontaosaston katsaus helmikuulta 1942, T–8362/9; Päämajan valvontaosaston katsaus maaliskuulta 1942, T–8362/10, NA (Reports of the surveillance section of the Finnish Military Headquarters, January, February and March 1942). The translated quotation is from the surveillance section's report for February 1942.

REFERENCES

Alkio, Paavo. 2003. *Sotatuomarin päiväkirjat: Katkelmia hänen päiväkirjoistaan*, ed. Erkki Rintala. Jyväskylä: Gummerus Kirjapaino Oy.

Bach, André. 2013. *Justice militaire 1915–1916*. Paris: Vendémiaire.

Bellamy, Chris. 2007. *Absolute War: Soviet Russia in the Second World War*. New York: Alfred A. Knopf.

Danielsbacka, Mirkka. 2007. *Kurittomuutta vai vastarintaa?: Tottelemattomuusilmiöt ja niiden kontrollointi jatkosodan alkuvaiheessa*. Unpublished MA thesis in Finnish and Scandinavian History, University of Helsinki.

Danielsbacka, Mirkka. 2008. Sotilaskurin rajoilla: Miehistön vastarinnan muodot ja merkitykset jatkosodan alkuvaiheessa. *Historiallinen Aikakauskirja* 106 (3): 269–284.

Danielsbacka, Mirkka. 2013. *Vankien vartijat: Ihmislajin psykologia, neuvostosotavangit ja Suomi 1941–1944*. Historiallisia tutkimuksia Helsingin yliopistosta XXXII. Helsinki: Unigrafia.

Donner, S.E. 1942. Hermotapaukset sodassa. *Medisiinari* 1942 (1): 4–14.

Ferguson, Niall. 1999. *The Pity of War*. New York: Basic Books.

Ferguson, Niall. 2004. Prisoner Taking and Prisoner Killing in the Age of Total War: Towards a Political Economy of Military Defeat. *War in History* 11 (2): 148–192.

French, David. 1998. Discipline and the Death Penalty in the British Army in the War Against Germany During the Second World War. *Journal of Contemporary History* 33 (4): 531–545.

Harinen, Olli. 1993. *Knut Pipping ja Väinö Linna sotilasyhteisön kuvaajina: Sosiologin ja kirjailijan havainnot suomalaisesta sotilasyksiköstä ulkomaisen tutkimuskirjallisuuden valossa*. Unpublished licentiate thesis in sociology, University of Helsinki.

Heinilä, Harri. 1997. *Vanhan rajan ylitys jatkosodan hyökkäysvaiheessa 1941: Jalkaväkirykmenttien miesten suhtautuminen siihen*. Unpublished licentiate thesis in political history, University of Helsinki.

Heinilä, Harri. 2006. Vanhan rajan ylitys hyökkäysvaiheessa 1941 jalkaväkimiesten näkökulmasta. In *Jatkosodan pikkujättiläinen*, ed. Jari Leskinen and Antti Juutilainen, 286–294. WSOY: Porvoo.

Jokipii, Mauno. 1987. *Jatkosodan synty: Tutkimuksia Saksan ja Suomen sotilaallisesta yhteistyöstä 1940–41*. Helsinki: Otava.

Jokisipilä, Markku. 2004. *Aseveljiä vai liittolaisia?: Suomi, Saksan liittosopimusvaatimukset ja Rytin-Ribbentropin –sopimus*. Bibliotheca Historica 84. Helsinki: SKS.

Juutilainen, Antti. 2006. Hyökkäys kolmelle kannakselle. In *Jatkosodan pikkujättiläinen*, ed. Jari Leskinen and Antti Juutilainen, 133–147. WSOY: Porvoo.

Keegan, John. 1993. *A History of Warfare*. London: Hutchinson.
Kivimäki, Ville. 2013. *Battled Nerves: Finnish Soldiers' War Experience, Trauma, and Military Psychiatry, 1941–44*. Tampere: Juvenes Print.
Kujala, Antti. 1995. *Venäjän hallitus ja Suomen työväenliike 1899–1905*. Historiallisia Tutkimuksia 194. Helsinki: SHS.
Kujala, Antti. 2009. Illegal Killing of Soviet Prisoners of War by Finns During the Finno-Soviet Continuation War of 1941–44. *Slavonic and East European Review* 87 (3): 429–451.
Kulomaa, Jukka. 1995. *Käpykaartiin? 1941–1944: Sotilaskarkuruus Suomen armeijassa jatkosodan aikana*. Helsinki: Painatuskeskus.
Lindstedt, Jukka. 1999. *Kuolemaan tuomitut: Kuolemanrangaistukset Suomessa toisen maailmansodan aikana*. Suomalaisen Lakimiesyhdistyksen julkaisuja A 221. Helsinki: Suomalainen Lakimiesyhdistys.
Loez, André. 2010. *14–18: Les refus de la guerre, Une histoire des mutins*. Paris: Gallimard.
Mälkki, Juha. 2008. *Herrat, jätkät ja sotataito: Kansalaissotilas- ja ammattisotilasarmeijan rakentuminen 1920- ja 1930-luvulla "talvisodan ihmeeksi."* Bibliotheca Historica 117. Helsinki: SKS.
Mann, Michael. 2012. The Sources of Social Power. *The Rise of Classes and Nation-States, 1760–1914*, Vol. 2. New York: Cambridge University Press.
Manninen, Ohto. 1980. *Suur-Suomen ääriviivat – Kysymys tulevaisuudesta ja turvallisuudesta Suomen Saksan -politiikassa 1941*. Helsinki: Kirjayhtymä.
Muttilainen, Olli. 1984. *Kieltäytymisrikoksista Suomessa jatkosodan 1941–1944 aikana*. Unpublished study in the research project Aikansa rikos [A Crime of Its Own Time], University of Helsinki.
Nuorteva, Jussi. 1987. *Suomen vankeinhoidon historiaa. Osa 4. Vangit – vankilat – sota*. Suomen vankeinhoitolaitos toisen maailmansodan aikana. Helsinki: Valtion painatuskeskus.
Overmans, Rüdiger. 2005. The Repatriation of Prisoners of War once Hostilities are Over: A Matter of Course? In *Prisoners of War, Prisoners of Peace: Captivity, Homecoming and Memory in World War II*, ed. Bob Moore and Barbara Hately-Broad, 11–22. Oxford and New York: Berg.
Pedroncini, Guy. 1967. *Les Mutineries de 1917*. Paris: Presses universitaires de France.
Pipping, Knut. 1978. *Komppania pienoisyhteiskuntana: Sosiologisia havaintoja suomalaisesta rintamayksiköstä 1941–1944*. Helsinki: Otava.
Redogörelse öfver Sveriges Socialdemokratiska Arbetarepartis Femte Kongress i Malmö 1900. Stockholm.
Rentola, Kimmo. 1994. *Kenen joukoissa seisot?: Suomalainen kommunismi ja sota 1937–1945*. Porvoo: WSOY.
Salminen, Esko. 1976. *Propaganda rintamajoukoissa 1941–1944: Suomen armeijan valistustoiminta ja mielialojen ohjaus jatkosodan aikana*. Keuruu: Otava.

Santa, Matti. 1997. *Impolan poppoo: Tyrvään komppanian rajua joukkoa.* Tyrvää: Tyrvään Sanomat.

Scott, James C. 1985. *Weapons of the Weak: Everyday Forms of Peasant Resistance.* New Haven and London: Yale University Press.

Smith, Leonard V. 1991. The Disciplinary Dilemma of French Military Justice September 1914–April 1917: The Case of the 5e Division d'infanterie. *The Journal of Military History* 55: 47–61.

Smith, Leonard V. 1994. *Between Mutiny and Obedience: The Case of the French Fifth Infantry Division during World War I.* Princeton: Princeton University Press.

Smith, Leonard V., Stéphane Audoin-Rouzeau, and Annette Becker. 2003. *France and the Great War 1914–1918.* Cambridge: Cambridge University Press.

Talvela, Paavo. 1977. *Sotilaan elämä: Muistelmat,* Vol. II. Jyväskylä: K.J. Gummerus Osakeyhtiön kirjapaino.

Vehviläinen, Olli. 2002. *Finland in the Second World War. Between Germany and Russia,* trans. Gerald McAlester. Basingstoke: Palgrave.

Ylikangas, Heikki. 2007. *Romahtaako rintama?: Suomi puna-armeijan puristuksessa kesällä 1944.* Helsinki: Otava.

National Archives (Kansallisarkisto), Helsinki (NA)

1. divisioonan kenttäoikeuden tuomioluettelot, pöytäkirjat ja asiakirjavihot 1941–1942 (T–18899).

JR 60:n arkisto (T–1716).

Päämaja, Tiedotusosaston valistus- ja viihdytystoimisto (T–8362).

Pirkka-Hämeen suojeluskuntapiirin kenttäoikeuden tuomioluettelot, pöytäkirjat ja asiakirjavihot 1941–1942 (T–18988).

Sotapäiväkirjat (JR 60).

Sotaylioikeus, asiakirjavihkot 1941–1942 (T–18823, T–18825).

Vakka-Suomen suojeluskuntapiirin kenttäoikeuden tuomioluettelot, pöytäkirjat ja asiakirjavihot 1941–1942 (T–18981).

CHAPTER 7

The Modern Welfare State

The welfare state is not an unequivocal concept, and its precise content and meaning often depend on the country and language concerned. In this book, it is a generic term for a system of government that emerged in the Western countries after the Second World War. In a welfare state, the state has at least some kind of social responsibility for its citizens (ensuring human, political and social rights) and public authorities are engaged in the redistribution of resources to at least some degree.

The welfare state is said to be one of mankind's most important and unique achievements, as it makes complete strangers participate in a mutual system of redistributing income, help one another and support this system voluntarily (Fong et al. 2005, pp. 277–302). On the other hand, the welfare state has been blamed for shifting the individual personal responsibility for one's life completely to the state, for making everyone a free rider and for paralyzing the natural human willingness to help others (Ostrom 2000). The following sections discuss the history of the welfare state, different models of the welfare state—Nordic (social democratic), conservative and liberal—and how the above two features that arise in discussion on the welfare state are part of the same requirement of reciprocity and human retributive moral sentiments.

© The Author(s) 2019
A. Kujala and M. Danielsbacka, *Reciprocity in Human Societies*,
https://doi.org/10.1007/978-3-319-96056-2_7

THE EMERGENCE OF THE MODERN WELFARE STATES

Throughout history, rulers and those in authority have protected their subjects against external and internal threats in return for taxes or labor provided by them. Subjects have also been entitled to expect from those above them at least some kind of succor for example in times of severe crop losses or famine. It was, however, only the modern welfare state that began to systematically redistribute resources and take on responsibilities previously assigned to families or individuals themselves, such as caring for those unable to work, the ill and the elderly.

The basis for the developments that ultimately led to the modern welfare state was laid when the lives of individuals and their families began to be insured against social risks of various kinds. Old-age pensions and accident and health insurance were included in the social insurance programs implemented by Chancellor Otto von Bismarck of Germany in the 1880s. They were, in principle, the first forms of public social insurance and social security for all citizens. Bismarck had to compete for the minds of the working class with the German Workers' Party which was still banned at the time (ban in force from 1878 to 1890). The aim of the social program was to mobilize the working class to help build a united German Empire and to have it bound through reforms with a semi-authoritarian state. The building of nation-states required the support of their citizens, which in turn was obtained by promising them more rights in return for increasing responsibilities (e.g. universal male suffrage in Germany in 1871). Health insurance (mandatory membership in sick funds for workers with two-thirds of costs paid from their contributions) and pensions for the elderly and victims of accidents, which had been decreed by Bismarck, originally applied to only part of the working class, and the state did not contribute to health-insurance costs. The extent of the reforms, however, improved after Bismarck and the first labor protection laws were passed. In Bismarck's pensions system, pensions were based on insurance, and they were contributory and status-related, with those earning more also receiving a larger pension. Imperial Germany followed a policy of negative integration or semi-authoritarian integration with regard to the Social Democratic Party. The party and the labor movement, in general, were allowed to operate legally, but they were prevented from being included in the centers of power (Wehler 1983, pp. 87, 134–140; 1995, pp. 902–915; Mann 2012a, pp. 502–503, 673–678; 2012b, pp. 288–289).

The evolution toward a nation-state and the two world wars of the twentieth century laid a basis for the growth of the responsibilities and power of public administration. The war years had assembled the people behind shared goals. Because of the war effort with which everyone identified, the burden had to be shared among the citizens of one's country in a way that was felt to be fair. As discussed in the Chapter 6 in the present book, the norm of reciprocity could be tested also in wartime conditions. Not everyone necessarily regarded sacrifices for the shared goal to be justified. It should be pointed out that the clear reduction of income differences and their process of remaining unchanged which took place in all developed industrialized countries ca. 1914–1980 were basically due to the destructive effects of the world wars, the depression of the 1930s and the fiscal measures of modern states (Piketty 2013).

During the Second World War, Great Britain, in particular, took a considerable step toward a welfare state leveling inequality among its citizens, while at the same time exploiting its colonies and their inhabitants (Collingham 2011, pp. 141–145; Pinker 2011, p. 658). In 1943, there was famine with resulting mass mortality in Bengal in India, for which Britain's Prime Minister Winston Churchill blamed the Indians themselves. In fact, Churchill's cabinet was largely responsible for the famine crisis in Bengal. It was exacerbated by the government's lack of action. Cargoes of foodstuffs shipped from Australia were directed to Britain instead of India. Food was hoarded to keep the standard of nutrition as high as possible for the British and to compensate for immense war debt (Mukerjee 2011, pp. 198–218, 272–275 and *passim*). The rationing economy functioned quite well in Britain during the Second World War and the standard of nutrition especially among working-class civilians improved, which may be one reason why civilian life expectancy in Britain grew during the First and Second World War at twice the rate of the rest of the twentieth century (Collingham 2011, pp. 384–385, 393–394; Wilkinson and Pickett 2009, pp. 84–85, 222). Working for the shared war effort was, however, also grounds for increasingly progressive taxation and, for example, duties on luxury goods. Under the emergency conditions of the war years, income disparity between various classes of society decreased, full employment was maintained, and social unity grew stronger (Wilkinson and Pickett 2009, pp. 84–85, 222).

In 1942, Lord William Beveridge presented his extensive program of social welfare policies for the United Kingdom. Known as the Beveridge

Plan, it included an ensured minimum level of subsistence for all citizens regardless of their social status in cases of unemployment or inability to work (Abel-Smith 1992). The plan also contained the idea of ensuring social security of last resort for old age and the founding of families. Beveridge proposed as means for achieving these aims social insurance, child benefits, free health services for all citizens and the maintaining of full employment. The plan soon began to be implemented and after the Second World War Great Britain became a forerunner in developments leading to the welfare state. It was, however, also among the first to dismantle the structures of the welfare state. Britain's early social security system provided flat-rate, means-tested pensions for the elderly poor from tax revenue, and was thus different from the insurance-based pensions system created by Bismarck (Mann 2013, pp. 129–166).

The welfare state practicing redistribution to adjust for income disparities and ensuring subsistence on a last-resort basis began to evolve in earnest after the Second World War. The two courses of development of the welfare state emerged from the German (Bismarckian) and the British (Beveridgean) models, respectively, the former being insurance-based and the latter means-tested. The Bismarckian model was gradually expanded to a growing number of citizens, while the Beveridgean model evolved along two different paths: the Nordic countries began to adopt a two-tiered income-based pensions system while in Great Britain the middle classes started to move toward privately funded pensions, which would later lead to heightened inequality as the poorer population remained within the sphere of diminishing means-tested support (Mann 2013, pp. 129–166).

The evolution of the welfare state was due not only to the overall democratization of developed Western societies but also to the challenge posed by the Soviet system and communism, the responses to which were social policy and systems of collective bargaining. A kind of unofficial social contract came into force in the developed capitalist countries. The Social Democratic labor movement became part of the prevailing political system in the Scandinavian countries and the Netherlands even before the Second World War. West Germany was governed by the Christian Democrats until the end of the 1960s but owing to the risk of resurgent national socialism and in order to prevent communism, workers were given a say in matters from the level of private companies to the administration of the German federal states long before the Social Democrats were included in the federal government. Increasing productivity based on technological development and improved education permitted the growth of real earnings for workers and functionaries, and Western Europe achieved a higher standard of living than in the "real socialism" of Eastern Europe.

The broad responsibility of the state for its citizens and a new principle of social security began to be emphasized in the Western countries. To cite Richard Titmuss's concepts (1963, pp. 75–87), a transition began from a residual and earnings-based model to an institutional one. In the residual model poor relief concerned only the poorest citizens and it was mostly charity. The state participated hardly at all in paying social benefits. The earnings-based model, on the other hand, was more clearly based on the individual's earnings in working life. The role of the state, in turn, began to gain considerable emphasis in the institutional model, and social policy came to include all citizens. The reforms did not explicitly aim at the kind of welfare state familiar to people today. The trajectory of developments could rather be described as one in which various reforms improving social security and opportunities for living that had been caused by pressure from surrounding society *came to lead* to the creation of modern welfare states. These states were thus also the results of political struggles and compromise (Kangas and Kvist 2013, p. 149; Moore 1978, pp. 3–48, 506–510).

Sweden was the leading nation in the evolution of the Nordic welfare states, although it did not have similar peaks of growth in progressive taxation as for example in Great Britain. This was no doubt partly due to the fact that Sweden took no active part in the war. Even after the war, there was initially more focus in Sweden on transfer programs than raising taxes. In Sweden, the level of uniform flat-rate national pensions was raised in 1946, followed in 1953 by universal health legislation corresponding to the British model. Active labor market policies began to be implemented in the 1950s and redistribution leveling inequality between the genders and classes of society increased in the following decade (Mann 2013, p. 134; Peterson 2012).

Finland, in turn, passed a national pensions act at an early stage, already in 1937, establishing an insurance-based pensions system and considerably expanding earlier social security based on poor relief (Hellsten 1993, pp. 54–79, 251–259). It was Finland's first reform in social policy that applied to all citizens, although the national pensions defined by it did not begin to be paid until after the Second World War. The notion that people who had made sacrifices for society would be more extensively entitled to social security did not gain ground even in Finland until the war years (1939–1945). After the Second World War the right to social security started to be referred to as a basic right of citizens (Kettunen and Petersen 2011; Kettunen 2011; Petersen 2011). Nonetheless, Finland lagged behind Sweden in the developments that led to the welfare state.

The social security of Finns was already improved through various reforms in the late 1950s and early 1960s, but the foundation of the present Finnish welfare state began to be laid in the years after 1966, when political power was exercised mostly by governments formed by left-wing parties and the political center—a situation that continued until the mid-1980s. The division of the educational system into secondary schools leading to higher education and elementary schools for farmers and workers stripped of "unnecessary" subjects was discontinued and replaced by a system of comprehensive schools for all young people of compulsory education age. Finland followed the reforms of Sweden, the forerunner in this respect. The influence of so-called conservative forces, however, was more prominent in Finnish legislation than in its Scandinavian counterparts (Kujala 2013, pp. 167–169, 196 and *passim*; Mann 2013, pp. 129–166).

The oil crisis of the early 1970s undermined faith in the regulation of an economy with its foundations created by the economic depression of the 1930s and the Second World War. At the same time, the international system of controlling the international economy and currency exchange rates, with the US dollar bound to gold and the exchange rates of other currencies defined in relation to the dollar collapsed when President Richard Nixon ended the gold convertibility of the dollar. Neoliberal economists demanded that the market economy was to be as free as possible from economic regulation in its development. They maintained that deregulation, the privatization of public operations and services, cutbacks on the social redistribution of income and the loosening of legislation and agreements for the protection of labor in the name of flexibility required by competitiveness would outrank all other models of economic policy in achieving worldwide economic progress. They also underscored the primacy of combating inflation and budget deficits in economic policy and worldwide free trade, i.e. the freest possible movement of goods, services, capital and labor. In keeping with so-called trickle-down theory, entrepreneurs were to be allowed to become rich with the least possible restrictions, because affluence would spread like manna from heaven to all parts of society and also improve the status of the poor in the developing countries. There is no denying that industry and commerce can, in fact, increase overall well-being, but in most cases, this requires redistributive action by the state, which was actually practiced in Nordic and West European societies.

Prime Minister Margaret Thatcher of Great Britain (in office 1979–1990) and President Ronald Reagan of the United States (1981–1989) began to implement neoliberal economic policies in their countries. This policy maintained that the market economy was to be allowed to operate freely upon its own terms, in other words as much as possible without the impediments of regulation by the state and the labor movement.[1] Thatcher and Reagan reduced the power of unions in their respective countries. The liberation of the movement of capital led to the increasing growth of multinational corporations and created a global economy. The economic policies of states have largely had to adapt to the terms laid down by the multinational corporations. This has been the case in Finland since the middle of the 1980s or from at least the early 1990s. The victory of neoliberalism also reinforced the economic bubbles that had always been part of capitalism and posed the question of whether the welfare state could be afforded any more. Also, the Soviet Union, which had challenged the market economy, ceased to be a player at the turn of the 1980s and 1990s. The welfare state, however, has managed to survive in Western Europe, with the exception of Great Britain, and it enjoys the support of large sectors of the populace and in principle the whole political spectrum. Even present British governments have not dared to tamper with the National Health Service, founded by a Labour government immediately after the Second World War and still widely popular (Mann 2013, pp. 57, 129–166).

THE TYPOLOGY OF WELFARE STATES

Gøsta Esping-Andersen's (1990) well-known typology of contemporary welfare states divides them according to three regimes: liberal, conservative (or corporatist) and social democratic. The classification is based on the internal political relations of power and labor-market practices of the countries concerned. Esping-Andersen later went on to add the notion of defamilization to his classification, with reference to how much the welfare policies of the state reduce the individual's dependency on the family (Esping-Andersen 1999). The typology of welfare systems thus came to be based on three institutions ensuring welfare: the family, the markets and public authorities. Esping-Andersen's classification also refers to the three models of state social policies outlined by Richard Titmuss (1983): marginal (or residual), contributory (industrial achievement-performance according to Titmuss) and universalist (or institutional redistributive).

Liberal systems of the welfare state—which could just as well be described as neoliberal, but Esping-Andersen's terms are applied here—underline efficiency and the responsibility of individuals to provide for themselves and their families with their earnings. The state invests relatively little in the social security of citizens, which is based on a marginal model of social policy with limited and means-tested benefits given only to those who are regarded as deserving them. There are only few public services and people take out private insurance policies for the majority of their welfare services. In the liberal model, equality generally means the equality of *opportunities*, not the equality of end results. The ideal is the greatest possible (upward) social mobility, giving everyone the opportunity to rise on the social scale through their skills and hard work. Among present countries, Great Britain, Ireland, the United States, Canada, Australia and New Zealand are closest to the ideal type of the liberal welfare state, albeit with less social mobility than in other welfare-state systems (Putnam 2015).

At present, the conservative (corporativist) welfare system is best represented by the Continental European countries Germany, France, Italy and Spain. In this system, social security is based on the role of employee, with social benefits tied to contributions via working life, i.e. the contributory (or Titmuss's industrial achievement-performance) model. The conservative welfare state model underlines the responsibility of the nuclear family for the welfare of its members. The employment of the provider (male) and the benefits attached to it will often provide the subsistence of the whole family. The state will repair the situation only when the family is unable to provide its own welfare (so-called subsidiary principle). This model is called "conservative" because it has a conservative ideological basis and includes the preservation of distinctions associated with the status of being an employee. The standard of entitlements is namely connected to earned wages. Except for education, there are few public services and the provision of welfare services is arranged with a system of insurance (though not through private insurance that is as distinctly market-based as in the liberal system).

The social democratic welfare state system is also known as the Nordic model, because the Nordic countries, including Finland, are closest to its ideal type. This system seeks to redistribute resources via taxation, to maintain full employment and to prevent poverty. Social benefits, or at least the majority of them, follow the principle of universalism, i.e. applying to all citizens being thus based explicitly on citizenship. In the liberal or conservative model, benefits are means-tested or based on the individual's role in the labor market. In the ideal version of the Nordic model, services are universal, of a high standard and funded through taxes. The aim of the social democratic welfare state system is the active reduction of inequality. Within this model, equality is generally understood as the provision of equal opportunities, which, unlike in the liberal model, includes the aim of equal results in the sense that the system will support the weakest individuals in all stages of their lives. The aim of equality of the social democratic welfare state system is well described by a definition formulated by the Indian economist Amartya Sen which is cited by the Swedish sociologist Göran Therborn (2013, p. 41). According to this definition, the basis of equality is the "equality of capability to function fully as a human being." This naturally includes subsistence, health and assistance in case of illness. It also includes the freedom to choose one's own path in life and the resources, knowledge and skills that it requires, which can be achieved through education.

Esping-Andersen's and Titmuss's typology of welfare states and their social policies lists the ideal types of these states. These types are not to be found anywhere in completely pure form and different countries usually have elements of all of them (Kangas and Kvist 2013, p. 151; Van Kersbergen 2013, pp. 139–147). The various types of welfare states are now closer to each other as the traditional welfare states and their social security systems have begun to break down. Esping-Andersen's classification, however, still serves as a good basis for a broad typology and facilitates studies of the characteristics of different welfare states.

Esping-Andersen's typology has had to be updated in recent decades also for the reason that the welfare states have been joined by the former socialist countries of Eastern Europe and a few East Asian countries. It is interesting to compare Japan with the western welfare states, because despite highly marginal social security, Japan has achieved high standing according many metrics of welfare and has even surpassed the Western countries (Wilkinson and Pickett 2009, pp. 183–184).[2] The Japanese model of the welfare has been described as both a hybrid combining the features of various systems and as a case apart among welfare states (Peng 2000, pp. 87–114; Sumino 2014, pp. 109–133; Takegawa 2010, pp. 53–67).

Reciprocity and Models of the Welfare State

All systems of the welfare state have their own principles regarding the recipients and terms of benefits. In all welfare states, the principles of distributing entitlements, however, are based on reciprocity, with different underlying assumptions depending on the model of the welfare state.

In the Nordic model, the state has traditionally been regarded as the main party responsible for both social security of last resort and extensive and comprehensive public services such as cost-free basic education and healthcare (Forma et al. 2007, pp. 51–52; Paloheimo 2010, p. 32). The idea behind universal entitlements is that everyone pays, and everyone benefits. In other words, paid taxes are returned to citizens in the form of public services. In order to function, however, this system requires a high degree of employment. Where the range and standard of public services are good and the pensions system functions well, even high taxes are generally accepted. Even before reaching adulthood, citizens of Nordic welfare states will have benefited from a large number of services provided by the state (child health centers, free education, general infrastructure etc.). After entering working life, they can feel that they are repaying some of these services in the form of taxes. On the other hand, the perspective can be shifted to the future and people can consider the taxes coming back to them later for example through day-care services and free education for their own children or care for one's elderly parents. In Finland, the notion of reciprocity has particularly been underlined in the care of the elderly. In the Nordic countries, the pensions system also calls for a kind of reciprocal agreement between different generations. Everyone takes their turn at helping since the younger generation pays for the pensions of older generations.

In the conservative contribution-based model, also known as the corporatist or Central European model, the reciprocity of contributions and received entitlements is more clearly evident: one receives in turn for what one has paid. Germany has been called the prime example of the Central European social-insurance state. In the social insurance state, social security is mainly implemented by dividing social risks collectively within occupations. Employees pay social insurance contributions from their wages, thus becoming entitled to a corresponding level of social security in case of illness, unemployment or retirement. Social security is thus paid for employees to benefit themselves and their families, and not by and for all citizens as in the ideal of the Nordic model. Moreover, the amount of benefits is based on the amount paid in. In this way, the system prefers vertical redistribution in accordance with the life history of the individual and the family rather than horizontal redistribution among different income groups. The social insurance-based system functions excellently and enjoys wide support in conditions of full (male) employment and stable family structures. The growth of unemployment and an increasing divorce rate will erode the functioning and legitimacy of the system, as growing numbers of people will not be caught in its safety nets. Cutbacks to social benefits (unemployment security) and growing numbers of poorly paid jobs are the reverse face of Germany's current economic miracle. More than one out of five full-time employed Germans are of low income according to German standards. Of 17 European states, only Lithuania has relatively more employees in the small-salary sector (earnings less than two-thirds of the median wage) (Clegg 2013; Leitner and Lessenich 2003; Mann 2013, pp. 135, 156–157; Weik and Friedrich 2014, p. 283).

Reciprocity between welfare-state benefits and paid taxes, i.e. the respective duties of the state and citizens is hardest to find in the liberal welfare states. In the liberal (Anglo-Saxon) model, individuals themselves namely bear the main responsibility for their own livelihood and welfare. The ideal of this model is a kind of night-watchman state that protects its citizens from external and internal threats with the military and police forces but does not distribute generous social benefits. In this model, the social benefits are of markedly means-tested nature. The term "welfare state" in the English-speaking countries refers more to a socially oriented state than a welfare state per se, following the definition of "welfare" as implying social security rather than overall well-being (Heikkilä 2009, p. 15). In Anglophone contexts, the "welfare state" has a different connotation than its literal equivalents in other languages, such as Finnish (*hyvinvointivaltio*) or Swedish (*välfärdsstat*), for it is identified as providing social security while at the same time seeking to control and direct the behavior of its citizens. There is the fear of the state becoming too closely involved with the lives of citizens, and therefore the notion of the welfare state in the broader sense is avoided.

In the liberal welfare states, the expectation of reciprocity is in fact associated more closely with opposition to the welfare state and the problem of free riders misusing entitlements than with the possible benefits of the welfare state and whether it is worthwhile to maintain it. The problem of parasitism highlights human retributive moral sentiments (commending and punishing) and especially their punitive aspect, since the undeserved use of welfare entitlements arouses considerable indignation in countries of marginal social policies, especially among the tax-paying middle class. Irrespective of conditions in society (i.e. an economic boom or recession), individuals are regarded as primarily responsible for their own fortune or lack thereof. This is why there is so much debate in liberal welfare states with means-tested social security about the poor who "deserve" to be helped and those who are poor because of their own "laziness" and do not deserve their benefits (Bowles and Gintis 2000; Leon 2012).

The notion of reciprocity is also problematic in the Nordic welfare state, where the state ensures social security of last resort. Why should anyone pay for someone else to be a free rider and receive basic social assistance from the state without the latter having contributed to it in any way? Attitudes about the responsibility of the state as the ultimate provider of social security, however, vary among different models of the welfare state. This is partly due to how much disadvantaged people are considered to be responsible for their own situation. Many studies in social psychology have shown that people have a marked tendency to shun those in abject conditions especially when the latter are felt to have contributed themselves to their situation (Pinker 2011, pp. 565–566; Zimbardo 2008, pp. 310–311). In the United States, generosity to the poor is closely connected to notions of the causes of poverty. Americans tend to be much more convinced than Europeans that poverty is due to the poor avoiding work. The fear of free riders is commensurate with the distance of classes of society from each other, or their perceived distance (Fong et al. 2005, pp. 278–279; Spicker 2013, pp. 193–201; Sumino 2014, pp. 109–133).

In liberal welfare states, universal social services and benefits are almost curse words because of the fear of parasitism. The actual abuse of benefits is a completely different matter. Disapproval of the far-reaching welfare state and public services "paralyzing" initiative is not necessarily based on any existing reality but is dictated more by attitudes. In Finland, for example, the abuse of benefits paid by the *Kela*, the

National Pensions Institute, appears in reality to be only a small problem. *Kela* pays out approximately 12 billion euros in benefits and entitlements per year, and the total sum of misused payments per years of which the authorities are aware is around 4 million euros, which means that payments on false grounds amount to only 0.03% of all *Kela* payments. Approximately one thousand people per year are suspected of the abuse of benefits. These cases are mostly related to unemployment allowances. The problem is not so much actual fraud (at least intentional) but rather the fact the people imagine cases of defrauding the system to be common. Social welfare services are questioned in Finland also because dealing with *Kela* and other public institutions is regarded as too difficult and bureaucratic. This is why there is most likely more people remaining without social benefits due to them by law than there are those who abuse the benefits system. Elderly people with limited means and without close relatives who are active enough will not necessarily have the energy to apply for benefits such as housing allowances and care support for pensioners, to which they would be entitled. Basic social assistance is most likely among the underused benefits provided by *Kela* (Kangas and Niemelä 2008; Kuivalainen 2007; Niemelä 2008, 2013).

It has been suggested that the passivizing influence of the welfare state extends to family relationships, assistance to family members and even to caring about them. The so-called "crowding out" hypothesis predicts that generous public support and services such as children's day care and care and service facilities for the elderly will diminish the responsibility that previously lay with the family, along with decreasing spontaneous assistance to family members and relatives and their care (Ostrom 2000).

In reality, however, this has not happened, and the course of events has instead been the opposite. Research has shown that in the South European countries, where public social services are scarcer than in Northern Europe, family members are helped more regularly (because this simply has to be done), but in the North European countries of extensive welfare services more people provide personal assistance than in the Mediterranean countries. Public services thus do not prevent relatives from helping one another. They may even increase the number of helpers by "liberating" more people to assist their relatives without being actually compelled to do so ("crowd in") (Albertini et al. 2007, pp. 319–334; Kohli 1999, pp. 81–104; Künemund and Rein 1999, pp. 93–121).

Or will state-provided benefits replace private charity and the activities of a civic society, as claimed by critics of the extensive welfare state?

The results of research also refute this assumption. They namely show that also in countries with generous social benefits people engage in volunteer work and make donations to charity (Danielsbacka et al. 2013). This has also been seen in historical reviews of changes over time in the ratio of public welfare services and private charity (Lindert 2014). Support from the state may even serve to increase private charitable activities (Lindert 2014; see also Heikkilä 2009, p. 79; Titmuss 1970, p. 225).

THE NORDIC MODEL

The universalist welfare state version known as the Nordic model takes the lead in almost all international comparisons. It is particularly commended for ensuring the welfare of citizens (see Partanen 2016). Despite this, and especially in Finnish debate, the functioning of the welfare state has been questioned for a long while. An often-negative discussion predominates in the media about growing income disparity, marginalization, poverty, distress and loneliness.[3] The above sections of this chapter address the history of welfare state systems and how the norm of reciprocity is included in the various systems at the theoretical level. We next go on to discuss the Nordic model in concrete terms, its strengths and failings and the role of the principle of reciprocity in relations both between citizens and between citizens and the state. We take as an example Finland, which is in many ways part of the Nordic "family" despite features and courses of development distinguishing it from its western neighbors.

Finland, still a poor country after the Second World War that was receiving assistance from international organizations, rose from "rags to riches" with exceptional speed, with per capita national income growing at a very fast rate in the 1950s and 1960s. Developments toward the welfare state, which began relatively late compared with other European countries, followed in the wake of economic growth. The example of the other Nordic countries, especially Sweden, was followed in creating the welfare state. Finland, however, did not achieve the level of its western neighbors until the 1980s. The Finnish welfare state was created with limited funds compared with Western Europe, and for this reason, it has been considered a lighter version of the Nordic model (Anttonen and Sipilä 2000; Kangas 2009, p. 42). Although Finland thus created a kind of "cut-rate version" of the Nordic welfare state, the achievement does not need to be looked down, for this "cheap model" appears to be converting economic success into welfare in efficient ways.

In 2017, Finland was ranked second among 128 countries in the Social Progress Index developed at Harvard University, despite being only 16th in terms of per capita gross domestic product. The Harvard researchers sought to make their metrics chart welfare as broadly as possible. The index considers three dimensions: basic human needs (nutrition, low infant mortality and personal security), the foundations of wellbeing (e.g. health and education) and opportunity (e.g. rights, freedoms and equality).

The other Nordic countries were also among the leading ten nations in terms of social progress, with Denmark coming first, Norway and Iceland third and Sweden eight. United Kingdom was ranked twelfth, Germany thirteenth, Japan seventeenth and the United States eighteenth. Among European countries, the lowest rankings were for Russia (67th), Kazakhstan (74th) and Azerbaijan (76th). As shown by the United States' 18th place in measured social progress while fifth in per capita GDP, economic success alone does not directly translate into social success. Up to a certain degree, however, economic success will correlate with social development. The poor countries of Africa were among the last both in comparisons of per capita GDP and on the index of measured social progress.[4]

Possibly the most widely noted international comparison commending the Nordic model in recent years is *The Spirit Level: Why Equality is Better for Everyone* by epidemiologists Richard Wilkinson and Kate Pickett (2009). In this book, Wilkinson and Pickett reiterate the "old truth" of fewer social and health problems in the Nordic countries and Japan than in most other rich countries, especially in liberal welfare states such as the United States and Great Britain. Their actual thesis, however, is that the presence of social problems correlates with income disparities within the country. The greater the income disparities, the more problems and vice versa.

Wilkinson and Pickett chose for their analysis 23 countries that they regarded as comparable from among the world's 50 richest nations. They excluded nations without comparable data on income disparity and ones with populations of less than three million, some of the latter being tax havens poorly suited to comparisons. They considered social and health problems with the aid of an index containing the following variables: life expectancy, teenage pregnancies, obesity, mental health problems, homicides, prison population size, trust ("most people can be trusted"), social mobility, education and infant mortality. The connections between the variables and income disparity were also considered individually.

According to Wilkinson's and Pickett's results the small income differences in the Nordic countries and Japan correlate with fewer social problems, while large-scale income disparity for example in the United States and Great Britain correlate with an abundance of social problems. The homicide rate in the United States (6 per 100,000 of population) is four times that of Great Britain (1.5 per 100,000) and 12 times the Japanese rate (0.5 per 100,000). With the exception of Finland,[5] the Nordic countries have a homicide rate of less than one person per 100,000. The prison population has also been steadily growing in the United States since the 1970s. According to Wilkinson's and Pickett's (2009, pp. 148–149, 246) data based on a United Nations survey of crime trends and systems of criminal justice, the United States has 4.5 times the number of prisoners (576 per 100,000 of population) compared with Great Britain (124 per 100,000) and 14 times the relative number of prisoners in Japan (40 per 100,000). According to data from the International Centre for Prison Studies of Great Britain, the United States has more than 700 prisoners per 100,000 people, giving the country a less than flattering first place internationally (Stiglitz 2013, pp. 19, 388). The French economist Thomas Piketty (2013, p. 765) points out that approximately 1% of adult Americans and over 5% of adult African American males were incarcerated in 2013. It is thus no wonder that in the United States public spending on prisons has grown six times faster than expenditure on public education. In some states, the amount of public funds for maintaining and building prisons is now equivalent to spending on tertiary education. Finland's prison population, on the other hand, has shrunk from being one of the highest in Western Europe in the 1950s (187 per 100,000 of population) to currently one of the lowest in Europe (68 per 100,000).[6] Also in the other Nordic countries, the numbers of prisoners are among the lowest in Europe.

In 2016, life expectancy in the United States (all: 78.5 years; males: 76.0 years; females: 81.0 years) was slightly lower than in Great Britain (all: 81.4 years; males: 79.7 years; females: 83.2 years), but significantly lower than in Japan (all 84.2 years; males: 81.1 years; females: 87.1 years). In the 2000s, mortality among the uneducated white population in the United States grew significantly in all age groups (25 to 64-year-olds), which has in fact led to lowered average life expectancy for all

Americans (Case and Deaton 2015, 2017). The mortality rate of uneducated white Americans has already exceeded that of African Americans, which has traditionally been higher. For example, in the 50 to 54-year-old age group in 1999, mortality among uneducated whites was 30% lower than among African Americans, while in 2015 it was 30% higher than among African Americans of the same age group (Case and Deaton 2017). Life expectancy in the Nordic countries is higher than in the United States, but the figures for both Denmark (all: 81.2 years; males: 79.3 years; women: 83.2 years) and Finland (all: 81.4 years; males: 78.7 years; women: 84.2 years) are quite close to both the American and British average life expectancies.[7] With regard to other metrics of welfare, Finland has been successful along with the other Nordic countries.

Wilkinson and Pickett (2009) observe the same point that is indirectly suggested by the above index of social progress. The economic growth of a country and the average growth of the income of its citizens have almost completely ceased to increase welfare in rich countries. Despite this, health and social problems within societies are still connected to income. Wilkinson and Pickett measure income disparity by comparing the income of the richest and poorest fifth of the population in a country. According to this metric, Japan, with the smallest differences of income, and the Nordic countries, with Finland immediately following Japan, are at the lower end of the income disparity scale. In both Japan and the Nordic countries, the richest fifth of the population is approximately four times richer than the poorest fifth, while in the United States the difference is over eight-fold.

According to Wilkinson and Pickett (2009, pp. 15–20, 135–136, 301–311), the success of the Nordic countries and Japan according to various metrics of welfare is thus due to their equal distribution of income. They maintain that all members of society benefit from low-income disparity, including the most affluent. This is shown by, among other things, the fact that in countries with small differences of income crime is at a lower level than in ones of major income disparity (see also Daly 2016). An increasing feeling of insecurity and the need to protect one's home behind walls and barbed wire hardly correspond to the interests of the rich either, not least because security always comes at a price. Finnish criminologist Janne Kivivuori (2013, pp. 366–368 [cit. p. 367]) observes in his book *Rikollisuuden syyt* (The Causes of Crime) that "it is difficult but possible to reduce the amount of crime; and presumably to increase it through more poverty and inequality in society." Although some crime is always due to universal human tendencies and competencies (individual factors), crime is still largely a social phenomenon. A welfare state combating social inequality can thus also reduce crime and create a greater feeling of security.

Another widely used metric of inequality is the Gini coefficient, measuring income equality throughout the population. The Gini coefficient can have values between zero and one (or alternatively between zero and one hundred. A coefficient of 0 implies completely equal income, i.e. everyone receiving the same amount, whole 1 (or 100) indicates extreme income inequality, with the richest person grabbing all income without leaving a red cent to anyone else. Japan had the same Gini coefficient as Finland had in 2012 before taxes and redistribution of income. With allowance for taxes and income redistribution, Japan was outranked by Finland and many other OECD countries, achieving a higher Gini coefficient. Although Japanese income redistribution to the needy is by no means of the same extent as in the Nordic countries, income disparity still remains at a low degree, for the gross earnings of Japanese higher income groups are in international comparison much closer to average earnings than in the United States or in many other countries. Moriguchi and Saez (2010, pp. 76–112) point out that the share of income of the top 1% in Japan has grown quite moderately since 1977. The small degree of income inequality in Japan is also due to the labor shortage from which the country has suffered since the 1960s. It tends to keep wages relatively high. Furthermore, the income of the top 1% in Japan has not significantly consisted of investment income since the Second World War. Instead, wages and salaries have had the largest and also growing share.

Being epidemiologists, Wilkinson and Pickett, however, paint a far too positive picture of equality in Japan with reference to the excellent health record of the Japanese. The equality index of the World Economic Forum's *Global Gender Gap Report* of 2017 ranks Japan clearly lower than the Nordic countries at 114th out of 144 countries, with the Nordic countries placed highest. Nor is Japan particularly well ranked in comparisons of proportion of people living in poverty and the incidence of childhood poverty, with the highest scores in this respect among the OECD countries.[8]

The Japanese model of the welfare state has been regarded as corporate-centered. Social security in Japan is based on lifetime employment with a salary structure reflecting the employee's process of setting up a family and life span (Esping-Andersen 1997, pp. 179–189). The Japanese welfare state has traditionally relied a great deal on the family and corporations. There have been no universal or generous state-provided social benefits in the country. In its social policies, the Japanese model of the welfare state emphasizes investment in economically profitable purposes, such as education[9] and public healthcare instead of offering a safety net for those unable to contribute to national wealth. The care of children and the elderly therefore remains largely the responsibility of women. Opinion surveys, however, show that in present-day Japan there is more support for generous public social security than previously, which may be due to recent unfavorable demographic, social and economic changes in Japanese society (Sumino 2014, pp. 109–133).

The Japanese population is aging at a very fast pace together with a drastically decreasing birth rate. The population is estimated to decrease from 128 million (in 2010) to 87 million by 2060. The increasing share of the elderly in the demographic structure leads to problems. The aging trend of the population is similar in many Western countries, but Japan is in the forefront of these developments. In addition, the cost of education has risen in Japan and the labor market has changed. As elsewhere, part-time work has increased in Japan, undermining the desire of firms and companies to have a commitment to their employees and to arrange social security for them. Lifetime employment and automatically raised pay are no longer self-evident. This has increased demands in Japan for the state to take greater responsibility to ensure welfare services (Goodman 2008; Peng 2000, pp. 87–114; Sumino 2014, pp. 109–133; Takegawa 2010, pp. 53–67).

In addition to the their overly positive description of Japan, Wilkinson's and Pickett's results have been criticized for their choice of inequality variable and countries to be compared, and also for using a simple correlation method and cross-sectional data (see e.g. Saunders 2010). Despite criticism and its occasional veracity, the connection of equality with welfare appears undeniable at least concerning some variables measuring risks the welfare of citizens. These were HIV/AIDS contagion, life expectancy, infant mortality and homicide. Using a body of data larger than Wilkinson's and Pickett's or that used by Peter Saunders, who had criticized the latter, and by applying adjusted regression models Heikki Hiilamo and Olli Kangas (2012) discovered statistically significant connections between the above measures of risks to welfare and income disparity. The connection of income inequality with higher male and female mortality, especially in the age-groups 1–14 and 15–49, was confirmed by Roberta Torre's and Mikko Myrskylä's (2014) study of 21 developed countries analyzing longitudinal data (from 1975 to 2006). According to this study, infant and young adult mortality are lower in societies of relatively even income distribution than in ones with less equal distribution. Torre's and Myrskylä's results suggest that income distribution appears to have a closer connection with mortality among young adult males than females. A society of greater equality actually corresponds to the interests of the more affluent population, because higher average life expectancy, lower infant mortality and a lower crime rate concern all citizens. It is also obvious that in international perspective the Nordic model of the welfare state is of good standard in many respects.[10] It aims at implementing equality among genders, classes of society and generations. What is the mechanism that generates welfare benefiting everyone in the Nordic model?

Trust

"The welfare state was not built upon the mutual trust of people," wrote Matti Apunen, head of the Finnish Business and Policy Forum (EVA) in the newspaper *Helsingin Sanomat* in spring 2013. He noted that, instead, the welfare state required its citizens to trust officials, "who rabidly lay down norms precisely because we do not trust other people."[11]

Finnish sociologist Antti Kouvo (2011; Kouvo et al. 2012) has studied the connection of the type of welfare state with how much unknown people or the institutions of public authorities are trusted. The results of data from extensive and representative questionnaires concerning Finland and other European countries clearly support earlier results. The countries whose welfare services are based on universalism, and especially those that also provide last-resort basic social assistance, are the best breeding ground for generalized trust. "Generalized trust" means to trust that fellow human beings unknown to each other do not want to harm one another explicitly or deliberately.

Along with generalized trust, the type of welfare state explains the institutional confidence of people, i.e. trust in the institutions of society, the government, the judiciary, parliament or the police. According to the World Values Survey of 2005–2009,[12] 58.9% of Finns and 68% of Swedes responded affirmatively to the claim "most people can be trusted." According to the European Social Survey of 2014, Finns were more trusting than ever before in the history of this survey (launched in 2002) and Finland was the second most trusting country in Europe.[13] An alarming decrease of social trust, including generalized trust, can, however, be seen among young Finns (ages 15–29) and in particular among boys and the youngest age groups (15 to 19-year-olds) (Myllyniemi 2017, pp. 39–42). This may suggest that in the future also the trust of Finns in other people will decrease. In the World Values Survey of 2005–2009, only 30.5% of Britons and 39.3% of US citizens felt that most people can be trusted. Nor did the 2005–2009 survey indicate trust in major companies among these citizens of Anglo-Saxon countries. The British score for a great deal or quite a lot of confidence in major companies was 36.6% of respondents compared to only 26.6% in the United States. The proportion in Finland was 45.3% and 50.9% in Sweden. Neither do people seem to trust the banking system in the United States. A questionnaire survey by American Express showed 29% of respondents said that they kept part of their savings in cash elsewhere than in a bank account. According to American Express, the withdrawal of savings from bank accounts became widespread with the outbreak of the economic crisis in 2008. The functioning of the market economy, or capitalism, is specifically based on mutual trust, i.e. the opposite party proceeding as expected and in a lawful manner.[14]

Individual factors, such as socioeconomic variables (education, employment, social class) and age, no doubt explain trust in other citizens and institutions to a great deal. In addition, personal experiences, for example, of discrimination, feelings of insecurity and low income erode both generalized trust and institutional confidence. According to research by Kouvo (2011; Kouvo et al. 2012), the fact, in particular, of having personally received means-tested benefits undermined the recipient's generalized trust in other people. This, however, was not the case when these benefits were felt to be sufficient and their availability was trusted.

The feeling of insecurity is closely associated with one's immediate environment and whether this environment produces this feeling. The so-called broken window theory predicts an increase of crime in environments that are dirty, untended and include general social disorder (Zimbardo 2008, pp. 25, 305). A setting of this kind gives the impression that no one is responsible, cares or watches over things. A study carried out in two housing areas of a British city supports this assumption. The trust of the inhabitants of the less reputable area in other, previously unknown, people was clearly lower than among the residents of the more highly regarded area. The same results have been obtained in similar questionnaire surveys. The cited study also showed that people react very quickly and instinctively to feelings produced by the immediate surroundings. The very fact of moving from a reputable housing area to a poorly regarded one is enough to lower the level of trust. When the test persons were sent to both areas and their level of trust was measured afterward with a questionnaire, the visitors to the poorly regarded area were clearly less trusting toward other people than those who visited the better area. The difference was almost as great as the difference measured between the actual residents of the respective areas. The good care of public space and the prevention of a social disorder in both richer and poorer housing areas and the prevention of socioeconomic segregation can promote the creation of an environment that feels safer and arouses trust (Nettle et al. 2014).

Kouvo's results show that in all types of welfare states the perception of citizens of whether the needy deserve their benefits is associated with generalized trust and whether the services provided by the state are felt to be equal and fair. The latter connection, in particular, was evident in the Nordic type of welfare state (Kouvo 2011). Institutional trust, for example, confidence in the fairness of taxation, was the main explanatory factor of generalized trust, i.e. trust in unknown fellow citizens. The perception of taxation as fair was also the main background factor of differences in the level of trust observed among citizens of Nordic and other European welfare states (Kouvo et al. 2012). Kouvo points out (2009), that an active civic society with non-governmental organizations is partly associated with generalized trust, but the relation of cause and effect is not unequivocal. It may also be possible that civic society in different types of states (e.g. liberal vs. universalist welfare states) creates generalized trust in different ways.

Research disproves Apunen's above-mentioned claim that the bureaucratic welfare state assumes that its citizens do not trust each other and that the authorities, therefore, "rabidly" issue norms and laws restricting personal freedom of action—as he puts it. As indicated by Kouvo's results, the universalist welfare state explicitly *produces* more trust between people than other types of the welfare state. Compliance with the law, achieved with the deterrent of severe prison sentences, is, in fact, more a characteristic of the liberal welfare states admired by Apunen—or dictatorships.

A great deal of trust in fellow citizens and the institutions of public authorities is also evident in Finnish society in poverty not usually being regarded as one's own fault but neither as the failing of society, which is opposite to attitudes in both former socialist countries and liberal welfare states. A definite majority of the Finnish population regards the causes of poverty to be external and structural factors independent of human characteristics, such as widespread unemployment, or inevitable setbacks such as bad luck and illness. Finns, however, differ from other Nordics in considering the individual to be somewhat more likely to be the cause of his or her poverty than is felt in Finland's western neighbors.

The prevailing system of the welfare society is nonetheless clearly associated with opinions on the causes of poverty. Who is asked is hardly of any consequence, because the respondent's background (education or income) does not appear to have much influence on the opinions of Finns regarding the reasons for poverty. Differences among Finns in this respect emerge only when the question concerns reasons for poverty among different sectors of the population. Finns namely see the causes of poverty in different ways depending on whether the question concerns the poverty of pensioners, families with children or immigrants. In slightly pointed terms, poverty is attributed to personal traits when speaking of immigrants and to the structures of society when referring to pensioners and families with children. The benefits officers of *Kela*, i.e. the people upon whose decisions the income of the neediest often depends, follow a way of thinking similar to the rest of the population. They, too, place more emphasis on structural causes and less to individual reasons when moving from immigrants to children with families and pensioners. Generally speaking, views to the effect that the poor are responsible for their own poverty clearly find more support among the general population than among benefits officers, who appear on all accounts to have more factual information about these matters than the average citizen. Differences of opinion regarding the reasons for poverty among different groups within the population are generally smaller among benefits officers than among Finns in general. The opinions of *Kela* personnel on the underuse or abuse of *Kela* benefits are also associated with their views on the reasons for poverty. Those who attributed poverty to personal reasons were also more concerned about the abuse of benefits, while those emphasizing the structural causes of poverty also underlined the insufficient use of benefits more than their abuse (Niemelä 2007, 2009, 2010).

Inequality most likely engenders or at least reinforces mistrust of other people. The further "others" are from "us" and the more divergent our lives are, the easier it is to maintain that not everyone is entitled to the same benefits. If poverty or being disadvantaged is also considered a possibility for oneself or if the poor are felt to be "us," it is easier to regard support for them as fair and in keeping with the norm of reciprocity. An environment providing security and small differences between groups of people will also make people regard other, unknown, people as partners in cooperation instead of a threat or as competitors. Collaboration, in turn, is based on mutual assistance. By trusting others, even unknown people, one can even improve personal health. It has namely been observed that trusting people live longer (Wilkinson and Pickett 2009, pp. 52–62). The considerable economic and social distance between whites and African Americans in the United States helps explain the undeveloped character of the American welfare state. Branko Milanovic (2016, p. 207) suspects that immigration to Europe from other continents may erode the hitherto existing feeling of belonging within populations and ultimately the European welfare state.

Social Mobility

Social mobility means opportunities for people to move up or down on the social scale during their lifetime, either in relation to people of the same age (intragenerational mobility) or to one's parents (intergenerational mobility). This has become possible in modern democratic societies in a completely different way than in the earlier hierarchical class societies. Present-day welfare states, in fact, seek to ensure the opportunity to influence one's own standing through personal ability by offering everyone equal opportunities, which is supported throughout the political spectrum, at least in principle. In present-day welfare states, the equality of opportunity and the promise that individuals can improve their status through hard work make the expectation of reciprocity a core factor of relations between the people and those in power in a completely new way. In earlier societies based on inequality, birth (class) generally defined the position of the individual and his or her descendants for all time to come. The authorities and rulers collecting taxes did not even promise the possibility of upward social mobility to the people. The lack of developed technologies, severe natural conditions and heavy taxation forced the common people to work hard, which, however, produced rewards in the form of rising in society in only extremely few exceptional cases. On the other hand, present-day society provides the opportunity of upward mobility as a reward for hard work, which also means that more can be demanded from society.

It is most likely impossible to completely eradicate nepotism from human societies. Moreover, some human traits are hereditary. Therefore, wealth and socioeconomic status will inevitably be passed on from parents to children in even the most egalitarian societies. It is, however, possible to have an effect on the extent of opportunities for upward social mobility regardless of birth. Social mobility has traditionally been part of the success of Nordic welfare states. In these countries, equality of opportunity has been sought by means such as educational and housing policies and by providing all citizens with an extensive system of social and health services of high standard. Especially for the post-Second World War baby boom generation in Finland, upward mobility on the social scale past the class status of one's parents was more the rule than the exception. At present, however, intergenerational mobility in Finland is no longer as self-evident as it used to be. In his study of differences of mobility between birth cohorts in Finland (2009), sociologist Jani Erola observed that increased relative mobility applied actually to only the cohorts born in the period from 1941 to 1965. The significance of the class status of parents has particularly grown for the youngest cohorts of the analysis, born in the period 1971–1975. Erola suspects that education will no longer provide cross-generational equality as effectively as previously. The expansion of education may result in its inflation, increasing cross-generational inequality rather than reducing it. The situation in Finland has not yet reached this stage, and Erola suggests as an explanation for reduced intergenerational mobility differences between cohorts in the initial stages of their working careers. Unemployment or insecure employment at this stage is reflected in the later working career and accordingly in class status, which generally becomes established by the age of 35. This also appears to be the case for the cohorts of the 1980s, who were prevented on the long recession of the 2010s from properly finding a place in working life and whose income levels, therefore, risk remaining lower than those of older age-groups.[15]

In the Nordic countries, the professional and class status of parents no longer defines, as a rule, the future and opportunities of their children. Family background, however, always has some impact on education and the choice of an occupation or profession, since social and cultural capital are also inherited along with economic resources (Sirniö 2016). Consequently, there are no grounds to claim that Finland is not a class society. It is, however, less of a class society where the affluence and means of parents define almost completely the opportunities of children to have, for example, health services or education of high standard (Putnam 2015). In the Nordic countries and Finland there is still considerably more intergenerational mobility than, for example in Great Britain or the United States (Hiilamo 2011, p. 96; Putnam 2015; Wilkinson and Pickett 2009, pp. 157–169).

The Finnish comprehensive school is one of the most important ways of ensuring social mobility. Alongside it, we must mention university-level education, which is still free and means that there are no economic obstacles to university studies for the children of less affluent families. All this, however, is due to basic education on an equal basis, provided for all children in Finland through the comprehensive school reform carried out in the 1970s. The public comprehensive school system and its teachers with their high level of education have made it possible to have only minor differences among Finnish schools in international comparison. The Finnish comprehensive school, sometimes known as "the equality-producing miracle," has received and continues to receive a great deal of international admiration. Its excellence has been noted in the international PISA studies of the skills of students in basic education. Carried out since 2000, the PISA studies assess at three-year intervals the skills of young people aged 15–16 in mathematics, science subjects, reading skills and problem solving. Finnish schoolchildren have achieved top results in the tests except for the most recent assessments. While Finnish schoolchildren still have high scores in the European context, Finland's overall ranking has dropped, which is due not only to improved skills elsewhere but also to a lower level of skills among Finnish schoolchildren. The drop in the ranking and variation in skills were considerable especially in science, which was the main PISA assessment area in 2006 and 2015 (Vettenranta et al. 2016, pp. 21, 34–36). Other disturbing signs for the Finnish comprehensive school system in the most recent PISA studies were the drop in the standard of the most poorly performing decile of Finnish schools (although inter-school differences are still very small in international comparison) and the clearly lower level of performance of boys compared with girls in both science subjects and reading skills (Kupari et al. 2013; Vettenranta et al. 2016, pp. 45–52, 57). The influence of the home background on learning results has also increased in Finland and regional inequality has begun to emerge, which had not been previously seen in Finland between the countryside and cities or between different regions of the country (Vettenranta et al. 2016, pp. 94–97).

Finland has led the Nordic countries in the PISA rankings and continues to do so. Basic education in Finland is of a considerably better standard than in Sweden, which has never been ranked very high in the PISA assessments. In Sweden (as also in Finland) the nine-year basic or comprehensive schooling is, however, free of cost, being organized by either the local municipality or a private so-called free school (*friskola*) approved by the state educational authorities. There are also private fee-paying schools in Sweden, but their numbers of pupils and students are small. On the other hand, the numbers of pupils and students at the comprehensive and high school level in the free schools have been growing throughout the 2000s. The free schools, which should be available to everyone regardless of background, have been accused of deliberately choosing pupils and students who perform better.[16]

In the PISA rankings, Sweden has remained below the average for the OECD countries in almost all tested areas. Differences between schools in Sweden have grown throughout the 2000s, which critics attribute to children being allowed to choose their school freely regardless of where they live. Critics of the system claim that "school shopping" has increased disparity, dividing schools into "good" and "poor." Freedom of choice ensures the children of well-to-do families a learning environment and schoolmates commensurate with their social status but is in conflict with Sweden's reputation of a model country of social equality, which it holds with due cause in many areas. The situation in Sweden, however, is not yet as alarming as in the United States, where the standards of basic-level schools vary greatly. This is due to their system of funding. Schools receive most of their funding from local government, whereby regional inequality is markedly reflected in the resources of schools.

Education in Great Britain is known to socially segregate pupils and students to a considerable degree. The majority of schoolchildren in the United Kingdom finish their compulsory education in the comprehensive schools originally introduced by Harold Wilson's Labour government in the 1960s. Prior to that, the eleven-plus examination at the age of eleven gave schoolchildren access either to higher levels of education or training for a trade, which maintained the traditional divisions of class.

At present, over 90% children in the United Kingdom attend a state-funded school free of charge and the remainder of less than 10% a private fee-paying school. Despite this, private schools educate the majority of the nation's leaders. A commission studying social mobility and childhood poverty noted in its report that elitism is still so ingrained in Great Britain that it could even be called the result of "social planning."[17] The elites of society are recruited from among a small group of people who have attended private schools, which usually require an upper-class background. For example, 71% of higher-level judges, 62% of higher officers in the armed forces and 50% of the members of the House of Lords have attended private schools.

An experiment was carried out in India in the early 2000s, measuring the problem-solving abilities of 11 to 12-year-old boys of higher and lower castes. So long as the boys were unaware of each other's castes, the lower-caste boys completed the tests as well or even better than the boys of higher castes. The roles changed once the boys' names, home villages and castes were revealed. The test results of the lower-caste boys deteriorated markedly. This phenomenon is not restricted to India or the caste system. In the United States, high school students were given a two-stage test in which the organizers stated that one part would test their abilities while the other stage would not. This had no effect on the results of white students, while the African-American students had poorer results when the test was stated to gauge their abilities (Wilkinson and Pickett 2009, pp. 113–115, 193–194). In other words, sharp inequality will make individuals of weaker social status underachieve in relation to their actual abilities, which means that society will not receive a full contribution in accordance with the capabilities of its members.

Universalism

The Nordic model of the welfare state has traditionally been based on the notion of universalism. The equality of opportunity that has been sought has been implemented by providing the same publicly produced services and equal benefits for all citizens regardless of their wealth. The idea behind universalism is for everyone to pay and everyone to benefit, which creates a commitment for all classes of society—especially the broad middle class—to support the welfare state. Extensive public services and income distribution are namely funded mostly by taxes, with the middle class as the main payer. If means-testing cutting back on benefits and services to a greater degree than at present is practiced, there is the risk of society gradually adopting the notion that the remaining social services are a marginal phenomenon only concerning the poor and they can be allowed to deteriorate.

Income tax in the Nordic welfare states is part of the system of redistributing income. It levels the amount of disposable income. On the one hand, taxation thus influences equality among citizens in terms of income distribution (though by no means all taxes are progressive). On the other hand, taxation, together with services provided by the state and the system protecting people against social risks, responds to expectations of reciprocity between the state and citizens. Public services and benefits funded with taxes are one of the mechanisms that maintain reciprocity in the universalist welfare state.

In Finland, the welfare state, enjoyed wide support among citizens regardless of political affiliation or socioeconomic status, both before and after the recession of the 1990s. Finns support both public income distribution and welfare services and have a critical view of measures that undermine them. Traditionally, the widest support is for services aimed at children and the elderly and their cutbacks, in turn, arouse the greatest disapproval (Paloheimo 2010, pp. 28–39; see also Jæger 2012, pp. 45–68). As observed by social policy expert Johanna Kallio (2010, pp. 14, 61, cit. p. 90) in her study of attitudes to the Finnish welfare state: "The social contract concerning the welfare state and its system of services is closely maintained by people of different generations and different social status. Finns want … to keep their universal and public system of welfare services, although private social security is being acquired more and income disparity has increased."

The Generational Transmissions in Finland research project monitors assistance and attitudes related to assistance between generations in families. It surveyed both in 2007 and 2012, i.e. before and during the most recent economic recession, the views of the two generations of Finns, the baby-boomers (born 1945–1950) and their adult children, on various familial obligations and the respective responsibilities of the family and society in the care of the elderly. According to the surveys, both generations regard the care of the elderly, especially their economic support to be the responsibility of society. Attitudes had hardly changed over the five-year follow-up period (Danielsbacka et al. 2013, pp. 52–53; Tanskanen and Danielsbacka 2009). In qualitative interviews in the same body of material, members of both generations raised the assumption of reciprocity associated with taxation:

> Well, it seems to me that since I've paid a fair amount of taxes, society should respond ... it depends on the situation, so if the children are in a good economic situation and they want to, out of their own heart, to do something, well that's quite OK. But somehow some of that tax money, having paid so much of it ... to get some of it back. (Female, born 1949)

> What you need for nutrition on a daily basis that's the responsibility of society. It is so that they [the elderly] have nonetheless paid in a few euros in taxes so maybe some of it could be got back. (Male, born 1974)

The idea of reciprocity between citizens and the state that is associated with taxation inevitably leads to the question of what welfare entitlements and services middle-class Finnish tax payers actually receive—or are entitled to receive—in return for the taxes paid by them. The welfare state expanded in Finland until the early 1990s. The economic recession of the 1990s led to a qualitatively different stage of the welfare state. New systems are no longer being constructed and instead, earlier ones are being modified and reduced. Emphasis on economic competitiveness on the one hand and increasing needs for social policy, on the other hand, have led to permanent austerity that has also altered welfare policies to have a rhetoric increasingly resembling a zero-sum game. Benefits for some mean the reduction of benefits for others. In Finland, the new stage of the welfare state, however, has not led to major or sudden institutional changes. Instead, it has marked a gradual shift toward municipal welfare services operating on the terms of the market and the conversion of universal benefits to becoming earnings-related (Kallio 2010, pp. 19–20, 25–26, 28–35).

In principle, public healthcare, regarded as a universal service is available to everyone in Finland, but in practice, health services have diverged. The working population has access to high-quality and fast occupational healthcare, while the public sector of this area operates slowly and is continuously deteriorating. Public specialized healthcare for serious illnesses, however, is still of a high standard and its proportion of co-payment is still reasonably low. There are, however, major regional differences in basic healthcare, because Finnish municipalities are responsible for organizing welfare service and the standard and extent of health services that can be provided for local residents often depend on the wealth of the municipality in question. Mergers of municipalities in recent years and increasingly larger municipalities inevitably mean that services cannot be offered to everyone, at least in nearby locations. This also means that not all Finns can be given care with equal speed. Completely self-funded health services and private health insurance have also become more widespread, which increases inequality.[18]

In 2017, a long-planned reform of the structure of social and health services aroused a great deal of debate in Finland. The purpose of the reform is to transfer responsibility for public social and health services from municipalities to larger administrative units (regions) and to reduce related costs and differences of welfare and health among citizens and to improve access to services and their equality. When passed, the so-called act on the freedom of choice included in the reform would allow users of services to choose more freely than at present between a social and healthcare center and some other service provider. It is this aspect of the reform that has aroused perhaps the greatest amount of criticism.[19] Many researchers and professors in this field have criticized the reforms under preparation for possibly having repercussions in reality that would be contrary to what was intended. Excessive reliance on outside contractors combined with the (optional) incorporation of public health services may magnify complexity, reduce performance, increase costs and impair accountability. Corruption can be covered up and taxes can be avoided by referring to trade secrets. Large amounts of public tax revenue are involved in health services and their use should be as transparent as possible.

Nor is it necessarily far-fetched to suggest that blaming the poor will expand to blaming the ill. The more health services diverge, the more will it be possible to blame the sick for various illnesses, such as obesity or lung cancer that are considered to be self-inflicted, and demand that they pay for their own care.[20]

CRACKS IN THE FAÇADE

A male resident of Helsinki who had knifed his drinking companion to death has been convicted of manslaughter in the Helsinki District Court and sentenced to 11 years in prison. [The 31-year-old] convicted man killed another male in his apartment in Käpylä in Helsinki last February. The man had been drinking before the incident and at the time of the homicide there were two other men in the apartment. [The convicted male] and the victim got into an argument in connection with which [the perpetrator] first hit the victim with his fist and then in the legs and neck with a kitchen knife. The convicted male said in court that he had been drinking for several days before the incident and previously almost daily. He had no recollection of how the victim had come to the apartment or of how the knife had come to be in the victim's neck.[21]

The Nordic model of the welfare state, which is discussed in the above sections, appears to be almost superior to others in international comparison. Its cracks and fissures, however, emerge upon closer inspection. The above minor news item published in the *Helsingin Sanomat* newspaper in the summer of 2011, tells of a crack in the façade typical of Finnish society, homicide. It describes the most typical kind of killing in Finland, committed in a home with the perpetrator and victim most likely known to each other, unemployed males living alone. At the time of the incident, both are intoxicated. The weapon is a knife, usually a kitchen knife, and other people are present. No one really recalls what happened. The incident takes place on a weekend. The homicide described in the article differs from the most typical pattern in that it was committed by a relatively young man, aged around 30. In most cases, both the felon and the victim are middle-aged.

Incidents of capital crime have been decreasing in Finland in the twenty-first century, but they still occur at a yearly average of 1.5 per 100,000 of population.[22] This is twice as much as in the other Nordic countries, where the annual average is less than one homicide per 100,000 people. The homicide rate in Finland is sixth highest in the European Union,[23] but still very low in overall international comparison, because the whole area of the EU is one of the least violent in the world.

In Finland, capital crimes are mostly committed among substance abusers who have become marginalized from working life. The intoxicants used by perpetrators and victims often include legal psychopharmaceutic medication for the treatment of mental health problems alongside alcohol. Most of the perpetrators are multiple offenders of violent crimes. The motives for homicides are mostly drunken arguments and there are rarely motives pointing to premeditation. The incidence of capital crime among other socioeconomic groups in Finland hardly differs from the rest of Western Europe. Capital crimes also have a distinct geographic distribution in Finland, occurring several times more in East and North Finland than in the western or southern parts of the country.

The difference is partly due to the fact that, owing to long distances from hospitals, ambulances reach victims too late in the north and the east (Lauerma 2014, pp. 81–92; Lehti 2014, pp. 3–7, 10, 12–13, 33). The high incidence of capital crime in Finland also offers a new perspective on the problem areas of contemporary Finnish society, although the significant homicide rate has its roots not only in present-day problems of society but also in the distant past in Finnish culture (Koskivirta 2003; Ylikangas 1999). Current high homicide statistics, however, are attributable to a clearly defined group of people who have marginalized from society (Niemelä and Saari 2013). The prevailing attitude to them appears to be that we have always had these drunks among us and nothing can be done to help them unless they themselves agree to use available social services. A kind of indifference to them is also evident in the fact that this group of people includes numerous victims of repeated violence.[24]

Foreign experts speaking in 2009 at a seminar organized by *Kela*, the National Pensions Institute of Finland, estimated that Finnish society is markedly divided among so-called insiders and outsiders. The social security system ensures relatively good benefits for insiders, i.e. employed people. These benefits include, in particular, health services and income-related unemployment benefits, while basic social security benefits for people outside the labor market and the sphere of income-related benefits are poor (Hiilamo et al. 2010, pp. 7–9). Homicides among drinking companions can be regarded as an extreme example of the effects of alienation, although the recent growth of inequality is not a direct underlying reason for capital crime in Finland.

Regarded as a universalist welfare state, Finland today appears to have two tiers of people: those able to partake of both the well-functioning system of services and income redistribution and those remaining without. The haves are the employed, clients of occupational healthcare and people entitled to income-related benefits and income redistribution. The have-nots are those who are not in working life and are outside the sphere of income-related benefits and have to manage on basic and minimum social security benefits.

In the early 2000s, social policy expert Heikki Hiilamo (2003) introduced the notion of the "bureaucracy trap" to describe a specific problem of the Finnish social security system related to the insufficiency of means-tested benefits. Short-term employment is actually not worthwhile in all situations. In the Finnish benefits system, other social benefits awarded in addition to unemployment benefits such as housing support or basic social assistance cannot be accommodated in practice to short periods of employment. The rigidity of the system leads to a situation of overlapping benefits and wages. Benefits are first paid in excess and then later recovered from the recipient, which means that a short period of employment will only lead to more income problems (Hiilamo 2011, pp. 62–67). Some of these bureaucratic or incentive traps have subsequently been removed, but researchers still criticize the point that the unemployed, especially recipients of basic social assistance and labor market subsidies for job seeking are often treated in an unnecessarily rough manner.[25] Antti Kouvo, who has considered the origin of trust in these contexts, has observed that those with experience of means-tested benefits will trust other people less. This, however, is not the case if these benefits are felt to be sufficient and their availability is trusted. The humiliation of the poor (some prefer to embellish this as "providing incentive") is thus counter-productive over the long term.

A core feature of the Nordic model has been a reasonable level of benefits and assistance, including minimum social security. Minimum social security benefits mainly apply to the very poorest and are strictly means-tested also in the Nordic countries. Basic social assistance, for example, is a minimum social security benefit. Benefits of this kind have traditionally been only small part of all social security benefits, but they have been important as assistance of last resort. The Nordic countries have been ranked internationally high in terms of minimum social security benefits and the poverty-reducing effects of their respective systems. The Nordic countries and Finland, however, display a course of development in growing income disparity that began in the 1990s, with growing numbers of poor people in society whose benefits continued to diminish. Relative poverty in Finland has grown at a record pace compared with other OECD countries,[26] as well as income disparity, which, however, is low in European perspective.

The Constitution of Finland (Section 19) notes that the state must be able to provide all citizens with necessary subsistence and care when individuals themselves are incapable of acquiring them. Basic social security is thus one of the duties of the welfare state. Basic social security entitlements in accordance with the constitution are basic social assistance, the basic per diem allowance for unemployment security, labor market subsidies, per diem allowances for illness and maternity or paternity and national pensions for inability to work, old age and the loss of a guardian. The constitution, however, does not define in any further detail the sufficient level of basic social security (Kangas et al. 2013, pp. 6–15).

Social policy expert Susan Kuivalainen has studied (2010) how Finland has managed with regard to the level and sufficiency of minimum or basic social security in comparison with Norway, Denmark and Sweden, considering developments from the early 1990s to 2005. The results show that Finland is still (or was at least at the time) a member of the Nordic "family," but the reason for this is that the level of minimum social security has sunk and poverty among welfare recipients has increased in all the Nordic countries. The situation in Finland is thus no exception. The Nordic basic social security systems, however, are still well placed in international comparison, because the level of basic social security has also gone down everywhere else and poverty among those dependent on it has increased. One of the main underlying ideas of politicians is to prevent basic social security from becoming an alternative with too much appeal. It has therefore been allowed to lag behind in the overall development of real earning, despite the fact that poverty has increased considerably, along with all its negative consequences, which have no doubt led to costs exceeding the achieved savings. This has probably also been a response to the disapproving moral views held by many about people on social assistance. The Nordic model is thus still in a special position compared with other forms of the welfare state, but the difference is no longer as great as it used to be. There may be considerable differences with regard to individual countries and not all the liberal welfare states can be classed together. In the United Kingdom, for example, the level of basic social security has increased during the twenty-first century, being even higher than in Sweden in 2010 (Kuivalainen and Nelson 2012).

Differences in Health

In his book *The Killing Fields of Inequality*, Swedish sociologist Göran Therborn (2013, pp. 10–19, 49, 132–136) analyses three types of inequality in the present world: inequality with regard to life expectancy and health, inequality of existence and human dignity and inequality of available resources. The Nordic welfare state has not been able to conquer the inequality of life expectancy and health. While average life expectancy in the Nordic countries and Finland is quite high in international comparison (e.g. approximately 82.4 years in Sweden and roughly 81.4 years in Finland in 2016),[27] but differences between socioeconomic groups are immense. In late 2007, average life expectancy of 35-year-old Finnish males in the lowest income quintile was approximately 13 years lower than in the top income quintile, and in 2013 the difference was estimated to be as much as 16 years. Among women, there is a seven-year difference in life expectancy between the highest and lowest socioeconomic groups. Also, the average male/female difference in life expectancy is roughly seven years, which is high when compared internationally. There are also regional differences of health and mortality. People in East and North Finland have poorer health than West and South Finnish, and they also die younger. The main causes of regional differences in mortality are cardiovascular diseases, accidental and violent death and alcohol-related deaths. Life expectancy increases only among higher income groups while it has remained the same in the lowest income quintile since the late 1980s (Mackenbach et al. 2008, pp. 2468–2481; Tarkiainen et al. 2013, pp. 21–27). The growth of differences in life expectancy in Finland appears to have subsequently stopped, at least between males of the top and bottom income quintiles, as life expectancy in the latter quintile began to improve in the 2010s especially because of fewer alcohol and violence-related deaths (Tarkiainen et al. 2017). Since the growth of life expectancy is particularly due to a lower rate of deaths from alcohol, one reason for it may be the increases of taxes on alcohol products carried out since 2008 after a reduction of these taxes in 2004. The reduction in 2004 was carried out contrary to recommendations from experts and it led to a considerable increased in mortality especially among the lowest socioeconomic groups (Herttua 2010). Developments in Finland in recent years have been opposite to those in America, where mortality among uneducated white has grown rapidly in the twenty-first century (Case and Deaton 2017).

Finland's National Institute for Health and Welfare has noted that major alcohol consumption and smoking explain approximately half of the health differences between social groups in the country. Differences of health are also explained by differences evident in other aspects of lifestyle from an early stage (Myllyniemi 2012, p. 48). Only approximately one out of ten senior high school students smokes, while the corresponding figure for vocational school students is 40%.[28] Smoking among young people is connected to school grades. The poorer the grades, the more common smoking is. Smoking is also strongly dependent on the home, as also children's nutritional habits, exercise and other pastimes. Obesity is also a class issue in the Western countries, attributable to the connection of class with lifestyle. Professional and vocational status has namely been found to have a clear connection with the weight index in almost all rich countries, including Finland. The index grows incrementally when moving from occupations requiring more education to ones requiring less education. Researchers have compared the connection of weight index with occupational status in Finland and Japan, respectively. It turned out that there is no such connection in Japan, which is likely due to the traditional diet of people in working-class occupations, which is low in calories in Japan but of high-calorie content in Finland (Silventoinen et al. 2013).

Differences in health between groups do not reflect only lifestyle differences. The Whitehall Study, which was launched in Great Britain in the 1960s (Marmot 2004) explored the influence of work-related stress on the mortality of civil servants at different levels of the professional hierarchy. The initial hypothesis of the study was that higher-ranking civil services were more likely to die of stress-related cardiovascular and other chronical illnesses. Surprisingly, opposite results were obtained. The mortality rate of employees at the lowest level, such as porters, was three times higher than that of higher-level officials, such as administrative managers. The greatest surprise was that differences of status in mortality remained despite allowance for lifestyle. The Whitehall researchers' results concerning the effects of socioeconomic status on differences in health is widely known. It has been explained with so-called stress theory, according to which stress associated with lower status leads to higher morbidity, thus lowering the average lifespan (Wilkinson and Pickett 2009, pp. 73–87).

In general, large income differences within a country are almost undeniably related to a lower than average life expectancy of its population. Differences in health within the population in Finland or elsewhere in the Nordic countries, however, have not completely followed recent changes in income disparity. When income disparity decreased in the 1970s and 1980s, differences in the health of socioeconomic groups did not, however, decrease as much income differences, while the sharp growth of income disparity that began in the 1990s has not led to equally dramatic increases in differences of health between various groups of the population. While these differences are growing, their increase has not become evident to completely the same degree as the growth of income disparity (Hiilamo 2010; Hiilamo and Kangas 2012).

RECIPROCITY UNDERLYING THE NORDIC WELFARE STATE

While the Nordic countries, including Finland, are not—nor have ever been—an unequivocally defined social paradise, they still stand out positively from the majority of other countries (Kvist et al. 2012, pp. 201–205). The level of equality between classes and genders alike is in many respects the best in the world. High-standard and equal basic education and a free system of tertiary education still ensure, especially in Finland, possibilities for social mobility. Mutual trust between citizens and trust in the institutions of society are at a high level in the Nordic welfare states.

The above sections discuss three aspects of responsibilities and expectations between authorities and the people that are important background factors of the support and viability of the Nordic welfare state:

Universal public services and taxation. Even high taxes are accepted if they provide in return universal social services of high quality. A universal system of services applies to as many people as possible. In other words, the system is supported partly because it corresponds to the interests of citizens. Trust in both other people and representatives of the authorities is an essential background factor of the universalist welfare state model, because individuals can regard activity for shared interests as fair if they can rely on others doing likewise (Heikkilä 2009, p. 102). The loss of trust also means the loss of a moral attitude to paying taxes. Tax evasion among ordinary citizens may be a protest against a system that is felt to be unfair (Barth et al. 2013). The human tendency toward reciprocity is a further explanation for the functioning of the universalist welfare state. The reciprocity of services and taxation in the welfare state also applies in the opposite direction. Highly affluent people fleeing to tax havens or changing their country of residence in order to avoid inheritance taxes meet disapproval because they are not "paying back" the education, healthcare and safe growth environment that they received free of charge from the state. They also show how they underrate the reliable conditions for business that have been created by the state.

The state has a duty to take care of the weakest. People want to have something in return for paid taxes, but at the same time, it is maintained that the state has a duty to take care of the weakest among us. Reciprocity between the state and the people is thus not only a purely interest-related matter, i.e. a strict balance between paid contributions and received benefits (Kallio 2010, p. 14–16; Svallfors 1997).

It is equally associated with a notion of fairness and equality according to which everyone must ensure the opportunity for a life of dignity. The Nordic model maintains that the ultimate responsibility for this lies with the state. In the Western countries, especially in the Nordic welfare states, the state has namely taken on responsibility for providing basic social security which was previously the duty of the family and of private charities. Unlike for example people in East Asia, Finns have no legally prescribed duty to take care of their aging relatives, and instead the right to basic social security ensured by the state is recorded in the Constitution of Finland. In Japan, for example, the state has no duty to provide any kind of safety net for its unproductive citizens, which means that the family (in practice women) are responsible for the care of both children and the elderly, which in turn is in keeping with the principle of Confucianism.[29] This, however, leads to situations where the needy without relatives or having relatives unable to support them will fall beyond all safety nets. In addition, the obligation to provide care often puts women in an untenable situation and may be a partial explanation for the decreasing birth rate in Japan.

The "social contract" between the state and the people (and between the strata and classes of society). Along with citizenship and its rights and obligations, the modern welfare state created a kind of reciprocal contractual relationship between the state and the people. Worldwide unrest in the twenty-first century, prevalent also in the European welfare states, partly stems from the unraveling of this social contract. The legitimacy of the welfare state of even the Nordic model may be at risk if the authorities turn a deaf ear to the aims of the people.

A consequence of increasing inequality is that the rich must invest more and more in arrangements to ensure their private security. This is in full progress in the United States, where differences of income are clearly greater than in the Nordic countries. In Finland and the Nordic countries, income disparity is at a moderate level compared with many other countries, but in both Finland and Sweden its rate of growth has been among the fastest in the Western countries. The growth of inequality leads not only to social unrest and rioting but also increases the malaise of citizens in general. The more equal a society is, the better the standard of welfare for everyone—not only the poorest. As discussed above, inequality in Finland is best reflected by the health of the most affluent and poorest elements of the population and differences in their respective life expectancies. Although not all the problems of welfare states can be attributed to income disparity, its connection with many social problems is obvious. The following sections discuss in further detail the unequal distribution of income and property and the developments that have led to the present situations and consider the American model of society from the perspective of reciprocity.

NOTES

1. On the definition of neoliberalism, see Mhone (2005, pp. 1625–1628), Outinen (2015, p. 29), Yliaska (2014, pp. 72–84).
2. Wilkinson's and Pickett's conclusions on social welfare in Japan are largely based on the excellent health of the Japanese. This, in turn, is due to the fact that in Japan also the lower socioeconomic groups follow a very healthy diet and the group-centered culture supports weaker individuals in many cases (though not always). The Japanese diet is healthy for reasons of tradition, and there are no class differences with regard to obesity, unlike for example in Finland. Silventoinen et al. (2013).
3. See e.g., *Helsingin Sanomat*, December 13, 2008 ("Suomi on rikkaiden maiden ykkönen tuloerojen kasvuvauhdissa"); *Helsingin Sanomat*, December 4, 2011 ("Tuhansien kuilujen ja railojen maa").
4. Social Progress Index 2017, http://www.socialprogressimperative.org/global-index/. Accessed July 15, 2018.
5. More on capital crime in Finland in the section *Cracks in the Façade*.
6. For example, the "Do Better – Do Less" report of a British commission on developing prisons and criminal sanctions cites Finland as an example, because Finland managed to reduce its prison population to one third while in Britain it had doubled over a period of 20 years. Commission on English Prisons Today. 2009. Do Better—Do Less: The report of the Commission on English Prisons Today, p. 12, https://d19ylpo4aovc7m. cloudfront.net/fileadmin/howard_league/user/online_publications/Do_Better_Do_Less_low_res.pdf. Accessed May 1, 2017.
7. Life expectancy data (from 2016): World Health Organization. World health statistics 2018: monitoring health for the SDGs, sustainable development goals, http://www.who.int/gho/mortality_burden_disease/life_tables/situation_trends/en/. Accessed July 15, 2018. On differences in health in Finland, see the section *Cracks in the Façade* herein.
8. UNICEF 2016; en.wikipedia.org/wiki/Poverty_in_Japan and sources cited on the webpage; *The Japan Times*, December 6, 2014 (Mark Schreiber, "Poverty takes on a new look in today's Japan"), http://www.japantimes.co.jp/news/2014/12/06/national/media-national/

poverty-takes-new-look-todays-japan; https://www.weforum.org/
reports/the-global-gender-gap-report-2017. Accessed July 15, 2018.

9. On the other hand, a good job or an executive position in Japan usually requires attending expensive private schools and studies in equally expensive private universities. As of 2012, the average annual cost of attending a private primary school in Japan was approx. US$ 10,000, https://en.wikipedia.org/wiki/Education_in_Japan. Accessed March 14, 2017. In this respect, Japan resembles the United States more than the Nordic countries, where public authorities pay to the costs of basic education and university studies.

10. The above comparison between the Nordic and other models of the welfare state does not consider ecological sustainability, an area where all consumption oriented Western countries need to make considerable improvements. See Hirvilammi (2015), Kasvio (2014).

11. *Helsingin Sanomat*, June 18, 2013 ("Odotettavissa huomenna: voimistuvaa liberalismia").

12. The Finnish and British surveys were carried out in 2005, and the Swedish and American ones in 2006.

13. *Helsingin Sanomat*, November 9, 2015 ("Luottamus kantaa suomalaisia").

14. http://www.worldvaluessurvey.org/WVSOnline.jsp. Accessed May 1, 2017. Only the United States and Sweden are listed in the results of the sixth round of the World Values Survey (compiled 2010–2014), but they indicate that the economic recession has eroded trust in other people. In the United States 35.1% and in Sweden 61.8% of respondents now responded affirmatively to the claim "most people can be trusted." On the other hand, the recession appears to increase trust in major companies: in the United States 33.5% and in Sweden 53.5% stated in 2011 that they have a great deal or quite a lot of confidence in major companies.

15. *Taloussanomat*, April 8, 2017 ("Minä vuonna synnyit? Katso, kuulutko voittajien vai häviäjien sukupolveen"), http://www.is.fi/taloussanomat/oma-raha/art-2000005160933.html. Accessed May 27, 2017.

16. *Turun Sanomat* 30.10.2013 ("SVT: Ruotsin vapaakoulut karttavat ongelmaoppilaita").

17. *The Guardian*, August 28, 2014 ("Closed shop at the top in deeply elitist Britain, says study"), http://www.theguardian.com/society/2014/aug/28/closed-shop-deepy-elitist-britain. Accessed May 1, 2017.

18. *Helsingin Sanomat*, April 22, 2014 ("Viimeisen ei tarvitse sammuttaa valoja"); *Helsingin Sanomat*, May 13, 2014 ("Sydäninfarktiin kuollaan herkimmin Lapissa").

19. *Yle uutiset* newscast, February 7, 2017 ("Professorit: Vapaudesta valita tuli mahdoton yhtälö—Talon voi polttaa vain kerran"), http://yle.fi/uutiset/3-9477663, February 27, 2017; *Helsingin Sanomat*, March 1, 2017 ("Miksi soten valinnanvapaudesta nyt väitellään? Tämä kaikki sinun tulee tietää").

20. Esko Aho, former Finnish prime minister and president of the Finnish Innovation Fund Sitra actually proposed this already in 2005, when he called for higher healthcare payments from patients who do not take care of their health but follow an unhealthy lifestyle. *Kauppalehti*, August 31, 2005 ("Esko Aho korottaisi hoitomaksuja kuntonsa laiminlyöjiltä"). Aho's proposal was widely criticized. Among other things, its unethical and unequal tone was condemned. *Helsingin Sanomat*, September 1, 2005 ("Arvostelijat moittivat Esko Ahon esitystä terveysapartheidiksi"). See also *Helsingin Sanomat*, January 26, 2014 ("Huono-osaisten auttaminen ei enää huvita").

21. *Helsingin Sanomat*, June 27, 2011 ("Ryyppykaverien riita Käpylässä johti rajuun puukotukseen").

22. *Helsingin Sanomat*, March 5, 2017 ("Suomalaisilla on nyt ainutlaatuinen tilaisuus: Henkirikoksia tekevä kossukansa voi jäädä historiaan"); June 23, 2016 ("Henkirikoksien määrä on lähes puolittunut 2000-luvulla – tutkijat ymmällään syistä").

23. Wilkinson and Pickett mistakenly suggest that Finland's high homicide rate is due to the large numbers of firearms in Finnish households (pp. 136–137), although in reality only around 3% of all homicides are committed with legally owned hunting weapons: Lauerma (2014, p. 183). Alcohol is a much more prominent reason for the high rate of capital crime.

24. *Helsingin Sanomat*, March 2, 2014 ("Väkivalta saa jatkua vuosia").

25. *Helsingin Sanomat*, April 26, 2014 (vieraskynäkirjoitus, Markku Laatu, "Höykyttäminen ei auta työttömiä eikä yhteiskuntaa"); on so-called incentive traps, see also *Helsingin Sanomat*, February 28, 2017 ("Kannustinloukut ovat pysyvä ongelma").

26. *Yle uutiset*, May 15, 2013 ("OECD: Suhteellinen köyhyys kasvanut Suomessa - Ruotsissa kehitys vielä rajumpaa"), http://yle.fi/uutiset/oecd_suhteellinen_koyhyys_kasvanut_suomessa_-_ruotsissa_kehitys_viela_rajumpaa/6643486. Accessed February 6, 2017.

27. Life expectancy data (form 2016): World Health Organization. World health statistics 2018: monitoring health for the SDGs, sustainable development goals, http://www.who.int/gho/mortality_burden_disease/life_tables/situation_trends/en/. Accessed July 15, 2018.

28. *Helsingin Sanomat*, April 22, 2014 ("Terveysongelmat kasaantuvat köyhimmille").

29. On the Confucian model of the family, see Therborn (2011, pp. 27–28).

REFERENCES

Abel-Smith, Brian. 1992. The Beveridge Report: Its Origins and Outcomes. *International Social Security Review* 45 (1–2): 5–16.

Albertini, Marco, Martin Kohli, and Claudia Vogel. 2007. Intergenerational Transfers of Time and Money in European Families: Common Patterns—Different Regimes? *Journal of European Social Policy* 17: 319–334.

Anttonen, Anneli, and Jorma Sipilä. 2000. *Suomalainen sosiaalipolitiikka*. Tampere: Vastapaino.

Barth, Erling, Alexander W. Cappelen, and Tone Ognedal. 2013. Fair Tax Evasion. *Nordic Journal of Political Economy* 38 (3): 1–16, http://www.nopecjournal.org/NOPEC_2013_a03.pdf. Accessed 27 May 2017.

Bowles, Samuel, and Herbert Gintis. 2000. Reciprocity, Self-Interest, and the Welfare State. *Nordic Journal of Political Economy* 26: 33–53.

Case, Anne, and Angus Deaton. 2015. Rising Morbidity and Mortality in Midlife Among White Non-hispanic Americans in the 21st Century. *Proceedings of the National Academy of Sciences of the United States of America (PNAS)* 112 (49): 15078–15083. https://doi.org/10.1073/pnas.1518393112.

Case, Anne, and Angus Deaton. 2017. Mortality and Morbidity in the 21st Century. *Brooking Papers on Economic Activity*, March 23. https://www.brookings.edu/bpea-articles/mortality-and-morbidity-in-the-21st-century/. Accessed 25 Mar 2017.

Clegg, Daniel. 2013. Central European Welfare States. In *The Routledge Handbook of the Welfare State*, ed. Bent Greve, 161–170. London and New York: Routledge.

Collingham, Lizzie. 2011. *The Taste of War: World War Two and the Battle for Food*. London: Penguin Books.

Commission on English Prisons Today. 2009. Do Better—Do Less: The Report of the Commission on English Prisons Today. https://d19ylpo4aovc7m.cloudfront.net/fileadmin/howard_league/user/online_publications/Do_Better_Do_Less_low_res.pdf. Accessed 1 May 2017.

Daly, Martin. 2016. *Killing the Competition: Economic Inequality and Homicide*. New Brunswick and London: Transaction Publishers.

Danielsbacka, Mirkka, Antti Tanskanen, Hans Hämäläinen, Inka Pelkonen, Elina Haavio-Mannila, Anna Rotkirch, Antti Karisto, and J.P. Roos. 2013. *Sukupolvien vuorovaikutus: Auttaminen ja yhteydenpito suurten ikäluokkien ja heidän lastensa elämässä*, Väestöntutkimuslaitos Tutkimuksia D 58. Helsinki: Väestöliitto.

Erola, Jani. 2009. Social Mobility and Education of Finnish Cohorts Born 1936–1975: Succeeding While Failing in Equality of Opportunity? *Acta Sociologica* 52: 307–327.

Esping-Andersen, Gøsta. 1990. *The Three Worlds of Welfare Capitalism*. Cambridge: Polity Press; Princeton: Princeton University Press.

Esping-Andersen, Gøsta. 1997. Hybrid or Unique?: The Japanese Welfare State between Europe and America. *Journal of European Social Policy* 7: 179–189.

Esping-Andersen, Gøsta. 1999. *Social Foundations of Postindustrial Economies.* Oxford: Oxford University Press.

Fong, Christina M., Samuel Bowles, and Herbert Gintis. 2005. Reciprocity and the Welfare State. In *Moral Sentiments and Material Interests: The Foundations of Cooperation in Economic Life*, ed. Herbert Gintis, Samuel Bowles, Robert Boyd, and Ernst Fehr, 277–302. Cambridge, MA and London: MIT Press.

Forma, Pauli, Johanna Kallio, Jukka Pirttilä, and Roope Uusitalo. 2007. *Kuinka hyvinvointivaltio pelastetaan?: Tutkimus kansalaisten sosiaaliturvaa koskevista mielipiteistä ja valinnoista.* Sosiaali- ja terveysturvan tutkimuksia 89. Helsinki: Kelan tutkimusosasto.

Global Gender Gap Report. 2017. https://www.weforum.org/reports/the-global-gender-gap-report-2017. Accessed 15 July 2018.

Goodman, Roger. 2008. The State of Japanese Welfare: Welfare and the Japanese State. In *Welfare State Transformations: Comparative Perspective.* ed. Martin Seeleib-Kaiser, 96–108. Basingstoke and New York: Palgrave Macmillan.

http://www.theguardian.com.

Heikkilä, Seppo. 2009. *Altruismi, vastavuoroisuus ja hyvinvointivaltio.* Sosiaalipolitiikan pro gradu -työ, Kuopion yliopisto.

Hellsten, Katri. 1993. *Vaivaishoidosta hyvinvointivaltion kriisiin: Hyvinvointivaltiokehitys ja sosiaaliturvajärjestelmän muotoutuminen Suomessa.* Helsingin yliopisto, sosiaalipolitiikan laitoksen tutkimuksia 2/1993. Helsinki: Hakapaino Oy.

Helsingin Sanomat.

Herttua, Kimmo. 2010. *The Effects of the 2004 Reduction in the Price of Alcohol on Alcohol-Related Harm in Finland—A Natural Experiment Based on Register Data.* Finnish Yearbook of Population Research XLV 2010 Supplement. Helsinki: Population Research Institute.

Hiilamo, Heikki. 2003. Sosiaaliturvan yhteensovittamisen kannustimet. *Kansantaloudellinen aikakauskirja* 99: 294–311.

Hiilamo, Heikki. 2010. Tuloerot repesivät – kärsivätkö kansalaiset? In *Hyvinvointivaltion suunta – nousu vai lasku?* ed. Heikki Taimio, 72–89. Helsinki: Työväen Sivistysliitto.

Hiilamo, Heikki. 2011. *Uusi hyvinvointivaltio.* Helsinki: Like Publishing.

Hiilamo, Heikki, and Olli Kangas. 2012. Väärien profeettojen jäljillä?: Kahdeksan erää tuloerojen vaarallisuudesta. *Yhteiskuntapolitiikka* 77 (2): 121–133.

Hiilamo, Heikki, Olli Kangas, Kristiina Manderbacka, Päivi Mattila-Wiro, Mikko Niemelä, and Lauri Vuorenkoski. 2010. *Hyvinvoinnin turvaamisen rajat: Näköaloja talouskriisiin ja hyvinvointivaltion kehitykseen Suomessa.* Helsinki: Kelan tutkimusosasto.

Hirvilammi, Tuuli. 2015. *Kestävän hyvinvoinnin jäljillä: Ekologisten kysymysten integroiminen hyvinvointitutkimukseen*. Sosiaali- ja terveysturvan tutkimuksia 136. Helsinki: Kelan tutkimusosasto.

Jæger, Mads Meier. 2012. Do We All (Dis)Like the Same Welfare State?: Configurations of Public Support for the Welfare State in Comparative Perspective. In *Changing Social Equality: The Nordic Welfare Model in the 21st Century*, ed. Jon Kvist, Johan Fritzell, Bjørn Hvinden, and Olli Kangas, 45–68. Bristol and Chicago: Polity Press.

Kallio, Johanna. 2010. *Hyvinvointipalvelujärjestelmän muutos ja suomalaisten mielipiteet 1996–2006*. Sosiaali- ja terveysturvan tutkimuksia. Helsinki: Kela.

Kangas, Olli. 2009. Onko Suomi enää pohjoismainen hyvinvointivaltio? In *Kurssin muutos: Kestävään kasvuun ja hyvinvointiin*, ed. Heikki Taimio. Helsinki: Työväen Sivistysliitto.

Kangas, Olli, and Jon Kvist. 2013. Nordic Welfare States. In *The Routledge Handbook of the Welfare State*, ed. Bent Greve, 148–160. London and New York: Routledge.

Kangas, Olli, and Mikko Niemelä. 2008. Väärinkäyttö syö sosiaaliturvan kanna-tuspohjaa. *Sosiaalivakuutus* 46 (3–4): 8–10.

Kangas, Olli, Mikko Niemelä, and Anu Raijas. 2013. Tutkimushankkeen lähtö-kohdat ja tavoitteet. In *Takaisin perusteisiin: Perusturvan riittävyys kulutuk-sen näkökulmasta*, ed. Olli Kangas, Mikko Niemelä, and Anu Raijas, 6–23. Helsinki: Kelan tutkimusosasto.

Kasvio, Antti. 2014. *Kestävä työ ja hyvä elämä*. Helsinki: Gaudeamus.

Kauppalehti.

Kettunen, Pauli. 2011. The Transnational Construction of National Challenges: The Ambiguous Nordic Model of Welfare and Competitiveness. In *Beyond Welfare State Models*, ed. Pauli Kettunen and Klaus Petersen, 16–40. Cheltenham and Northampton: Edward Elgar.

Kettunen, Pauli, and Klaus Petersen. 2011. Introduction: Rethinking Welfare State Models. In *Beyond Welfare State Models*, ed. Pauli Kettunen and Klaus Petersen, 1–15. Cheltenham and Northampton: Edward Elgar.

Kivivuori, Janne. 2013. *Rikollisuuden syyt*. Helsinki: Kustannusosakeyhtiö Nemo.

Kohli, Martin. 1999. Private and Public Transfers between Generations: Linking the Family and the State. *European Societies* 1: 81–104.

Koskivirta, Anu. 2003. *The Enemy Within: Homicide and Control in Eastern Finland in the Final Years of Swedish Rule 1748–1808*. Studia Fennica Historica 5. Helsinki: Finnish Literature Society.

Kouvo, A. 2009. Missing Link Between Trust and Participation? In *Civic Mind and Good Citizenship—Comparative Perspectives*, ed. A. Konttinen, 114–127. Tampere: Tampere University Press.

Kouvo, A. 2011. The Sources of Generalized Trust and Institutional Confidence in Europe. *Research on Finnish Society* 3 (1): 29–40.

Kouvo, A., T. Kankainen, and M. Niemelä. 2012. Welfare Benefits and Generalized Trust in Finland and Europe. In *The Future of the Welfare State. Social Policy Attitudes and Social Capital in Europe*. ed. H. Ervasti, J.G. Andersen, T. Fridberg, and K. Ringdal, 195–213. Cheltenham and Northampton: Edward Elgar.

Kuivalainen, Susan. 2007. Toimeentulotuen alikäytön laajuus ja merkitys. *Yhteiskuntapolitiikka* 72 (1): 49–56.

Kuivalainen, Susan. 2010. Kestääkö suomalainen vähimmäisturva pohjoismaisen vertailun?: Vertaileva analyysi vähimmäisturvan tasosta ja sen köyhyyttä ehkäisevästä vaikutuksesta neljässä Pohjoismaassa 1990–2005. *Yhteiskuntapolitiikka* 75 (4): 377–388.

Kuivalainen, Susan, and Kenneth Nelson. 2012. Eroding Minimum Income Protection in the Nordic Countries?: Reassessing the Nordic Model of Social Assistance. In *Changing Social Equality: The Nordic Welfare Model in the 21st Century*, ed. Jon Kvist, Johan Fritzell, Bjørn Hvinden, and Olli Kangas, 69–87. Bristol and Chicago: Polity Press.

Kujala, Antti. 2013. *Neukkujen taskussa?: Kekkonen, suomalaiset puolueet ja Neuvostoliitto 1956–1971*. Helsinki: Tammi.

Kupari, Pekka, Jouni Välijärvi, Leif Andersson, Inga Arffman, Kari Nissinen, Eija Puhakka, and Jouni Vettenranta. 2013. *PISA 12 Ensituloksia*. Opetus- ja kulttuuriministeriön julkaisuja 2013: 20.

Künemund, Harald, and Martin Rein. 1999. There is More to Receiving than Needing: Theoretical Arguments and Empirical Explorations of Crowding In and Crowding Out. *Ageing and Society* 19: 93–121.

Kvist, Jon, Johan Fritzell, Bjørn Hvinden, and Olli Kangas. 2012. Nordic Responses to Rising Inequalities: Still Pursuing a Distinct Path or Joining the Rest? In *Changing Social Equality: The Nordic Welfare Model in the 21st Century*, ed. Jon Kvist, Johan Fritzell, Bjørn Hvinden, and Olli Kangas, 201–205. Bristol and Chicago: Polity Press.

Lauerma, Hannu. 2014. *Hyvän kääntöpuoli*. Helsinki: WSOY.

Lehti, Martti. 2014. *Henkirikolliuuskatsaus 2014*, OPTL:n verkkokatsauksia 36/2014. https://helda.helsinki.fi/handle/10138/152607. Accessed 27 May 2017.

Leitner, Sigrid, and Stephan Lessernich. 2003. Assessing Welfare State Change: The German Social Insurance State Between Reciprocity and Solidarity. *Journal of Public Policy* 23: 325–347.

León, Francisco José. 2012. Reciprocity and Public Support for the Redistributive Role of the State. *Journal of European Social Policy* 22: 198–215.

Lindert, Peter H. 2014. Private Welfare and the Welfare State. In *The Cambridge History of Capitalism. The Spread of Capitalism: From 1848 to the Present*, ed. Larry Neal and Jeffrey G. Williamson, Vol. II, 464–500. Cambridge: Cambridge University Press.

Marmot, Michael. 2004. *The Status Syndrome: How Social Standing Affects Our Health and Longevity*. London: Bloomsbury.

Mann, Michael. 2012a. *The Sources of Social Power. The Rise of Classes and Nation-States, 1760–1914*, Vol. 2. New York: Cambridge University Press.

Mann, Michael. 2012b. *The Sources of Social Power. Global Empires and Revolution, 1890–1945*, Vol.3. New York: Cambridge University Press.

Mann, Michael. 2013. *The Sources of Social Power. Globalizations, 1945–2011*, Vol. 4. New York: Cambridge University Press.

Mackenbach, Johan P., Irina Stirbu, Albert-Jan R. Roskam, Maartje M. Schaap, Gwenn Menvielle, Mall Leinsalu, and Anton E. Kunst. 2008. Socioeconomic Inequalities in Health in 22 European Countries. *The New England Journal of Medicine* 358: 2468–2481.

Mhone, Guy C. Z. 2005. Neoliberalism. In *New Dictionary of the History of Ideas. Vol. 4. Machiavelism to Phrenology*, ed. Maryanne Cline Horowitz, 1625–1628. Farmington Hills: Thomson Gale.

Milanovic, Branko. 2016. *Global Inequality: A New Approach for the Age of Globalization*. Cambridge, MA and London: The Belknap Press of Harvard University Press.

Moore, Barrington, Jr. 1978. *Injustice: The Social Bases of Obedience and Revolt*. London and Basingstoke: Macmillan.

Moriguchi Chiaki, and Emmanuel Saez. 2010. The Evolution of Income Concentration in Japan, 1886–2005: Evidence from Income Tax Statistics. In *Top Incomes: A Global Perspective*, ed. A.B. Atkinson and T. Piketty, 76–170. Oxford: Oxford University Press.

Mukerjee, Madhusree. 2011. *Churchill's Secret War. The British Empire and the Ravaging of India During World War II*. New York: Basic Books.

Myllyniemi, Sami. 2012. *Monipolvinen hyvinvointi. Nuorisobarometri 2012*. Nuorisotutkimusverkosto/Nuorisotutkimusseura, julkaisuja 127. Helsinki: Hakapaino.

Myllyniemi, Sami. 2017. *Katse tulevaisuudessa. Nuorisobarometri 2016*. Nuorisotutkimusseura, julkaisuja 189. Helsinki: Grano Oy.

Nettle, Daniel, Gillian V. Pepper, Ruth Jobling, and Kari Britt Schroeder. 2014. Being There: A Brief Visit to a Neighbourhood Induces the Social Attitudes of that Neighbourhood. *PeerJ* 2:e236: 1–20. https://doi.org/10.7717/peerj.236.

Niemelä, Mikko. 2007. Oma vika, epäonni vai rakenne? Väestön mielipiteet köyhyyden syistä. *Yhteiskuntapolitiikka* 72 (6): 585–598.

Niemelä, Mikko. 2008. Perceptions of the Causes of Poverty in Finland. *Acta Sociologica* 51: 23–40.

Niemelä, Mikko. 2009. Does the Conceptualisation of Poverty Matter? Empirical Example of Non-generic Approach of Poverty Attributions. Online Working Papers 3/2009. Helsinki: Kela. https://helda.helsinki.fi/handle/10138/14176. Accessed 27 May 2017.

Niemelä, Mikko. 2010. Kelan etuuskäsittelijöiden näkemykset köyhyyden syistä. *Janus* 18 (4): 337–354.

Niemelä, Mikko. 2013. Mielipiteet toimeentuloturvaetuuksien kohdentumisongelmista ja niiden ratkaisukeinoista. In *Toimeentuloturvan verkkoa kokemassa: Kansalaisten käsitykset ja odotukset*, ed. Ilpo Airio, 112–137. Helsinki: Kelan tutkimusosasto.

Niemelä, Mikko, and Juho Saari. 2013. *Huono-osaisten hyvinvointi Suomessa*. Helsinki: Kelan tutkimusosasto.

Ostrom, Elionor. 2000. Crowding Out Citizenship. *Scandinavian Political Studies* 23: 1–14.

Outinen, Sami. 2015. *Sosiaalidemokraattien tie talouden ohjailusta markkinareaktioiden ennakointiin: Työllisyys sosiaalidemokraattien politiikassa Suomessa 1975–1998*. Helsinki: Into Kustannus Oy.

Paloheimo, Heikki. 2010. Hyvinvointivaltion kannatus ja äänestyskäyttäytyminen. In *Hyvinvointivaltion suunta – nousu vai lasku?* ed. Heikki Taimio, 20–39. Helsinki: Työväen Sivistysliitto.

Partanen, Anu. 2016. *The Nordic Theory of Everything. In Search of a Better Life*. New York: HarperCollins.

Peng Ito. 2000. A Fresh Look at the Japanese Welfare State. *Social Policy and Administration* 34: 87–114.

Petersen, Klaus. 2011. National, Nordic and Trans-Nordic: Transnational Perspectives on the History of the Nordic Welfare States. In *Beyond Welfare State Models*, ed. Pauli Kettunen and Klaus Petersen, 41–64. Cheltenham and Northampton: Edward Elgar.

Peterson, Martin. 2012. Pathways of the Welfare State: Growth and Democracy. In *Transformations of the Swedish Welfare State: From Social Engineering to Governance*, ed. B. Larsson, M. Letell, and H. Thorn, 23–37. Basingstoke: Palgrave Macmillan.

Piketty, Thomas. 2013. *Le capital au XXIe siècle*. Paris: Éditions du Seuil.

Pinker, Steven. 2011. *The Better Angels of Our Nature: Why Violence Has Declined*. New York: Viking.

Putnam, Robert D. 2015. *Our Kids: The American Dream in Crisis*. New York: Simon & Schuster.

Saunders, Peter. 2010. *Beware False Prophets: Equality, the Good Society and the Spirit Level*. London: Policy Exchange.

Silventoinen, Karri, Takashi Tatsuse, Pekka Martikainen, Ossi Rahkonen, Eero Lahelma, Michikazu Sekine, and Tea Lallukka. 2013. Occupational Class Differences in Body Mass Index and Weight Gain in Japan and Finland. *Journal of Epidemiology* 23: 443–450.

Sirniö, Outi. 2016. *Constrained Life Chances: Intergenerational Transmission of Income in Finland*. Publications of the Faculty of Social Sciences 26. Helsinki: Unigrafia.

Social Progress Index 2017. http://www.socialprogressimperative.org/global-index/. Accessed 15 July 2018.

Spicker, Paul. 2013. Liberal Welfare States. In *The Routledge Handbook of the Welfare State*, ed. Bent Greve, 193–201. London and New York: Routledge.

Stiglitz, Joseph E. 2013. *The Price of Inequality*. London: Penguin Books.

Takanori Sumino. 2014. Escaping the Curse of Economic Self-Interest: An Individual-Level Analysis of Public Support for the Welfare State in Japan. *Journal of Social Policy* 43: 109–133.

Svallfors, Stefan. 1997. Worlds of Welfare and Attitudes to Redistribution: A Comparison of Eight Western Nations. *European Sociological Review* 13: 283–304.

Takegawa Shogo. 2010. Liberal Preference and Conservative Policies: The Puzzling Size of Japan's Welfare State. *Social Science Japan Journal* 13: 53–67.

http://www.taloussanomat.fi.

Tanskanen, Antti, and Mirkka Danielsbacka. 2009. Perheen vai yhteiskunnan vastuu?: Suurten ikäluokkien auttamisasenteiden tarkastelua. *Janus* 17: 20–35.

Tarkiainen, Lasse, Pekka Martikainen, and Mikko Laaksonen. 2013. The Changing Relationship between Income and Mortality in Finland, 1988–2007. *Journal of Epidemiology and Community Health* 67: 21–27.

Tarkiainen, Lasse, Pekka Martikainen, Riina Peltonen, and Hanna Remes. 2017. Sosiaaliryhmien elinajanodote-erojen kasvu on pääosin pysähtynyt. *Suomen Lääkärilehti* 72 (9): 588–593c. http://www.potilaanlaakarilehti.fi/site/assets/files/0/09/07/074/sll92017-588.pdf. Accessed 25 March 2017.

Therborn, Göran. 2011. *The World: A Beginner's Guide*. Cambridge: Polity Press.

Therborn, Göran. 2013. *The Killing Fields of Inequality*. Cambridge and Malden: Polity Press.

Titmuss, Richard M. 1963. *Essays on "The Welfare State"*. London: Unwin University Books.

Titmuss, Richard M. 1970. *The Gift Relationship: From Human Blood to Social Policy*. London: Allen & Unwin.

Titmuss, Richard M. 1983. *Social Policy: An Introduction*. London: Allen & Unwin.

Torre, Roberta, and Mikko Myrskylä. 2014. Income Inequality and Population Health: An Analysis of Panel Data for 21 Developed Countries, 1975–2006. *Population Studies: A Journal of Demography* 68: 1–13. https://doi.org/10.1080/00324728.2013.856457. Accessed 27 May 2017.

Turun Sanomat.

UNICEF. 2016. Fairness for Children: A League Table of Inequality in Child Well-Being in Rich Countries. In *Innocenti Report Card 13*, UNICEF Office of Research: Innocenti, Florence. https://www.unicef-irc.org/publications/830/. Accessed 27 May 2017.

Van Kersbergen, Kees. 2013. What Are Welfare State Typologies and How Are They Useful, if at All? In *The Routledge Handbook of the Welfare State*, ed. Bent Greve, 139–147. London and New York: Routledge.

Vettenranta, Jouni, Jouni Välijärvi, Arto Ahonen, Jarkko Hautamäki, Jenna Hiltunen, Kaisa Leino, Suvi Lähteinen, Kari Nissinen, Virva Nissinen, Eija Puhakka, Juhani Rautopuro, and Mari-Pauliina Vainikainen. 2016. *PISA: Ensituloksia. Huipulla pudotuksesta huolimatta.* Opetus- ja kulttuuriministeriön julkaisuja 41.

Wehler, Hans-Ulrich. 1983. *Das Deutsche Kaiserreich 1871–1918. Deutsche Geschichte.* ed. Joachim Leuschner. Bd. 9. Göttingen: Vandenhoeck & Ruprecht.

Wehler, Hans-Ulrich. 1995. *Deutsche Gesellschaftsgeschichte.* Bd. 3. *Von der "Deutschen Doppelrevolution" bis zum Beginn des Ersten Weltkrieges 1849–1914.* Munich: Verlag C. H. Beck.

Weik, Matthias, and Marc Friedrich. 2014. *Der grösste Raubzug der Geschichte: Warum die Fleißigen immer ärmer und die Reichen immer reicher werden.* Taschenbuch 60804. Köln: Bastei Lübbe Taschenbuch.

Wikipedia.

Wilkinson, Richard, and Kate Pickett. 2009. *The Spirit Level: Why Equality Is Better for Everyone.* London: Penguin Books.

World Health Organization. World Health Statistics 2018: Monitoring Health for the SDGs, Sustainable Development Goals. http://www.who.int/gho/mortality_burden_disease/life_tables/situation_trends/en/. Accessed 15 July 2018.

World Values Survey. http://www.worldvaluessurvey.org/WVSOnline.jsp. Accessed 1 May 2017.

http://yle.fi/uutiset.

Yliaska, Ville. 2014. *Tehokkuuden toiveuni: Uuden julkisjohtamisen historia Suomessa 1970-luvulta 1990-luvulle.* Helsinki: Into Kustannus Oy.

Ylikangas, Heikki. 1999. Reasons for the Reduction of Violence in Finland in the 17th Century. In *Crime and Control in Europe from the Past to the Present*, ed. Mirkka Lappalainen and Pekka Hirvonen, 165–173. Helsinki: Hakapaino.

Zimbardo, Philip. 2008. *The Lucifer Effect: Understanding How Good People Turn Evil.* New York: Random House Trade Paperbacks.

CHAPTER 8

Inequality in the United States and Other Industrialized Countries

In an interview for the Finnish newspaper *Helsingin Sanomat* in 2015, the American economist Jeffrey Sachs, special adviser to UN Secretary-General Ban Ki-moon gave an unembellished account of the state of his own country: "The United States is a corrupt political system" … "The top executives of Wall Street money market funds make a billion dollars a year and yet pay the lowest taxes. How can that be possible? It is possible because politicians protect them, because they are major donors to election campaigns." "And we call that democracy."[1]

The preceding chapters of this book have discussed manifestations of reciprocity in historical and present societies. One of the factors that erodes reciprocity is economic inequality, which often underlies social inequality. We next address the historical background of disparities of income and wealth and their connection with policies implemented in society. In his 2013 book, *Le capital au XXIᵉ siècle* (*Capital in the Twenty-First Century*), French economist Thomas Piketty outlined the main courses of development in income and wealth disparity over the past 200 years. The book aroused a great deal of attention, because it demonstrated how the division of income in the developed countries over the past 30 years has begun to evolve toward the great degree of inequality that prevailed in the nineteenth century. Piketty regards the process of increasing equality from the First World War to 1980 as only an interim stage.

According to Piketty, there was a great deal of economic inequality in the Western European countries and Japan on the eve of the First World

© The Author(s) 2019
A. Kujala and M. Danielsbacka, *Reciprocity in Human Societies*,
https://doi.org/10.1007/978-3-319-96056-2_8

War, with the top decile (top tenth, or top 10%) controlling approximately 90% of property or wealth (with capital income playing a major role) and 45% of national income. Those possessing the largest amount of wealth are not necessarily the ones with the highest incomes, although this is partly true. A similar division of income and wealth has in fact existed since the beginning of the nineteenth century, most likely even longer. At the beginning of the 1910s in France and Sweden, the top percentile (the top one hundredth or top 1%) alone controlled 60% of wealth in France and Sweden, and 70% in Great Britain. In the United States, there was somewhat less concentration of income and wealth in the top decile of the population.

The material damage of the world wars, the loss of foreign investments by private individuals, a low level of savings, the depression of the 1930s, low values of stocks and real estate, inflation and fiscal (taxation) measures applied in the war years and by modern states to large amounts of assets and large incomes wiped out a considerable portion of the wealth and investment income of the European and Japanese elites (especially the top 1%) and leveled the distribution of income and wealth. In France and Germany in 1980, for example, the share of pre-tax income of the top 10%[2] was slightly more than 30%, but 35% in 2010. The share of overall wealth of the top decile of Europeans shrank to 60% in the 1970s and 1980s, after which it has increased slightly. A new feature compared with the situation prior to the First World War is the increased share of the wealth of the following 40%. In relative terms, the lowest 50% owns almost as little (under 5%) as they did before the First World War.

In the 1950s and 1960s, the United States had a more unequal distribution of income than Europe, but it was more equal than before this period or since. In 1980, the share of the top 10% of income was slightly less than 35%, but by 2010 it was over 45 or almost 50%. The share of the top 1% rose in the United States from 10% in 1980 to 18 and even 20% in 2010. With regard to its top percentile in terms of income, the United States is now on a par with the most unequal countries in the world, such as Argentina, South Africa and Colombia.[3]

In the period from 1947 to 1973/1974, the real pre-tax income of all American households grew approximately to an equal degree in relative terms. From the 1970s to the mid-2000s, on the other hand, the higher the income the income group, the faster the speed of growth of pre- and after-tax income (Jacobs and Skocpol 2005, p. 4; Bartels 2008,

p. 9; Hacker and Pierson 2011, p. 23).[4] Between 1979 and 2010, the proportion of the American middle class (the sector of the population with disposable income between 25% below and 25% above median income) shrank from one-third to 27% and its average income decreased from 80% of the mean to 77%. In 2010, proportion of the middle class in Sweden, the Netherlands and Germany in relation to the whole population was larger than in the United Kingdom and the United States, where the middle class has considerably shrunk in relative terms since the 1980s.[5] The reasons for this can be found in the economic policies pursued in these countries.

The data of the Congressional Budget Office (CBO) mentioned in note 4 shows how the top income earner percentile has increased its income to an inordinately greater degree than other income earner groups. Present-day inequality in the United States is based in particular on the considerable increase of income acquired by the top 10 and 1% from salaries and increasingly from capital income among the very richest. According to Piketty, this cannot be explained by technology or merits, because the same technology has not led to corresponding inequality in the distribution of income in Continental Europe or Japan. The radical reduction of taxation of highest income and significant rise of pay for executives have not led to any greater improvement of productivity in the Anglo-Saxon countries than in Continental Europe or Japan, where changes in taxation and executive pay were not as great. Neoliberal tax policies cannot be justified with improved productivity which they have not generated. The concentration of income is not associated with social mobility in the sense that broader circles than the elites could have high income at least at some stage of their working careers. On the other hand, the purchasing power of the minimum wage in the United States was at its highest in 1969 and approximately one-third lower at the beginning of 2013. This is simply a question of the ability of different classes of society to negotiate more income for themselves. If this trend continues, the top 10% will earn as much as 60% of all income by the year 2030. Will the majority of Americans continue to accept this? In other words, what will this mean for stability in society?

With regard to recent developments (1980–2010) in income distribution, the other English-speaking countries resemble the United States more than the Continental European countries, but the top 1% of the former, however, has not managed to raise their share of income (pre-tax income) to be as high as in the United States. In Japan and

France, the growth of the top percentile's share of income in the same period remained relatively small (Piketty 2013, pp. 392, 482–533 and Figs. 9.2–9.9).

In Sweden, the share of income of the top decile grew from almost 25% to slightly under 30% in the period 1980–2010. In 1980, the top percentile in Sweden had only a 4% share of national income, but by 2010 it had reached 7%, or nine including realized capital gains. When the latter are included, the considerable rise of the top percentile's share of income in Sweden between 1980 and 2010 resembled developments in the United States and other English-speaking countries and stood out from the stability of Continental Europe. The main explanation for this is less tax on capital income than on earned income (Piketty 2013, pp. 503–507, 512–513, 747; Roine and Waldenström 2010, pp. 299–331; Therborn 2013, pp. 126–128; Bourguignon 2013, p. 38). The wealthy have on average more capital income and prefer to convert earned income into capital income. Even today, Finland and Sweden are countries with a relatively even distribution of income, but since 1980 or at the latest since 1990 income disparity has grown more in them than in many other developed countries.[6]

The growth of disposable income among all income-earner deciles and the highest-earning 1% in Finland in 1966–2007 shows that between 1966 and 1990 the lower the decile, the faster annual growth was, with least annual growth for the top percentile. Between 1990 and 2007, however, the order of annual growth for the respective deciles became completely the opposite. This was also reflected in how much each decile increased their overall income between 1990 and 2007. The income of the top 1% grew by 209% and of the top decile by 84%, but the income of the lowest decile by only 8% (see Fig. 8.1). Developments in income distribution in Finland over the past 40 years bear considerable resemblance to post-war American income distribution. In Finland, income disparity, which had still been slightly decreasing in the 1970s, began to grow in the 1990s. This was partly due to the economic recession of the period, which resulted in a large number of long-term unemployed people.

Markus Jäntti, Marja Riihelä, Risto Sullström and Matti Tuomala explain the recent growth of inequality in income distribution in Finland and the considerable increase of income for the top 1% with the reforms of taxation enacted in 1993, which expanded the taxational basis of capital income, raising taxes on capital gains or sales profits and lowering

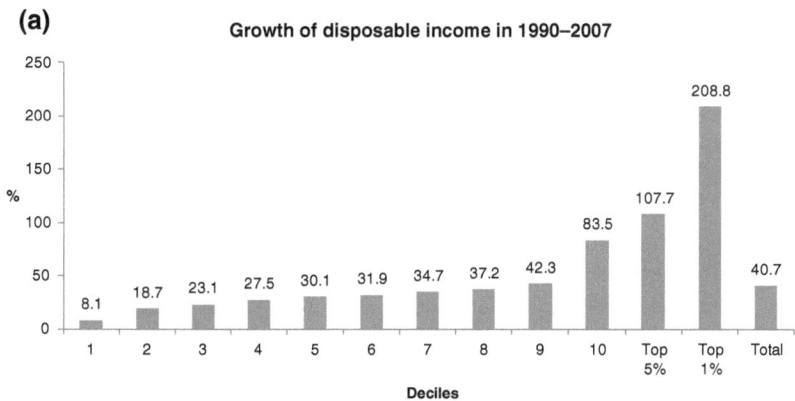

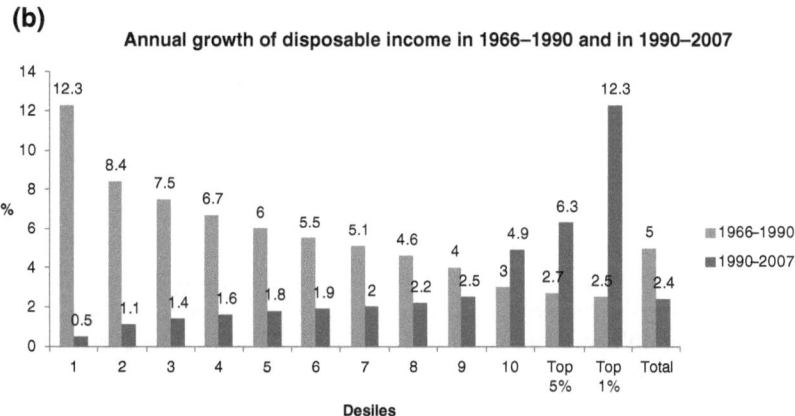

Fig. 8.1 a, b Real disposable income growth by deciles, top 5 and 1% and total (*Source* Riihelä et al. 2010, p. 8. In their most recent study [2015, p. 159], Riihelä, Sullström and Tuomala present again the lower figure, but with the latter period of comparison ending in 2012 instead of 2007 and thus displaying the effects of the recession)

them on income from dividends and implemented the differentiation (reduction) of the taxation of capital income. A wage earner with a good income will pay more taxes than a person with capital income at the same level of income. While progression in state income tax has been increased in recent years, it does not correspond at all to the lowering of the highest marginal taxes in the 1990s. Since the beginning of the 1990s, capital income in Finland have been taxed at a flat rate (from initially 25 to 30% in 2018 and currently 34% for capital income in excess of €30,000). In addition, income from dividends is partly tax-free. It is still profitable in terms of lower taxes to have large income in the form of capital rather than earned income. The municipal tax, social security and pensions insurance contributions and all indirect taxes are flat-rate taxes, but various deductions provide progression in municipal taxation. The proportion of flat-rate and almost flat-rate taxes of all taxation has grown. There is no municipal tax on capital income.

In 2007, capital income accounted for 62% of income for the top 1% (as opposed to only 14% in 1990), and as much as 91% for the top one thousandth. This means that for the very highest income groups in Finland, the tax burden (total tax ratio or taxes collected by the national economy in relation to Gross Domestic Product) no longer grew with increasing income but instead decreased, i.e. taxation became regressive. Regressive taxation applies a different standard to the highest incomes, i.e. they are in principle taxed more leniently than other income. Among the top percentile of earners, 50% of all capital income were realized capital gains (sales profits) and 36% were income from interest and dividends (in 2007).[7] The gap gained by the rich from ordinary wage earners was not due solely to preferential taxation but also to greater wage disparity. In the 1990s, the relative difference between the wages of executives and other employees grew from 14-fold to 32-fold (the executives of the Nokia corporation were not included in the comparison) (Hänninen 2014, p. 102).

In 1999–2000, good years for the Finnish economy, the capital income of the top group of earners grew markedly, with Nokia executives, in particular, receiving immense options that are taxed as earned income. At the time, and again around 2007, income disparities in Finland peaked, as measured with the Gini coefficient and the share of income of the top 1% of earners. In the 2000s, however, income disparity has no longer follower a similar rising trend as in the 1990s. The occasional slowing of the economy has also reduced disparity. Nonetheless, in 2013, which was a poor year for the economy, the top-earning 10% managed to increase its relative share of income, which was due to growth in capital gains. This highest-ranked decile earned 23% of all income, i.e. almost as much as the total for the lowest-earning

40%. On the other hand, the share of the 10% with most income was even higher in 2007 (26%).[8] The crises caused by the financialization of the world economy have at times reduced the capital income of the richest sector of the Finnish population, who have also suffered from them. The lower end of the income scale has of course suffered much more because of unemployment, among other reasons.

While the more lenient taxation of capital income as opposed to earned income in Finland was originally due above all to pressure from international competition in taxation (the fear of capital flight), it created in practice a modern-day "tax-exempt nobility" of the rich. When Finland was part of Sweden until 1809, the nobility or "lords temporal" (*världsligt frälse*) were granted partial tax exemption and the tax burden was placed above all on the peasants. The privileges of the present-day "tax-exempt nobility" are in contradiction with the requirements of equal or impartial taxation and social justice in general. Tax reforms carried out in Norway in 2004 lowered taxes at the upper end of the income scale and changed taxation so that it was no longer profitable to convert earned income into capital income. As a result, income disparity in Norway is currently lower than in Finland.[9]

Owing to technological progress and increased productivity, income distribution was equalized during the twentieth century (ca. 1910–1980). These factors permitted rising real incomes for the working class. Piketty underlines, however, that income distribution is ultimately a political issue that is not caused by any purely economic mechanisms. A good example of this is how low-income groups improved their relative status in France during a period of over a decade that began in 1968. Social and political unrest had the result that the purchasing power of the minimum wage grew as much as 130% between 1968 and 1983, while all wage earners saw only an average improvement of 50% in their purchasing power. Along with France, real income for workers in Great Britain, West Germany, Italy and Finland grew from the late 1960s to the early 1970s considerably faster than previously (Horn 2009, pp. 193–194). In actual fact, post-Second World War income disparity in Finland, when measured with the share of income of the richest 1%, was greater than in the other Nordic countries and continued to grow in the late 1950s, when the labor movement was divided and not involved in government. The distribution of income in Finland did not begin to resemble conditions in Sweden and Norway until the 1970s, when governments headed by left-wing and center parties implemented incomes policies that reduced income disparity (Roine 2014, pp. 31–33; Jäntti 2006, pp. 245–260; Kujala 2013, pp. 250–256, 327–328).

The Serbian-American economist Branko Milanovic published in 2016 a study on worldwide and inter-and intranational inequality. Because the reciprocity between the elites and the common people functions only within a single country at a time, we focus here on only the latter inequality. Milanovic emphasizes, however, with due cause that focus on a single country is becoming increasingly artificial and distorts reality.[10] He maintains that there are malign and benign forces that reduce inequality. The former are wars and internal conflicts and the latter include social pressure and politics (the labor movement and left-wing and centrist parties), widespread education, the service needs created by an aging population and low-skill-biased technological development. Along with openness or globalization and politics, technological progress usually belongs to the factors that promote inequality. Modern technologies provide more highly paid expert work as well as work for low wages, thus reinforcing the extremes of the income scale at the cost of its center. Globalization, in turn, has brought cheap labor from China and elsewhere in Asia to compete with the labor force of developed countries for jobs in industry, which benefits employers when negotiating wages with the latter (Milanovic 2016, pp. 56, 76 and *passim*).

According to a theory developed by Simon Kuznets in the 1950s, mean income grew in the early stages of industrialization, but inequality increased. Later, as income continued to grow, inequality began to decrease. Kuznets's graph describing this resembles an upside-down letter U. Developments in the leading Western countries over the past 30–40 years appeared to refute Kuznets's theory, but Milanovic rehabilitated it with his notion of recurring Kuznets Waves. Milanovic presents graphs of several countries in which the Gini coefficient of disposable per capita income describing inequality first rises as GDP per capita increases, but then begins to decrease as economic growth continues (First Kuznets Wave). Milanovic maintains that the developed Western countries have been in the rising stage of Second Kuznets Wave. His analysis, however, shows that inequality in income distribution has increased only slightly in Spain, Germany, Japan and the Netherlands. These results may be partly due to the fact that, unlike analyses of increases of income in different groups and their mutual relations, the Gini coefficient is more sensitive to changes in the center of the distribution than in the top and lowest income groups and will under-react to increases of income in the top 1%. Nonetheless, Milanovic's graphs undeniably indicate the same as Piketty's analysis with its focus on the top income groups: disparity of income distribution has not significantly increased in many Continental European countries or Japan over the past 30 years.[11] We regard it as quite obvious that this is due to the policies that slowed the growth of large incomes in these countries, unlike in the United States and the United Kingdom. Technology, globalization, extensive education and the needs of the aging population have largely similar effects in both groups of countries (see also Fig. 8.2).

According to Milanovic, the long-term analysis shows that economic growth by no means requires increasing income disparity. He regards the present-day United States as a plutocracy approaching a system of one-dollar one-vote and warns that high inequality sets in motion destructive forces, and that the damage and suffering caused by them will ultimately lower inequality. He maintains that the plutocracy supports globalization but sacrifices the foundations of democracy. Populism aiming at acquiring power in Europe tries to preserve a simulacrum of

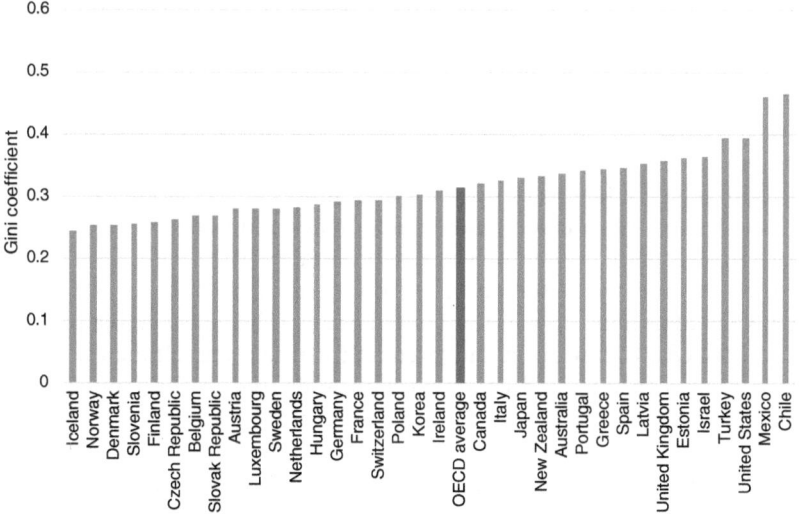

Fig. 8.2 Gini coefficient of disposable income after taxes and transfers, 2014 or latest available year (*Source* Based on data from OECD [2017], "Income inequality" [indicator], http://dx.doi.org/10.1787/459aa7f1-en. Accessed 24 Mar 2017)

democracy while reducing exposure to globalization (Milanovic 2016, pp. 89, 98, 189–211).

Along with income disparity, the internal distribution of wealth in countries is another source of inequality. Piketty has published perhaps the most astounding information about this. Just like the growth of income disparity, deepening differences of wealth undermine the experience of reciprocity. The share of wealth of the top decile in the United States is currently 70%, and of the top percentile 35% (as opposed to only 2% for the lowest 50%). The median net wealth of Americans is lower than that of the Spanish or the Taiwanese. The United States is an extremely wealthy nation, but with wealth concentrated in the hands of a relatively smaller group than in most other countries. In France, the top decile currently controls over 60% of wealth and the top 1% controls over 20%. At present, the richest one-thousandth (4.5 million people) of the world's population controls 20% of the world's wealth. Fortunes are accumulated considerably faster than average wealth. This discrepancy is so significant that according to Piketty's calculations the richest one-thousandth will own 40–60% of the world's wealth within 30 years if the course of development does not change. A situation like this would most likely be politically untenable.

It should also be pointed out that sizeable earned income will generate large amounts of wealth that are inherited by the following generation. Accordingly, Piketty suggests that developments will partly lead to the emergence of an idle class of rentiers of the kind that was influential in Europe in the nineteenth century and until the First World War.

In the post-war decades, the United States and Great Britain, in fact, had an exceptionally high marginal tax rate (70–90%) on the highest earned income and inheritance. On the other hand, there was a capital gains tax of at most 25% in the United States. The considerable progression applied in taxation in the twentieth century was ultimately due in all countries to wars and economic upheavals, but in the United States progression in taxation was originally raised also because the government did not want the major inequality of income and wealth of European nations in the New World. In the 1980s, the top marginal tax rates in the United States and Great Britain were radically lowered in the spirit of neoliberalism, and the highest salaries and largest amounts of wealth began to grow at a completely different pace than the wages and wealth of the following 90%. It now became much more worthwhile for heads of corporations and other members of the financial elite to increase their salaries than before, when marginal tax would channel most of the rise in pay to the government.[12] In 1965, the earnings of the president of an American corporation were equivalent to the average income of a total 24 employees. In 2010, this ratio was 243:1. In Japan it is 16:1. A discrepancy of this order cannot be explained by the special skills of executives, because the same expectations are placed on Japanese executives as on their American colleagues (Stiglitz 2013, pp. 4, 26, 394).

Prior to the First World War, inequality was due to the slow growth of national income, which was slower than the growth of return on capital. On the eve of the First World War, capital (mainly private wealth) in Europe was equivalent to national income over a period of almost seven years, in 1950 only two years' worth of national income, but in 2010 five years of national income. In the United States, this ratio has continuously varied between slightly under and over four years. The years from 1913 to 2012 were exceptional in world history as the only period when the rate of return on capital was less than the growth of production (and even then, only after taxes). In the Continental European countries, the period of strong economic growth from the late 1940s to the 1970s coincided with the prominent economic role of the state, which explains the continuing European popularity of the mixed economy model as opposed to the United States or Great Britain.

Economic growth has slowed in the twenty-first century. Its significant component is the growth of population which has now almost ceased especially in Europe. According to Piketty, a higher return on capital, a higher saving rate and limited economic growth will lead to the growing importance of large amounts of wealth and increasing inequality (the return of an idle rentier elite as in the nineteenth century), unless corrective measures are undertaken. Piketty also argues that the larger the amount of wealth, the higher the return on capital will be. This, too, will increase disparities of wealth. The twentieth century's process toward greater equality will thus risk remaining a kind of historical interim stage. The growth of private capital is also partly due to privatization and rising prices of shares and real estate.

According to Piketty, the growth of economic inequality and the problems it causes for economic growth and social stability should be countered with a worldwide progressive tax on capital, which could begin to be implemented within the European Union. Individual states readily begin to compete over tax reductions to attract investments, which means that no individual country can have the role of trailblazer.

All assets should be registered, also in so-called tax haven states. According to conservative estimates, almost 10% of the Gross World Product is hidden outside official registers in tax havens. Naturally, no taxes are paid on this capital to its countries of origin. In other words, its owners benefit from free trade, the free movement of capital and the services of public authorities at the cost of the businesses and citizens who still pay their taxes. The present debt crisis of the EU countries is a special phenomenon, because private wealth in Europe is equivalent to as much as five years' worth of national income, ranking thus among the highest in the world. In the post-war decades, many states had large amounts of net capital, but currently, these states have as much or even more debt than collectibles due to privatizations. If inflation remains low (which is the policy of the European Central Bank), the reduction of the debt of European states and the cutbacks on public spending that it requires will take decades, which is not a very positive perspective for society. Piketty regards his own proposal as a better solution (Piketty 2013).

The British economist Mark Blyth, who is also active in the United States, maintains that instead of cutbacks and austerity much better means to manage the bank crisis, the public deficit and the debt problem would be to raise taxes on the wealthiest and to return funds hidden in tax havens to be taxable. He maintains that many mainstream economists have taken this view. Those who have benefited from tax cuts and bail-outs should pay higher taxes (Blyth 2015, pp. 242–244, 270).

Piketty admits that his proposals of an annual tax on capital and the worldwide monitoring and regulation of the economy are not easy to carry out, and he calls them a useful utopia. We maintain that Piketty's suggestions can only be put into practice after a future financial bubble has caused an even worse crash of the world economy than was seen in recent years. Also in the past, only necessity caused by major setbacks has led to fundamental changes of course.

The capital tax could also be a solution to the problems of maintaining the welfare state, although its actual purpose, according to Piketty, would be to halt growing inequality and to regulate capitalism. The regressive taxation of highest income (especially capital income) that has formed in the present tax systems of the developed countries should anyway be restored to progression, because the lax taxation of large incomes erodes the legitimacy of the political system and undermines the foundation of the welfare state. A third basis for taxation could be a progressive inheritance tax. On the other hand, Piketty maintains that the total tax rate cannot be easily raised to any great degree especially where it is already high (as in rich and productive nations such as the Nordic countries).[13]

Piketty points out, however, that "[s]ome income disparity is needed to provide economic growth and innovation." Societies must decide to what extent they will accept disparity to avoid its becoming a problem of them.[14] He is not an opponent of either the market economy or globalization, but he feels that they should be made to serve the interests of the majority of the population and of humankind as a whole. Piketty rejects the suggestion that the market economy automatically maintains a balance in income distribution or equilibrium of any other kind, seeking to restore it after disturbances. On the contrary, his calculations show that without corrective political measures disparities of income and wealth distribution will continue to grow unabated.

THE ECONOMIC CRISIS OF EUROPE AND FINLAND

We discuss here only briefly the Euro crisis that beset the European Union in recent years, because it involved the unwillingness the governments of Germany and other rich European nations to help Greece, Portugal, Spain and Ireland to manage their debt burden rather than any reciprocity of the state and its citizens. The states of Greece and Portugal and private investors in Ireland and Spain[15] had become overloaded with debt, because of the low-interest rates in these countries caused by the illusion of stability created by the common currency. The prevailing view of the debt crisis is that the governments of Germany and France saved the banks of their own countries—and Great Britain—with the joint bailouts of the Eurozone countries. The leading European banks that had provided loans to the countries of Southern Europe were larger in relation to their respective national economies and thus harder to salvage than the American banks had been. The banks' receivables from Southern Europe were transferred to the stability funds of the Eurozone countries and the governments of the latter (i.e. their taxpayers) and the International Monetary Fund.

Fearing defeat at the polls, European politicians did not agree to a major write-down of the debts, although it has become obvious in recent years that Greece, in particular, will not be able to pay its debts. The South European countries were required to reduce spending on social security and to sell assets. The result was a major drop in the standard of living, mass unemployment and a social crisis in Greece, Spain and Portugal. Greece has been left hanging by a thread as a warning to other Eurozone countries against gathering too much debt. The various European governments declared that they were thus defending the interests of their own taxpayers, with the aim of preventing right-wing populists from benefiting from the Euro crisis. What happened? The crisis, which had simmered for years without being resolved destroyed the confidence of investors and citizens in the economic prospects of Europe. Cutbacks in spending stifled economic growth and led in all the Eurozone countries to a social crisis similar to Southern Europe, though less pronounced. The dissatisfaction of citizens helped right-wing populist parties increase their support to be larger than ever since the Second World War.[16]

According to Mark Blyth, the European Union copied the German model of economic management. In this model, the role of the state is not shunned as it is among American neoliberals. The state has a duty to maintain competitiveness and the freedom of competition and to implement a so-called social market economy (the German model of the welfare state), but not active counter-slump policies increasing consumption and demand. The central bank must be as independent as possible of political decision-makers, and its main duty is to keep inflation as low as possible. Low inflation is especially in the interest of investors. According to the prevailing way of thinking in Germany and the European Commission, this model is sited to all the EU member countries, especially those of the Eurozone. If a country is in difficulties with regard to its competitiveness and debts, they can be overcome by keeping to fiscal discipline and following joint rules on debt, i.e. cutbacks on expenditure and austerity policies. Blyth refers to the German model as *ordoliberalism*, a liberalism of order. The problem, however, is that not all Eurozone countries can in any way be copies of Germany, which has refined its competitiveness to the extreme. A surplus balance of trade in one country is inevitably reflected as a trade deficit in another country. If several countries simultaneously implement austerity policies reducing purchasing power, the products of none, including Germany, are sold and the economy of all of them suffers (Blyth 2015, pp. 135–143).

Alexander Stubb of the conservative National Coalition Party, who was prime minister of Finland's multi-party government in 2014 and 2015, was once asked in a television interview what he thought about ordoliberalism. Stubb, who holds a Ph.D. from the Department of International Relations at the London School of Economics, replied: "Excuse me, what?" A prime minister who implemented ordoliberalism in Finland was not aware of the name of his policy or its place in economic debate. The invisible hand of the economy carried out its work in this way in the economic policies of the prime minister of Finland.

In the fall of 2008, when the United States found itself in a banking crisis and economic recession, the governments of European countries, including Finland, began to stimulate their economies, which increased the amount of public debt. When the economic plight of Greece, Spain and Portugal was revealed in late 2009, European countries moved from stimulation policies to strict fiscal discipline and cutbacks on spending. It was imagined until 2012 in Finland that there were no particular problems in the country's own economy. In reality, Finland had entered a recession, which proved to be of record length and difficulty. In addition to problems of economic cycles there were also structural problems of the economy. The Finnish economy did not begin a period of more considerable growth until 2017.

In the early 2000s, Finnish forest industry companies spent very large sums of money on American and European business acquisitions which turned out to be unprofitable. It was realized only too late that the growth of electronic media led to excess production of printing paper and newsprint causing the prices of these products to crash. Over the past decade, Finnish companies in this sector have radically reduced their output of paper. The development of new products had been neglected for years, and good sales items still remain to be found.

The management of the Nokia mobile phone corporation imagined that the role of the world's leading mobile phone manufacturer could be maintained. This hubris was reflected negatively in product development. Nokia was late in developing competitive smartphones and was outpaced by its competitors. The decline of Finland's electronics and forest industries significantly reduced the country's revenue from exports and taxes, while a worldwide recession hampered exports in general.

The long-term sustainability gap of public finances in Finland is caused by, among other things, the aging of the population or the weakening of the dependency ratio (the ratio of children and pensioners to the population of working age) and a rate of employment that is too low in comparison with, for example, the other Nordic countries. The sustainability gap is an estimate of the savings in expenditure that are needed to prevent the country from eventually getting uncontrollably into debt and being instead able to meet its promises of services and pensions for its citizens. The gap is based on so many assumptions of the future that it should not be made at least the only or principal guideline of economic policy.

After 2008, the general government gross debt percentage of GDP in Finland grew quickly, reaching 61.4% in 2017 (63.5% in 2015). According to the EU's Treaty of Lisbon and Stability and Growth Pact, the public debt to GDP ratio should not exceed 60%. This figure is not based on economics but is instead the average for EU member countries at the time of the signing of the Maastricht Treaty in 1992. In 2017, the debt to GDP ratio of Germany was 64.1, of Sweden 40.6, of the UK 87.7 and of Greece 178.6% (the EU average was 81.6 and the Eurozone average was 86.7). Germany, however, has been able to reduce its public debt over the course of several years, while Finland has tried in vain until 2016 to halt the growth of public debt. Finland's general government deficit percentage of GDP reached 3.2 in 2014, which exceeded the 3% ceiling permitted by Treaty of Lisbon and the Stability and Growth Pact. Exceeding this figure is regarded by the European Union as a more serious breach of ruled than breaking the 60% limit on debt to GDP. In 2017, the deficit sank to 0.6%, to the relief of the Finnish government. The deficit in the United Kingdom was 1.9% (http://ec.europa.eu/eurostat. Accessed July 5, 2018).

The above figures apply to gross debt, for which the European Union has laid down limits. But when considering the net public debt to GDP ratio, i.e. including the assets of the public sector in the calculation, Finland has more wealth, mostly in the form of pension funds, than debt. In 2014, there were a few oil-producing countries and three developed industrialized countries, Norway, Finland and Sweden, with more assets than debts. The net debt of Finland and Sweden, the difference between gross debt and financial assets was approximately −50% of GDP, and over −200% for Norway. This information is based on IMF calculations (http://blog.hse-econ.fi/?p=6897, Akateeminen talousblogi. Roope Uusitalo. Accessed March 4, 2017).

Finland's multi-party government of 2011–2014, which also included left-wing parties, tried keep the state economy in balance with moderate increases of taxes and cutbacks of expenditure, including on education. The following government (2014–2015), with Alexander Stubb as prime minister, was in office during the parliamentary election campaign period and hardly achieved anything. The right and center government of Prime Minister Juha Sipilä (Center Party, the populist Finns Party[17] and the National Coalition Party) took office after the parliamentary election in the spring of 2015. It has cut back on funding for research and development, universities, vocational schools and high schools and children's day care, in addition to reducing the term of income-related (i.e. higher) unemployment benefits from 500 to 400 days. The aim of managing an economic crisis with "purging" reductions of expenditure explicitly belongs to the repertoire of right-wing parties. All of Finland's political parties, however, state that they wish to preserve the welfare state.

The Sipilä government threatened employee organizations with forced legislation that would have allowed negative exceptions to collective bargaining agreements. In order to preserve the freedom of organizations to negotiate agreements and avoid the planned legislation, Finnish unions agreed to negotiate with the government on reduced terms. In the spring of 2016, Finnish unions, employer organizations and the state entered into the so-called competitiveness agreement. Working hours were increased, mainly by a symbolic amount, and wages were not raised. Social security costs were transferred from employers to employees and holiday-related pay to public sector employees was reduced. The agreement was meant as a signal to international credit rating agencies and investors that there was a consensus in Finland regarding solutions to economic problems, above all halting the growth of public debt. At present, it appears that the agreement did not create the desired numbers of new jobs, i.e. improve employment (it is improving thanks to the growth of Finland's economy), or solve the sustainability problem of the public economy. Owing to tax reductions, the degree of debt of the public economy has barely diminished. This begs the question of how seriously Finland's present government, scaring the public with debt, is actually concerned about debt, as it appears to prefer tax cuts to decreasing public debt.

Moreover, tax relief for large income earners is, in Euros, much larger sums of money than the mites given to low-income groups. The multi-party governments in power in Finland during the previous parliament tried to level income disparities with their economic policies. The Sipilä government, on the other hand, reduced not only unemployment benefits but also other social welfare entitlements paid to the needy. Sipilä's standard reply to criticisms of his economic policies is that painful cutbacks affecting everyone have been necessary, but in reality the painful cutbacks have not affected the classes of society to which the prime minister himself belongs. According to calculations by the information services of the Finnish parliament from 2017, the present government's policies will increase income disparity in the period from 2015 to 2018.[18]

In February 2017, the Confederation of Finnish Industries canceled all agreements at the central or national labor-market organization level,[19] including one that secures the role of local shop stewards. The local agreements sought by the Confederation require shop stewards representing employees. Even the agreement requiring advance notification of industrial action was canceled. This is not necessarily an insurmountable problem, because the same agreement points are included in the agreements of many unions and organizations and can be included in stipulations where formal agreements do not yet exist. The employers wanted to underline with their actions that the following round of labor-market negotiations will no longer take place at the central organization level but will instead be specific to unions and sectors of industry. The employers wish to have agreements on working conditions made as close as possible to the level of individual firms and companies, because they are more powerful in those contexts than the unions—or ideally to be negotiated between companies and individual employees. This is about power rather than money. The Finnish industrial sector is by no means intimidated by the fact that the former round of negotiations at the union level in 2008 became far too expensive for both it and the public authorities. Rising costs were not yet an issue when employers were given the possibility to negotiate at the union level that they had sought. The Finnish culture of collective bargaining agreements and the trade union movement are, however, strong factors, and it is not likely that Finland would be adopting American practices in which the labor movements and employees have no say in matters. In any case, it is a cause of concern that the government and the industrial sector do not particularly appreciate societal consensus underlying collective agreements that has existed in Finland since 1944.[20]

Some economists maintain that years of cutbacks in public spending and the stagnation of real income have not moved Finland from the economic recession but have instead only prolonged it. A low-interest rate and the above-mentioned net assets of the public sector could have permitted a moderate increase in borrowing and economic stimulation policies. Stimulus policies in the United States under President Barack Obama put the economy back on its feet, but the indecision of the European Union, the European Central Bank and European governments in the management of the Euro crisis and austerity policies kept Europe in the red for several years. It was only through the policy of purchasing government bonds begun by the European Central Bank and the various national central banks in 2015 that conditions were created for some kind of growth. For a long while, Finnish exports, which consisted mostly of investment products after Nokia ceased to make mobile phones, thus did not have particularly good prospects in Europe, their main market area, regardless of Finland's own economic policies. In any case, it is obvious that there was no need to reduce research and development funding or expenditure on education and social security and that there would have been room for investments in infrastructure. Economic stimulation would have created more jobs, increased tax revenue, reduced the sustainability gap and ensured the existence of welfare services.

Since 2001, fixed investments in Finnish industry have remained at a lower level than before and investment in research and product development has decreased over the past six years. Limited investments have led to the erosion of industrial capital and the loss of jobs. Finland's forest and technology industries alone have lost 50,000 jobs over the past ten years, and 100,000 have been lost in Finnish industries as a whole. It is clear that decreasing numbers of well-paid jobs and moderate pay rises have eroded purchasing power and the conditions for growth. In 2015, however, fixed investments began to grow, and the worst investment recession now appears to be in the past. Finland's GDP in 2016, however, was still smaller than in 2008, unlike in neighboring Sweden, which wisely kept its own currency and did not adopt the euro. When Finland's economy trod water and declined and there were insufficient conditions for exports, companies concentrated on paying out dividends. The fact that instead of investing, companies pay out their profit as dividends to shareholders is a phenomenon typical of all Western countries.[21] There is hardly a single developed industrialized nation that has not lost a considerable part of its potential economic growth because of the finance crisis and recession of recent years.

In Finland, Prime Minister Sipilä's government has unconditionally refused to raise direct taxes. One can only wonder why industrialized nations combating economic problems, including Finland, allow the considerable amount of tax planning and tax evasion that is practiced by international corporations through legally permitted internal loans and pricing procedures. According to former Federal Chancellor Christian Kern of Austria, Amazon and Starbucks pay less taxes in Austria than a sausage stall.[22] Profits and revenue are thus not taxed in the countries where they have been generated but in countries of exceptionally low taxes or they disappear into tax havens with no tax revenue obtained from them by tax authorities at the national level. Multinational corporations, including ones of Finnish origin, avoid taxes by having in one country of operation very little sales, no labor costs or assets, but large profits on which low taxes are paid. Conversely, the company will have hardly any profits in another country, even losses, but despite this a large volume of sales, labor costs and investments in physical assets. The company will thus transfer profits to be taxed in a country of low or non-existent taxation. Time will show how far the recent measures of industrialized nations to combat tax planning and the use of tax havens will lead.

In the system created by international competition in taxation the requirement of the impartial and fair treatment of all national actors, which should apply in matters of taxation and would be expected to improve predictability usually associated with the market economy, remains a dead letter. In 2013, the median corporate tax paid by major corporations in Finland was 6.76%. The official corporate tax rate at the time was 24.5%. The actual tax burden for small and medium-sized enterprises was 21–24% in the period from 2009 to 2013 (*Helsingin Sanomat*, February 7, 2015 [Katja Boxberg, "Suuryhtiöt maksavat vähiten yhteisöveroa"]). The rent-seeking phenomenon is also known in Finland.

Over the past 25 years, income disparity has increased in both Finland and Sweden, although the Nordic countries still have relatively minor differences of income. Some politicians and market-fundamentalist think tanks defend the growth of income disparity on the grounds that it would promote economic growth. The OECD, on the other hand, sees the matter in completely opposite terms: increasing income disparity, which has been present in all of its member countries impedes economic growth in a statistically significant way. In the majority of OECD countries, income disparity is greater than ever before during the past 30 years. Negative impact on economic growth is caused by the fact that in their economic distress the poorest 40% of income earners do not acquire sufficient education for their children. The needy fall behind even more and important potential for economic growth is lost.

To promote economic growth, the OECD recommends not only efficient and sensibly focused redistribution through taxation and transfer of income, but also an investment in employment, good jobs, high-standard education and healthcare and the broad participation of women in working life (OECD 2014, 2015).

THE AMERICAN MODEL—WINNER TAKES ALL

People in most countries no doubt cherish the view—usually incorrect—that their own country is in some way unique and stands out in a positive sense from all other countries. The myth of the so-called American dream lives on tenaciously in the United States. It maintains that anyone, with enough hard work and enterprise, can rise from rags to riches, in contrast with the countries of Europe and Asia where people are born unequal and there are major and insurmountable obstacles to rising in the social scale. This notion had some basis in truth in the nineteenth century, but no longer during the past century, and especially not after the 1980s. Research shows that in the United States intergenerational income mobility (the incomes of parents vs. children) is lower than in Western Europe. Social mobility of this kind is greatest in the Nordic countries, Australia and Canada. It is also higher in Germany, Spain and France than in the United States. Italy and the UK are ranked lowest in this respect among the rich industrialized countries (Noah 2013, pp. 35–37 [28–43], 200; Therborn 2013, s. 120; Wilkinson and Pickett 2009, pp. 157–169).

The level of education of American parents is also a good indicator of whether or not their children will have a college or university education. In 2012–2013, the cost of attendance per semester at Harvard University was USD 54,000 (tuition plus accommodation etc.) or USD 38,000 (tuition). The average income of the parents of students at Harvard corresponded to the income bracket of the richest 2% of Americans. America's leading universities do not clearly state the grounds on which they choose their students. It is obvious that donations from parents to the university play a major role in this context.[23] Also in Finland, the children of academically educated parents are markedly overrepresented among university students, but cost-free university education improves the opportunities of children from non-academic and poor families to acquire a university degree, thus promoting social mobility. We must bear in mind that the most equal educational opportunities possible for the children of all classes of society will also promote economic growth by allowing the most gifted people to serve in leading positions in society and the economy. If family money dictates whose children become the leaders of the future, the result will be poorer not only for the economy but also with regard to social equality (Bourguignon 2013, p. 85).

Americans have aptly been described as conservative egalitarians. The fact that Americans also support equality is by no means surprising, considering how embedded reciprocity is in human behavioral tendencies. In 2007, 72% of Americans considered income disparity in their country to be too great. Even the majority of those who considered themselves to be upper class (less than 2% of the population) held this view. The majority of the population (61%) felt that the system favored the rich, and only 36% considered the system to be fair. According to another opinion survey, 92% preferred income distribution of the Swedish kind and only 8% supported the American model of income distribution. These surveys were conducted in the early 2010s. According to an opinion survey conducted in April 2011, 64% of Americans supported the raising of taxes on high-income earners to balance public spending and income.

It is a completely different matter, however, that Americans have highly limited information about income disparity in their own country. When citizens were asked to give the average annual incomes of the heads of corporations, income 28 times smaller than in reality was given as an answer.[24]

American political scientists Jacob S. Hacker and Paul Pierson use the phrase "winner takes all" to describe the policies implemented in their country over the past 30 years. Tax reductions in favor of the wealthy and corporations have led to a situation in which the 400 richest households paid taxes in 2007 at the rate of 16.6%, while the average rate for all taxpayers was 20.4%. This was, of course, due to the lower rate of taxation on capital income as opposed to wages and salaries. Between 1979 and 2007, the average tax rate of the highest-earning 1% decreased from 37 to 29.5%. Among all American taxpayers the change was only from 22.2 to 20.4%. In 2013, the tax rate for the top 1% had, however, risen to 34%.[25]

American investor Warren Buffett is one of the world's five wealthiest people. He also enjoys telling the unembellished truth. According to him, "[t]here's been class warfare going on for the last 20 years and my class has won." Buffett finds it outrageous that he pays taxes on his immense income at the same or lower rate than his secretary. Until 2009, this rich investor was a major owner of the Moody's rating agency, but he says that he does not believe at all in the ratings produced by these agencies. Buffett has also calculated that in 2009 the 400 richest Americans earned USD 97,000 an hour, over twice as much as in 1992 (Stiglitz 2013, pp. XII, 225 [quote], 421; Hacker and Pierson 2011, p. 229; Weik and Friedrich 2014, p. 181).

The dismantling of economic regulation began at the turn of the 1970s and 1980s in sectors protected against competition where it could be justified more readily, but it went on to become a general trend of policy. The minimization of regulation in financing proved to be one of the most dubious measures. The economic cycles of capitalism became more pronounced and no lessons were learned from the IT bubble of the turn of the millennium. The Glass–Steagall Act, which was passed in 1933, maintained a difference between investment banks managing the wealth of individuals and institutions and ordinary commercial and savings banks. Investment banks had to handle the savings that they received and the loans that they issued through commercial banks and in keeping with the regulations on commercial banks (which meant that only the latter could generate new money by providing credit). This meant that the risk-taking involved in large-scale investments was isolated from the rest of the economy and the money of ordinary citizens. In 1999, this act, which in reality was being circumvented, was ultimately repealed and banks were also released from the restrictions that had applied to investments with the deposits of other people or other parties. The protections of deposits (i.e. knowledge that the government would step in if necessary) remained in force and actually promoted investments of a gambling nature (Stiglitz 2013, pp. 112–114, 489). Bankers are worried only about the failure of their own investments, not those of other investors (Hacker and Pierson 2016, p. 90).

In order to expand business, the finance sector developed various kinds of opaque investment products, such as derivatives, that bet on different results for securities and guarded against the financial failure of the object of investment. Derivatives are non-transparent, i.e. completely unpredictable in terms of content and impact because of bank secrecy. In other words, no one knows what obligations or chain reactions they can lead to in the worst-case scenario. When the economic crisis finally erupted, everyone wanted to get rid of securities of decreasing value, which made the downward spiral worse. Mutual trust and credit, essential to financing, became negative because no one knew what skeletons were in the opposite party's cupboard. The credit recession brought the wheels of the economy to a halt. Buffet has candidly called derivatives "weapons of mass financial destruction."

Joseph E. Stiglitz, winner of the Nobel Memorial Prize in Economics awarded by the Central Bank of Sweden (there is no actual Nobel Prize in Economics) regards derivatives as insurance products or gambling instruments rather than investments. According to US law, however, they were to be primarily compensated in case of bankruptcy before the claims of other creditors, not to mention the wages of employees, even where bankruptcy was due to derivatives, as had often been the case. When the finance bubble burst in 2008, the US government indemnified holders of derivatives. The bailout of the AIG insurance corporation alone was greater than the sum of welfare spent on the poor in America between 1990 and 2006. In many cases, bankers were even allowed to keep their bonuses, which they had hardly deserved in view of the situation that they had caused. On the other hand, autoworkers were persuaded to accept lower pay in order to save their industry. It was worth taking large risks in investments because society would generously provide assistance when risks materialized. In good years, investors culled profits and in poor years taxpayers would reimburse losses.[26]

According to the German journalists Matthias Weik and Marc Friedrich, the above situation was like the return of communism that had been buried 20 years earlier with "privatized profits and socialized losses." The words of Erich Honecker, former party leader of the German Democratic Republic, when leaving for exile in 1993 proved to be a prophecy: "Communism is not dead. It has only lost a battle" (Weik and Friedrich 2014, pp. 80, 120).

The finance sector also marketed so-called mortgage-backed securities, which included along with other securities subprime mortgages summarily awarded to the poor. These loans were aggressively offered to people with no possibility to pay interest or amortization. This completely immoral practice is known as predatory lending. In the spirit of the unfounded optimism of the period, credit rating agencies gave the mortgage-backed securities high ratings and naturally, bets were made on the failure of repaying mortgages. The investors who made the mistake of buying these securities (also known as toxic assets) suffered major losses when their value finally collapsed, while insiders betting on the outcome made sizable profits.

But not all investors are by any means, speculators. There are many private individuals, responsible financial institutions and pensions funds in this sector that seek good, but stable returns and security for their funds. The crises and instability caused by irresponsible actors do not correspond to the interests of these investors.

A telling example of the indifference or fraudulence of lenders and rating agencies is a USD 724,000 mortgage given to a Mexican strawberry picker, which was resold as a triple-A security, because the man had a clean credit record, having only recently moved to the United States. Earning 14,000 dollars a year, strawberry picker would have to pick for a fair number of years before the mortgage would be repaid in full. The success of repayment was naturally completely irrelevant for the original lender and the agency that rated the security. The responsibility of these agencies for their ratings lasts as long as the receding taillights can be seen.

Financial institutions, speculators and individual investors maximized returns with debt leverage, i.e. primarily financing their investments with debt. Old debts were paid with new debt. The house of cards stood as long as investors and lenders maintained faith in the loan-fueled get-rich automaton.

Investment market expert and guru André Kostolany had a great deal of experience of stock exchange investors with a herd mentality whose ability to make informed decision had been blurred by the desire to get rich: "I would go to the stock exchange every day, because nowhere else in the world can you see so many idiots per square meter as you can find there" (Weik and Friedrich 2014, pp. 60–86, 179–182, quote p. 76).

When Alan Greenspan was the chairman of the Federal Reserve, the central bank of the United States (also known as the Fed), from 1987 to 2006, the overall amount of dollars in cash, deposits, securities, dollar-based government bonds, Eurodollar reserves and dollar reserves of non-European countries grew from approximately 3.6 trillion (thousand billion) to 10.3 trillion dollars. The worldwide value of finance derivative trade was five trillion dollars in 1990, and over 700 trillion in 2011. Over this period, the volume of the world economy grew from 22 trillion to 69 trillion dollars. These figures are from German sources. According to the Finnish economist and Member of Parliament Timo Harakka, the value of derivatives at the end of 2012 was 632 trillion dollars, nine times the value of industrial production in the world. The multiplied value of securities and the considerable growth of debt greatly increases the instability of the worldwide market economy (Weik and Friedrich 2014, pp. 22–35, 131–133, 186–190; Patomäki 2013, pp. 43–49; Harakka 2014, p. 83; Mann 2013, p. 328).

Greenspan gave assurances that a new economic bubble could be avoided. This was possible for a while but only because the middle class and the poor in America lived beyond their means. In a society of uneven income distribution, the middle class and the poor tend to imitate the lavish consumption of the rich at the cost of keeping their own finances in balance. Economic growth during the first decade of the twenty-first century and the rise in the standard of living of the middle class and the poor were only based on over-indebtedness. The continuous rise in the prices of housing served as collateral for the debt. Housing, however, became overpriced and its demand and value began to decrease in 2006. The bubble finally burst in September 2008. Millions of Americans lost their jobs or their homes in foreclosures, not being able to afford the costs of managing their debt (Stiglitz 2013, pp. xlvii, 15–17, 106–114, 137–139, 149, 171, 239–257, 291–293, 309–310, 337–338). Nearly 40% of American families' home equity disappeared between December 2006 and December 2008. The total debt of financial institutions, however, had been two and a half times greater than the total housing debt (Hacker and Pierson 2011, p. 2; Patomäki 2013, p. 35).

According to Stiglitz, the financial industry, unlike for example manufacturing industries, does not create anything new. It only redistributes wealth, i.e. transfers it to the richest. Paul Volcker, former chairman of the Fed, has pointed out that the innovations of the finance sector have not promoted economic growth or the good of society, the only exception being automatic teller machines. According to other information, the profits of the financial sector in 2007 were as much as 40% of all corporate profits, while other sources define it as 27% (the largest rise since 1980, when this figure was 13%). By 2011, the proportion had again risen to 30%. In 2007, over a third of the total of wages paid in New York City were earned in Wall Street (cf. one eighth in 1972) (Hacker and Pierson 2011, pp. 46, 66, 228–230; Stiglitz 2013, pp. xxxi, 45–59, 400; Noah 2013, p. 156). François Bourguignon (2013, p. 85) underlines the point that channeling credit predominantly to those with the most economic power and contacts will erode potential for developing the economy. Many of those who might have the most to contribute to the economy do not belong to the elites. This is highly true of the hegemony of the financial sector and its effects.

At the beginning of 2008, 56% of General Electric's profits came from the financing sector. Before the crisis of 2008, General Motors' financing section generated between 60 and 90% of the corporation's profits. The cobbler just couldn't stick to his last. Even these traditional manufacturing giants expanded into financing, because this was the sector where money was being made.[27] After the crash of 2008, the US federal government had to bail out the American automobile industry.

The 1% that increased its income at the cost of the rest of society includes along with bankers, executives of other sectors and leading entrepreneurs. Major corporations and their executives have lost their connection with society and they are no longer interested in the stakeholder perspective of taking employees, society and the state into consideration. The only aim now is to maximize shareholder value. There is no such thing as truly free and total competition, nor do the normal laws of the market economy apply. The term rent seeking refers to acquiring revenue that is higher than could be obtained in a situation of free competition. It is done by influencing the government and its economic policies through lobbying and campaign contributions. Tax, corporate and bankruptcy legislation and the policies of subsidies and privatization of the government give preference to the economic elites. The society also supports them by selling underpriced oil-drilling and mining rights. Corporations can obtain loans on better terms than others and can restrict competition in many ways, which the supporters of neoliberalism do not, however, consider to be a problem. Nonetheless, the elites have not exhibited any greater sense of social responsibility, focusing instead on minimizing their own taxes and increasing their income, with due success. Regardless of how poor the results are, the elites will always reward themselves generously (Stiglitz 2013, pp. xxxii–xxxiii, xl–liii, 7, 35–64 and *passim*; Hacker and Pierson 2016, pp. 92–94, 176–180, 270–333; Mann 2013, s. 384–385).

Since 1989, the financial sector has predominated among the one hundred American corporations providing the most funding for political activities, having donated more than the total provided by the energy, healthcare, defense and telecommunications sectors. The situation has a come a long way from the early 1970s, when the political activity committees of unions made larger campaign contributions than the corresponding committees of corporations. Because of advertising fees charged by television channels and other media, the costs of America's presidential and congressional elections reached astronomical proportions by the twenty-first century. Campaign contributions of this size can only come from financial institutions, major corporations and the wealthiest citizens. At the same time, earlier ceilings placed on campaign funding have been removed. In 2012, the richest 0.01% of Americans, paid 40% of electoral campaign funding (compared with 15% in 1980). Massive mud-slinging campaigns can lead to defeat at the polls for uncomfortable candidates (Democrats or moderate Republicans) (Hacker and Pierson 2011, pp. 116–124, 227 and *passim*; 2016, pp. 220–269; Stiglitz 2013, pp. 164–167).

Branko Milanovic regards as naive the idea that the rich make campaign donations without trying to promote the policies that they want to see implemented. Neither do they throw their money away in business without expecting returns on it.[28] It was discovered in the fall of 2017 that many of the major donors of the Republican Party were unsatisfied with the party's inability to carry out the reforms that they regarded as important. One of them stated the following in an email: "The GOP (i.e. Republican) leaders should know, no movement on remaining agenda: tax reform, infrastructure, deregulation, etc. means no funding from supporters like me."[29] The tax overhaul passed by the Republicans in Congress in December 2017 considerably reduced corporate taxes and also provided tax reductions for private citizens, which were much more generous for the rich than for average citizens. To the Democrats it was quite obvious who benefited from the tax reform: "What this is all about is nothing more than the Republican party very generously rewarding their wealthy campaign contributors," Senator Bernie Sanders said. "Let's call this out for what it is: Government for sale" (Senator Elizabeth Warren). Moreover, the tax overhaul also benefited the senators and House members themselves, most of whom belong to the richest 1%. If the Republicans remain in power, the increase to the budget deficit resulting from diminished tax revenue will be corrected by dismantling the social security of ordinary citizens.[30]

The victorious progress of the financial industry was based on neoliberalism, which is a current of economic thinking, not a conspiracy. If it had been a mere conspiracy it would never have achieved such a leading role over the past 30 years. We should not, however, ignore the energy with which American businesses began to fund and lobby politicians in the late 1970s. According to a Russian saying, free cheese is offered only in mousetraps. The main objective was to acquire tax reductions for companies and taxpayers, especially the highest earning ones among the latter. President Ronald Reagan argued that tax cuts for the rich would lead to growing tax revenue as they would promote economic activity. The result, however, was diminished tax revenue and a deficit in government finances, which President Bill Clinton of the Democratic Party turned into a surplus. The tax reductions especially benefiting the richest end of the taxpayer scale that were implemented by President George W. Bush in the early 2000s had the same effect as Reagan's tax cuts. Moreover, the cuts increased pressure to reduce investments in education, technology and infrastructure, meaning that they were in this sense only detrimental to the economy. The principal benefits of tax cuts went to their recipients and the financing sector, which needed clientele for its investment products.

Stiglitz estimated that a fifth of the federal budget deficit of 2012 was due to Bush's tax cuts, 15% by the wars in Iraq and Afghanistan started by Bush, 16% by the stimulus package of the economy, and 48% by an underachieving economy resulting from the housing bubble and the recession to which it led (Stiglitz 2013, pp. 142, 144, 260–264, 314, 420, 432).

Political scientist Larry M. Bartels has demonstrated how American senators of the 1980s and 1990s (Republicans more than Democrats) were more inclined to vote according to the opinions of voter groups in their constituencies the higher the income of these groups. The views of the lowest-earning third had no effect whatsoever on the senators. Almost all the senators and most members of Congress belonged to the highest-earning 1%. According to Bartels, income disparity has grown especially during the terms of Republican presidents. There has been higher unemployment but less economic growth in these periods than under presidents of the Democratic Party (the comparison covers the years 1947–2005).

Martin Gilens, on the other hand, shows that the opinions of the lower half of the income scale had no effect on policies implemented between 1981 and 2002 (with chronology extending from 1964 to 2006 in some matters) if they differed from those of the higher income groups. Policy, as implemented, is a different matter than the Senate's voting behavior studied by Bartels. In situations of conflict between voter groups, the views of the top 10% were reflected in implemented policy, particularly in economic policy and matters of religion. With impending elections and generally in situations of close competition, however, the opinions of all voter groups were important, but when time had passed after elections and one party predominated, the even-handed approach disappeared. According to Gilens, the idea that the Republicans are for the rich and the Democrats defend the poor, is too black and white and thus incorrect. Gilens, who rejects unduly categorical notions of only the interests of the richest Americans being significant in politics, ends his book, however, by pointing to the increase of economic inequality in his country over the past 30 years: "Further concentration of political influence among the country's affluent threatens both the perception and the reality of a shared political community so central to the health of even the modestly democratic republic we currently enjoy."[31]

Of the Republican presidents, Dwight D. Eisenhower and Richard Nixon still followed the welfare state policies laid out by Franklin Delano Roosevelt's New Deal, no doubt mostly because it was still the prevailing way of thinking in the post-war decades. Eisenhower regarded attempts to revoke Roosevelt's social reforms as foolish and doomed to fail, and he considered unions to be part of industrial life in America. Nixon promoted consumer and environmental protections and supported a more radical healthcare reform scheme than the later Obamacare (Hacker and Pierson 2016, pp. 149–155). George H. W. Bush was far too moderate for extreme Republicans. Moreover, he and his predecessor Ronald Reagan had to raise taxes despite having promised the opposite in their election campaigns. Nonetheless, the Republican Party drifted further and further to the right in the 2000s. The southern states had traditionally voted into Congress Democrats, who were often on the right and served as a bridge between the two parties. When they finally retired, they were replaced by right-wing Republicans, who were no longer bridge-builders.

In the Republican Party primaries of the 2010s, the Tea Party movement, which had emerged in 2009, has sought to replace moderate candidates with similarly thinking extremists. The candidates and elected members of Congress were required to promise that they would under no circumstances raise taxes. The budget deficit had not previously been a cause of concern for the Republicans, but when President Barack Obama's stimulus package and other bills concerning the economy went before Congress the party was interested only in cutting social welfare expenditure and reducing taxes. The political elements that had previously made compromises across the aisle with the Democrats were no longer present.

Relying on their minority position to block legislation in the Senate, the Republicans threatened the federal government with insolvency. The government would have been unable to pay in a normal manner salaries and pensions and other expenditure legislated by Congress. The representatives of the party did not agree to raising the debt ceiling, but called instead for tax cuts, the canceling of tax raises on the rich and cutbacks on social welfare spending. A crisis of this kind took place first in 2011 and again in 2013. Especially after the Democrats lost the House of Representatives to the Republicans in the midterm elections in the fall of 2010, and previously their 60-vote supermajority in the Senate, it became almost impossible to have amendments to legislation passed in Congress. The filibustering procedure allowed in the Senate to delay or block voting gives the political minority (40 senators out of 100) power that it does not have in most other developed counties. By taking Congress hostage in this way, the Republicans tried to prevent the Obama administration from functioning and also block his re-election. The latter attempt failed, but the trust of the public in Congress and politicians was reduced to a great deal (Hacker and Pierson 2016, pp. 239–269, 315–336; Mann and Ornstein 2012, pp. ix–103).

In the US Senate, small and often predominantly rural states with a larger white population than the national average, are entitled to two representatives just like the larger states. The Republicans benefit from this situation. The polarization of the electorate and the political parties is also reflected in the elections for the House of Representatives. Rural voting districts usually choose Republicans for the House, while the Democrats are preferred in the big cities, which are ethnically more diverse than the countryside. After the midterm elections of 2010, the Republicans drew the boundaries of the voting districts in the states which they had won in a way that benefited them. The term "gerrymandering" applying here refers to assembling the supporters of the opposing party into a few large voting districts, primarily containing the voters only one party. The supporters of one's own party are placed in districts where they have a sufficient majority, while the opposition has nonetheless considerable voting support. As a result, the latter votes are "lost." In the election for the House of Representatives in 2012, the Democrats received 51% of the vote, but the Republicans gained 54% of the seats. As electoral districts have become homogenous and "safe" for either party, the Republicans have found it easier to become right-wing than in a situation where they would have concentrated in winning the votes of citizens of the political center.[32]

Strict local requirements of voter registration and identification placed on exercising the vote maintain low voter turnout and, in practice, favor the more affluent white population over African Americans and Hispanics. In the US midterm elections of 2010, voter participation among the young and non-white population (overall turnout 38%) decreased considerably from the elections of 2008 (turnout 62%), which led to a Republican victory. American voter participation, in general, has decreased since the 1960s and is now lower than in many West European countries. The poor, the uneducated and non-whites are, of course, considerably overrepresented among the sleeping voters, ultimately to their own detriment. As a well-known saying in Washington puts it: "If you're not at the table, you're on the menu." The turnout in the 2012 presidential election was an acceptable 58%, but in the midterm elections of 2014, in which the Republicans won the Senate and thus gained control of both chambers of Congress, was only 37%. In the United States a result even as poor as this is not questioned, but, viewed from the outside, extremely low turnout damages the legitimacy of the representative political system of the United States.

In many states, only a small and select minority participated in the presidential primaries of 2012. In the Republican primaries, white evangelical Christians aged over 45 are considerably more active than the population on average.[33] Evangelicals are selectively pro-life, they oppose the right to abortion on religious grounds but not the death penalty. They also believe in the literal interpretation of the Biblical account of creation rather than modern science. Nor does their Christian faith prevent them from maintaining exaggerated enemy scenarios or engaging in hate speech. A large portion of the American population is oriented politically more in accordance with extreme conservative Christian values than on the basis of income, education or class.

The Tea Party movement, representing older and on average wealthier white conservative, in many cases evangelical Christians, wants to reduce spending on education for young people of a more progressive mindset than theirs and welfare for the more ethnically diverse population, because the poor (i.e. African Americans) supposedly do not pay taxes but are instead supported by hard-working people. Pensions, however, must not be privatized to commercial institutions, even though extreme Republicans of the political elite would like to do so in their enthusiasm for privatization. The Tea Party movement regards strong government to be more than acceptable when reducing illegal immigration with radical measures. Many of the members of this movement had their political awakening in Barry Goldwater's 1964 presidential campaign with its spirit of opposing the civil rights movement and big government.[34]

Reducing the power of the federal government is a fundamental article of faith for the present Republican Party.[35] Neoliberals have spread on a worldwide basis the misconception that, unlike private business, government or public authorities cannot promote economic growth at all through their own investment and efforts. They ignore the fact that the considerable economic growth of the United States in the twentieth century was based on the growth of productivity, which in turn was due to education provided by the authorities and technological progress and inventions produced by federal funding. The latter included high-tech materials, semiconductors, satellite communications, GPS, computers and the internet. Stiglitz regards government investment in education, research and infrastructure as multipliers that stimulate economic growth to a great deal. The Republicans in South Carolina either do not or do not want to know that for every tax dollar paid by a resident of the state to the federal government, Washington pays over five dollars from tax revenue back to the state. In Mississippi, the ratio is 1:2.34.[36]

A special feature of the United States are news channels openly declaring the views of either leading party. It is quite commonly maintained that, for example, the news of the arch-conservative Fox channel is often mostly propaganda. Accordingly, the media that was most opposed to Obama spread the unfounded and outright ridiculous claim that the presidential healthcare reform included orders on so-called death panels with the task of deciding on euthanasia. The idea of the death panels was introduced by Sarah Palin, Republican vice-presidential candidate in 2008, and was joined by fellow party members including John Boehner and Newt Gingrich. Palin's allegations of euthanasia also applied to the British NHS, which aroused a great deal of indignation in the UK. Death panels were chosen as the "Lie of the Year" in the United States.[37]

A further sign of the level of knowledge of citizens is that half of all Americans imagine foreign aid to be one of the largest items of expenditure of the federal budget (in reality it amounts to only 1% of the budget). Thirty-five percent of the population are unaware that Obamacare and the Affordable Care Act are the one and the same. According to Hacker and Pierson, swing voters shifting their loyalties between the parties and lauded by the media as knights of democracy are ignorant people who decided their political standing on the most superficial ground.[38] There is thus no need to wonder why many Americans cannot connect the recent impasse of their political system with the extreme Republican trend threatening to paralyze the federal government if cuts to taxes and spending are not agreed to.

In the 1970s, American unions were still a counterweight to businesses, but since the Reagan era, the unions have been completely disarmed especially in the private sector. Nothing similar has happened in Canada on the other side of the border (Hacker and Pierson 2011, pp. 56–61, 186–187; Schlozman et al. 2012, pp. 87–94, 360–361). The Walmart retail chain, the largest private employer in the United States, employs 1.4 million people, but they do not include unionized employees, because this is not permitted by the company (Noah 2013, pp. 125–128). Workers are usually denied freedom of association only in countries where also other democratic rights are infringed.

Where the degree of unionization is low, workers lack the power to bargain for raises in pay. Unlike in other developed countries, wages in the United States have not risen at the same pace as productivity, and the influence of unions on the atmosphere of society has been eliminated. According to a study by economists Florence Jaumotte and Carolina Osorio Buitron of the International Monetary Fund, the decline of unions and unionization explains approximately half of the growth of income disparity in the developed industrialized nations between 1980 and 2010 measured with both the Gini coefficient and the growth of the relative proportion of the top 10% of income earners. No other factor has had such major impact on this. The weakening of unions has led to the growth of the proportion of the income of the richest earners at the costs of other income earner groups (Noah 2013, pp. 128–129, 134–143, 201; International Monetary Fund 2015). In the United States, the change in this direction was naturally greater than on average in the developed industrialized countries.

According to Stiglitz, the bailout of the financial system was necessary as such. The major actors in particular (with the exception of Lehman Brothers) were saved because they were too large go bankrupt. The method that was applied with the bailouts was a different matter. The government provided bailouts for financial institutions and received shares in these banks to approximately half the value of the bailouts. Securities (government debt and troubled private assets—toxic assets) were purchased from the banks or mortgage lenders. The Fed loaned massive sums of money to banks, which went on to loan them at higher rates. There could hardly have been an easier way to make profits. Shareholders and creditors did not have to take economic responsibility for their mistakes as required in a market economy and fraudulent bank executives (there were also honest ones) were not made legally responsible for their misdeeds, as would be required by the rule of law.

In the rescue of the financial system, a considerable portion of private debt turned into public debt. When the worst crisis had passed, the financial sector recovered and the old style of derivatives ("weapons of mass destruction") and excess bonuses continued as if nothing had happened. Since the regulation of the financial industry was left to the industry itself and remained highly insufficient because of Republican opposition, new bubbles and crashes are not only possible but also probable.

Those who lost their jobs and their homes in foreclosures received government "bailouts" with a tiny measure while they had been given to banks in abundance. The result was, of course, a great deal of bitterness toward the political establishment in Washington. The decrease in the purchasing power of citizens prolonged the recession.[39]

The growth of income disparity in the United States has undermined the realization of reciprocity between the government and the people and likewise between the economic elites and ordinary Americans. The chosen policy does not prevent disparity from growing and instead promotes it. The duty to pay taxes is passed on to the ordinary citizens, who, however, receive very little in return from the government.

Considering the neoliberal trend that has lasted for over 30 years, it is no surprise that the American welfare state which was even originally more limited than its European counterpart has been shrunk to an absolute minimum and its safety nets for people in distress are much smaller than on the other side of the Atlantic. The American model was built for a society of full employment where share prices never go down, much less collapse. Normal unemployment security in America is only for six months. In 2011, only 38% of the unemployed received support, and 44% had not received a cent of unemployment assistance (Stiglitz 2013, pp. 12–15, 29). In 2012, 47 million Americans depended on federal food stamps. The overall uncertainty of life increased as unemployment grew. With the outsourcing of formerly regular jobs, some have been forced to become more or less ostensible entrepreneurs, which means that the companies for which they work have also outsourced their losses to them. The pensions of many people are bound to share prices on the stock market. The recession of 2008 was a severe blow to them (Noah 2013, p. 54; Stiglitz 2013, pp. 15–16, 221–222, 285).

In 2014, most households were poorer than in 1987. As a result, voters punished Obama and the Democrats in the 2014 midterm elections, although the economic bubble had been allowed to develop when Obama's Republican predecessor and the Republican Congress were in power and although the American economy had recovered to a great deal under Obama and through his policies.[40] Despite new jobs and low unemployment, wages and purchasing power remained stagnant, which paralyzed economic growth. The low-wage model functions poorly even in the United States.[41]

Owing to limited social welfare benefits, private social welfare (charities and donations) has a greater role in the United States than in Europe. In 2013, private individuals and non-profit organizations donated a total of approximately 335 dollars to various charities in the United States. This is roughly 2% of GDP. Most of the donations, approximately one-third, go to religious organizations and their charitable work.[42]

Seen from the American perspective, the European welfare state has crowded out the desire of individuals to help their fellow man,[43] while the supporters of a far-reaching welfare state regard Americans as having surrendered to the arbitrariness of charitable organizations, which can direct assistant to only the "deserving" poor or more agreeable groups of people needing help. In reality, private charity has not disappeared from countries with generous social welfare benefits, nor is there any reasonable obstacle to sufficient public social security coexisting with private charitable work. Private charities, however, cannot completely replace social security provided by the state.

Prior to the Affordable Care Act reform, which Obama managed to get passed at the beginning of his term despite considerable opposition, there had not been a public system of health insurance in the United States, where employers have traditionally arranged health insurance for employees. In 2006, up to 46 million people or 18% of the US population had no health insurance (the figure for 1979 was only 15%). Many people lacked the means or initiative to acquire health insurance or were denied it by insurers who regarded them to be too ill. The new system had to be implemented via private insurers, because any government-run system was socialism to the Republicans (as also the welfare state and the mixed economy of the Nordic countries). American medical science undoubtedly leads the world, but the country's private and commercial healthcare system is two and a half times more expensive per capita than the average for the developed countries. In other developed countries, the state uses its considerable negotiating power to keep healthcare costs reasonable, while in the United States the government is expected to leave profitable private business alone. The results of the expensive American system, however, are poor because it does not cover all citizens and because there is also considerable inequality in the country in other respects as well. Americans have one of the shortest life expectancies of the developed countries. In addition, the size of income disparity between the states of the union correlates positively with life expectancy (greater disparity means shorter life expectancy). Infant and child mortality (under 1-or 5-year-olds) is higher in the United States than in Cuba, Belarus or Lithuania, not to mention the countries of Western Europe. There is a major and growing difference in the respective life expectancies of the rich and the poor in the United States,[44] but as discussed above, this is also the case in Finland.

The US government supports through its tax system the housing for wealthy Americans four times as much as the poor receive public housing benefits (Stiglitz 2013, p. 371). The federal government provides the highest level of social welfare for the retired population. The Social Security and Medicare systems initially met with strong opposition, but they have become popular over time. On the other hand, the development of social security for young people and the working population has been neglected. In the mid-1960s, however, President Lyndon B. Johnson tried to expand the American welfare state, but he directed his reforms at special groups such as the retired and the poor without aiming at social welfare services for the population as a while. The system was under-resourced from the outset. The economic conditions for services did not improve even later, because the necessary funds were consumed by the war in Vietnam and the problems of the economy caused by it. Also, the coinciding and later rise of neoconservatism, based on an undercurrent aimed against the African American population, undermined support for social welfare services in Congress and more broadly in society as a whole.[45]

As mentioned above, Branko Milanovic in his 2016 book (pp. 199–211) described the United States as a plutocracy that supports globalization, while its democracy has deteriorated into the rule of money. Populists opposed to globalization are in turn trying to gain power in Europe and there is the risk of democracy turning into a mere staged front. How then should we regard the administration of President Donald Trump, who took office at the beginning of 2017, which combines plutocracy with populist opposition to globalization? Trump is ordering companies to move jobs back to the United States at the risk of suffering punitive customs duties. If Obama had suggested something similar, the Republicans would have branded him a supporter of state socialism or a communist.

In their book published in 2012, Thomas E. Mann and Norman J. Ornstein write that "one of the two major parties, the Republican Party, has become an insurgent outlier—ideologically extreme; contemptuous of the inherited social and economic policy regime; scornful of compromise; unpersuaded by conventional understanding of facts, evidence, and science; and dismissive of the legitimacy of its political opposition" (2012, p. xiv). It appears to be the case that when a party's extremist thinking develops far enough, the party can rapidly undergo a metamorphosis in which its former tenets turn into their opposites.

Trump outshadowed his Republican competitors in the 2016 presidential primaries. Populism ("brash conservatism") overran conservatism. Trump could lie and promise as much as he liked, and make his supporters scream for Hillary Clinton to be put in jail. Until now, threatening political opponents with prison has belonged of the repertoire of Third-World operetta dictatorships, not one of the world's oldest democracies. Trump's misogynistic rhetoric and actions did not lose him the support of women or evangelical Christians. It is obvious that Trump's supporters knew that he lied, and many of them no doubt disapproved of his behavior. Nonetheless, they regarded his promises of making American great again and reducing the power of politicians and Wall Street more important than his minor failings. The latter did not matter if illegal Mexican immigrants and other bad hombres are deported and China, Japan, Mexico and Germany can be stopped from exploiting the United States. The worldview of many of the supporters of the Republican Party is just as Manichean as that of extreme political movements in general.[46]

Trump's antics while running for the presidency boosted sales for American mass media, which the latter did not mind. They did not begin to take the risks that he represented seriously or to oppose him until the final stages of the presidential campaign. Trump was given a great deal of free publicity and Hillary Clinton spent much more money on her campaign than her opponent. Those among the American super-rich who did not fund Clinton or Trump focused on making sure that Congress would go to the Republicans.

The attitudes to Russia of many supporters of the Republican Party have also changed since the days of Ronald Reagan. A third of them have a positive view of Russia's authoritarian leader Vladimir Putin. It is hard to say whether this is due more to the admiration of strong leaders typical of populists or Trump's positive references to Putin, all the possible reasons for which are not yet known. In any case, this has come a long way from conservatism. Instead of Putin, conservatives admire politicians like Winston Churchill, who keep to democratic procedures and have an old-fashioned respect for speaking the truth and also respect the freedom of a critical press as part of the democratic system. It has been claimed that Trump's campaign promoted Russian interference in the 2016 presidential election and that the easing of sanctions on Russia would have been the price for electoral assistance, but it is best to wait for official investigations to be completed before any conclusions.[47] In any case, it has come to light that Russia used a massive social media campaign to spread disinformation discrediting Clinton and consequently supporting Trump and destabilizing American society in general.[48]

Clinton received 2.9 million more votes than her competitor, but in comparison with the 2012 presidential election Trump won six states from the Democrats: Michigan, Wisconsin, Pennsylvania, Florida, Ohio and Iowa, thus gaining a clear majority in the electoral collection. The three first-mentioned states went to Trump with a very small majority of the vote. Had Clinton campaigned more in these rust-belt states, especially in Wisconsin and Michigan, which she neglected, instead aiming at Arizona, Florida and Georgia, she might have won. Clinton received the overwhelming majority of the African American vote, but 29% of Hispanics and Asians voted for Trump. Seven out of ten non-college-educated white males voted for Trump and six out of ten non-college-educated white women. Both demographics included more Trump voters than among white males or females on average.

Trump's success presumably indicates the fact that uneducated disadvantaged whites who are afraid of competition from African Americans, Hispanics and Asians want to restore white supremacy after an African American president. So long as poor whites are employed, the conflicting relationship of employer and employee will inevitably play a role in their attitudes. When unemployment sets in or well-paid industrial work is replaced by work for low wages, the party favorable to the workers or unions (or immigrants) readily become scapegoats (this has also been the case in Finland). It is an outright absurdity that the poor and uneducated sector of the American populace believes that an unscrupulous real-estate investor like Trump, who has not paid taxes in years because of lax laws, will bring the plutocracy to heel and restore lost jobs. Research has shown that mortality is rising among uneducated white and has surpassed the mortality of all African Americans in the United States. The issue here is of real distress for poor whites caused by the dismantling of the American welfare state to which Trump reacted better than Clinton did. Hillary Clinton's long political career, lack of charisma and her close relationship with Wall Street prevented her from creating the kind of winning coalition Obama had. Poor electoral success among uneducated whites was a serious warning to the Democrats in view of the future. The average Republican voter, however, was richer than the average Democrat. This is partly due to the fact that the majority of younger citizens and non-whites voted Democrat. The Republicans won the majority in both the House of Representatives and the Senate.[49]

According to the Columbia Journalism Review, Trump's supporters received their information from an insulated media system that evolved around the Breitbart website. They went on to spread their view on social media, while closing their eyes and ears to established media outlets. The worldview that was accepted and disseminated by Trump's supporters was disinformation partly blended with correct information to improve credibility. The importance of completely false news was smaller than assumed.[50] There is nevertheless due cause to doubt the latter conclusion (see notes 47 and 48).

In 2017, Trump's and the Republican Party's voters had their first experience of how well the president and the party dominating the House of Representatives and the Senate could keep their campaign promises. Obamacare was repealed with the votes of the Republicans in the House but owing to dissension within the majority party a repeal decision that could come into force has not been reached in Congress as a whole. On the other hand, the individual mandate included in Obamacare, which imposes a financial penalty on people who do not get health insurance, was overturned as part of the tax reform. The Tax Bill remained the Republicans' only major reform of legislation in all of

2017. According to the estimate of the CBO, repealing the individual mandate will increase the number of uninsured people by 13 million by 2027. Health insurance premiums will rise.[51] Only a part of the Republican members of the House of Representatives belongs to the extreme faction that absolutely calls for cuts to social welfare spending and lower taxes for the wealthy. But it is not to be expected that in its budget policies the Republican-majority Congress will fulfill Trump's campaign promises of leaving main items of social security expenditure untouched, especially since the tax reform will increase public debt and the budget deficit. Many of the federal benefits are in fact likely to be scrapped.[52]

The UK vote for Brexit in June 2016 reflects a rise of populism similar to Trump's electoral victory. According to studies, people without acquaintances outside their own locality who do not travel were more likely to vote for leaving the EU than those with a broader social network. The majority of votes in the large cities, Scotland and Northern Ireland opposed Brexit. Poor voters, in particular, felt that they had nothing to say about immigration or other social problems and that politicians do not care about them (naturally not all supporters of Brexit were marginalized individuals). The supporters of Brexit felt that Britain was going in the wrong direction. In places with few immigrants who often remained unknown, immigration was felt to be a particular problem. There were many who felt that the availability of social services was at risk. People voted as much in terms of subjective feelings as they did on the basis of age, income or place of residence.[53]

A survey carried out in ten EU countries showed that all of them had more supporters of ending immigration from Muslim-majority countries than there were opponents to this idea. The elderly, lower education and rural dwellers were the most opposed to Muslim immigration. It was only in Britain and Spain that supporters for ending immigration numbered less than half of the respondents. The attitudes of the Germans and the French, for example, were more negative than those of the British.[54] Continental Europeans thus have no cause to consider themselves more tolerant than the Americans or the British.

It appears quite plausible that the "Arab spring" created by globalization, cuts in public spending and growing inequality in the developed industrialized countries became channeled into rising support for right-wing populism. In the United States, though not in Europe, right-wing populism joined a considerable portion of most disadvantaged members of society in the same camp as its richest members. In the French and Dutch elections in the spring of 2017, right-wing nationalism, however, lost votes. In countries such as Poland, Hungary, Turkey and Russia, with a weak democratic heritage, conservative and aggressive nationalism is government policy, but the underlying reasons are mostly different than in the developed Western countries.

NOTES

1. *Helsingin Sanomat*, January 9, 2015 (Jeffrey Sachs interviewed by Annukka Oksanen). Sachs' message to the Nordic countries was: "Here in Scandinavia, you have the best-functioning society in the word. Don't destroy it." Regarding Sachs's career, it should be mentioned that in 1985 the leaders of Bolivia began to apply, upon his recommendation, shock therapy in response to a debt crisis and hyperinflation. The national currency was devalued, and its value was allowed to float, price and wage regulation was terminated, and public expenditure and the wages of government employees were cut. Klein (2011, pp. 244–246), Dunkerley (2007, pp. 146–158).

2. Piketty (2013, pp. 400–401). Factor income (market income) is earned income plus capital income. Gross income (pre-tax income) is market income plus government transfers received. Disposable income (after-tax income) is gross income minus taxes.

3. Piketty (2013, pp. 183–249, 375–598 and Tables 7.1–7.3 and Figs. 8.1, 8.5–8.6, 9.2–9.9 and 10.1, 10.3–10.6).

4. Cumulative growth in average inflation-adjusted after-tax income, by pre-tax income group, from 1979 to 2013 was 192% in the top percentile, in a completely different class than for all other income groups in the United States. https://www.cbo.gov/sites/default/files/114th-congress-2015-2016/reports/51361-HouseholdIncomeFedTaxes_OneCol.pdf, p. 42. Accessed February 20, 2017. According to OECD data, approximately 47% of the increase of pre-tax income between 1975 and 2012 went to the top 1%. Keeley (2015, p. 33). Real disposable income of the lowest decile of income earner households and the corresponding median income of all households decreased between 2007 and 2011, but despite the recession the income of the top decile increased. OECD (2015, pp. 106–107). On the UK, see Atkinson (2015, p. 105).

5. Milanovic (2016, pp. 194–197).

6. According to the Gini coefficient comparison: Bourguignon (2013, p. 38), Atkinson (2015, p. 81), OECD (2015, p. 24). In Finland, the share of income of the top decile of income earners was 20% in 1981 and

26% in 2007. The share of income of the top percentile was some 3% in 1981 and almost 7% in 2007. This was gross income, i.e. before taxes and other paid transfers (social security and pensions insurance contributions) but including received transfers such as pensions and social welfare assistance (progressive taxes and paid income transfers decrease the inequality of income distribution). The same trend also emerges in disposable income, although the shares of income of the top decile and centile are slightly smaller than the above after taxes and income transfers. Riihelä et al. (2010, p. 9).

7. Riihelä et al. (2010, pp. 20–23) (1–36). Also, Jäntti et al. (2010, pp. 371–411), Riihelä et al. (2015, pp. 144–186).

8. Riihelä et al. (2010, pp. 9–10, 14); *Helsingin Sanomat*, December 19, 2014 ("Tuloerot kasvoivat viime vuonna"); http://pxweb2.stat.fi/Dialog/varval.asp?ma=270_tjt_tau_117&path=../database/StatFin/tul/tjt/&lang=3&multilang=fi.

9. http://no.wikipedia.org/wiki/Skatt_i_Norge. Accessed February 20, 2017; OECD (2015, pp. 20, 56). See also Aaberge and Atkinson (2010, pp. 448–466).

10. Ireland's Gross Domestic Product is thus 20% larger than its Gross National Product, which consists of only the earnings of Irish citizens. Most of the returns on investments by foreigners in Ireland go most likely to tax havens. Luxembourg is a location for widespread and more or less opaque financial activities and the country's GNP is only two-thirds of its GDP. Milanovic (2016, p. 237). In 2012, more foreign investments flowed into tiny Luxembourg than into both France and Germany combined, the largest economies of the Eurozone. *International New York Times*, November 15–16, 2014 ("Uphill battle to end global tax havens").

11. Milanovic (2016, pp. 4, 46–47). On the Gini coefficient, see Atkinson (2007, pp. 19–20).

12. Piketty (2013, pp. 183–198, 375–392, 404–747, 793–834), Hacker and Pierson (2016, pp. 36–37) (median net wealth), Blyth (2015, p. 242). On the other hand, when the highest marginal tax rate in the United States was 70% in 1979, the realized income tax rate for households of the top 0.01% of earners was a highly reasonable 21%, which means that there must have been various loopholes in taxation. Noah (2013, pp. 110–111).

13. Milanovic does not believe that large-scale intranational redistribution is possible any more in a world with free movement of capital from one country to another. He would reduce inequality with high inheritance taxes, a capitalism of the workers and the people and equal educational opportunities. Milanovic aims at a society with low inequality of

market incomes (earned income and capital income) and a relatively small state. Countries of this kind are South Korea, Taiwan and Japan (2016, pp. 217–222). We can ask, however, if the high inheritance tax is any easier to carry out than Piketty's tax on capital. A third leading name in recent income distribution studies, the British economist Anthony B. Atkinson suggested in his last book (2015) before his death a number of concrete measures for increasing equality. The OECD (2015), in turn, urges focusing on the lowest 40% of income earners (households), whose incomes have lagged behind since 1985 compared with both the top income groups and the average rate of development. The poorest 40% have hardly been able to benefit from recent economic progress, and the absolutely poorest 10% even less.

14. *Helsingin Sanomat*, June 14, 2014 (Piketty interviewed by Petri Sajari).
15. When the crisis broke out, the Irish and Spanish states had relatively little debt and were by no means close to the 60% ceiling laid down for public debt, which Germany and France had exceeded in several years, thus breaking the rules of the monetary union. The states of Ireland and Spain did not become highly indebted until they had taken on responsibility for private sector debt.
16. Blyth (2015), Stiglitz (2016), Harakka (2014); http://www.spiegel.de/wirtschaft/soziales/eurokrise-so-geht-es-italien-griechenland-spanien-irland-portugal-und-zypern-a-1136013.html. Accessed March 4, 2017. The present debt crisis of the European Union is a special phenomenon, because European private wealth is the equivalent of up to five years' worth of national product and is among the highest in the world in this respect. Piketty (2013, pp. 285–291, 884).
17. The Finns Party (Fi. *Perussuomalaiset*) regarded the reduction of tax on motor vehicles as their major victory. This tax reduction mostly benefits the buyers of expensive automobiles, in other words quite other people than supporters of the Finns Party. The Finns Party split in June 2017. The majority of the party's parliamentary group established a new political party, Blue Reform, as the Finns Party remained in the hands of the minority of the parliamentary group. The Finns Party joined the political opposition and became even more pronounced in its opposition to immigration than previously. The majority of party's supporters also support this line. The parliamentary group of the Blue Reform is a group of generals without troops. Because of them, the Sipilä government still has a small majority in the Finnish Parliament.
18. *Helsingin Sanomat*, September 8, 2017 (Teija Sutinen, "Budjetti kääntää   tuloerot   kasvuun"); http://vasemmisto.fi/wp-content/uploads/2017/09/Eduskunnan-tietopalvelu_2017_09.pdf. On   debt and intimidation with debt, see http://labour.fi/ptblogi/2017/05/31/

velka-meill-on-aina-vieraanamme and the same http://www.labour.fi/
ptblogi/2017/09/07/suomen-velkaraja-on-viela-kaukana/.
19. The Confederation of Finnish Employers recognized employee organizations as equal parties at the beginning of 1940, when Finland was
defending itself against the Soviet invasion in the Winter War of 1939–
1940. The recent cancellation of various agreements at the central federa-
tion and organization level eroded mutual trust more than it affected the
content of agreements.
20. The industrial sector maintains that Finland's collective bargaining system
and the rules of working life are too rigid and need to be made more
flexible. In late 2016, the OECD estimated the Finnish labor market
to be flexible. Lasse Laatunen, a retired executive and director of the
Confederation of Finnish Industries and the architect of the confederation's social policy positions does not regard the rules and regulations of
working life in Finland to be any more inflexible than in other countries.
Laatunen, a true expert in this area, feels that there are individual differences running both ways among countries, but he does not believe that
"a model superior to all others could be found somewhere." *Helsingin
Sanomat*, November 25, 2016 ("OECD kehuu Suomen työmarkkinoita
joustaviksi") and January 2, 2015 ("Suurpäätösten kummisetä jättää val-
lan," both articles by Teemu Luukka).
21. Between 2003 and 2012, 500 major corporations listed by Standard and
Poor's used 54% of their profits for stock payback and 37% for dividends.
Stock payback benefits shareholders just as much as dividends. Less than
10% of profits remained for investments. Hacker and Pierson (2016,
p. 282).
22. http://bbc.com/news/business-37259278. "Amazon and Starbucks pay
less tax than sausage stall, says Austria." Accessed March 5, 2017.
23. Piketty (2013, pp. 774–778). President Donald Trump's son-in-law and
senior advisor Jared Kushner was admitted to Harvard after his father
made a considerable donation to the university.
24. Hacker and Pierson (2011, pp. 151–155), Stiglitz (2013, pp. 159–160,
184–185), Skocpol and Williamson (2012, p. 233), Bartels (2008, s.
127–161), Schlozman et al. (2012, pp. 52–68), Hacker and Pearson
(2016, p. 197).
25. Stiglitz (2013, s. 90—91); https://www.cbo.gov/sites/default/files/114th-
congress-2015-2016/reports/51361-HouseholdIncomeFedTaxes_OneCol.
pdf, p. 32. Accessed February 20, 2017.
26. Stiglitz (2013, pp. xxiii–xxiv, 43–49, 61, 72, 84, 97, 106–111, 126–139,
212, 308–311, 316–317, 320, 399, 423), Blyth (2015, pp. 24–32,
43–44), Mann (2013, pp. 322–331, 344–347).

27. Noah (2013, p. 156). In 2015, General Electric decided to focus on manufacturing and to terminate most of its financing operations, which had seriously destabilized the corporation during the last economic crisis. *International New York Times*, April 11–12, 2015 (Andrew Ross Sorkin and Michael J. de la Merced, "In big shift, G.E. plans to phase out finance arm").

28. Milanovic (2016, p. 189). See also http://highline.huffingtonpost.com/articles/en/mercers/. Accessed March 18, 2017. Super-rich campaign backers Robert and Rebekah Mercer (who have funded also Cambridge Analytica) moved from Ted Cruz's camp to support Trump, bringing Steve Bannon along with them to be involved in Trump's campaign. The Mercers, however, placed conditions on opening their purse strings: "If Mr. Trump had told Billy Bush, whoever that is, earlier this year that he was for open borders, open trade and executive actions in pursuit of gun control, we would certainly be rethinking our support for him. ... We are completely indifferent to Mr. Trump's locker room braggadocio."

29. http://www.politico.com/story/2017/10/05/republican-donors-trump-mcconnell-anger-243449. Accessed October 6, 2017.

30. https://www.huffingtonpost.com/entry/democrats-outrage-gop-tax-cuts_us_5a39ff6be4b025f99e132495?ncid=inblnkushpmg00000009; https://www.theguardian.com/us-news/2017/dec/16/bernie-sanders-tax-bill-republicans-trump; http://www.taxpolicycenter.org/sites/default/files/publication/149851/2001628-distributional_analysis_of_the_tax_cuts_and_jobs_act_as_passed_by_the_senate_1.pdf. Accessed December 20, 2017.

31. Bartels (2008, especially pp. 32–35, 49, 62, 252–282), Gilens (2012, especially pp. 82, 101–104, 167, 172–174, 189–208, 221–252, quote p. 252), Schlozman et al. (2012, pp. 249, 232–262). See also Hacker and Pierson (2016, pp. 194–196).

32. Hacker and Pierson (2016, pp. 256–259), Saarikoski and Saarikoski (2016, pp. 112–113). Former US Attorney General Eric Holder aptly describes the undemocratic nature of gerrymandering: "We have a system now where politicians are picking their voters, as opposed to voters making selections about who they want to represent them." http://www.independent.co.uk/news/world/americas/barack-obama-ready-to-roll-return-politics-eric-holder-us-attorney-general-former-us-president-a7605076.html. Accessed March 2, 2017. https://theguardian.com/us-news/2017/jun/25/partisan-gerrymandering-republicans-2016-report. Accessed June 25, 2017.

33. Hacker and Pierson (2011, *passim*), Stiglitz (2013, pp. 164–168, 445–446), Schlozman et al. (2005, pp. 19–71; 2012, p. 309) (quote). Also, electoral districts voting for a single representative and assured seats for

the other party passivize voters in non-presidential midterm elections. The American electoral system contains many elements that passivize voters, some of them deliberately, such as strict voter registration and identification requirements. http://www.theguardian.com/commentis-free/2014/nov/05/midterm-massacre-boosts-republican-2016-demo-crats. Accessed November 5, 2014.

34. Skocpol and Williamson (2012, *passim*) (on the Tea Party movement). On Goldwater see Kabaservice (2012, pp. 80, 87–115).

35. In the 2010s, opposition to the federal government led to a situation where its non-defense discretionary spending (adjusted for inflation) was one eighth lower in 2016 than in 2010. In 1989, there was one federal worker per 110 other Americans; in 2013 the ratio was 1:150. Cuts on spending and the reduction of the federal workforce make it difficult and even impossible to carry out work successfully, which is reflected in services provided for citizens. Among others, the Internal Revenue Service has suffered from reduced government spending. Nonetheless, every dollar spent on the IRS produces six dollars in recovered taxes and every dollar for tax audits on high earners recovers 47 dollars. Over the long term, all cuts to research and development, infrastructure, conservation of the environment, education and healthcare spending will have the effect of slowed or completely non-existent economic growth. One of the obstructionist methods of Republicans in the early 2010s was to defund legislative reforms that had already been decided, thus preventing them from coming into force. Hacker and Pierson (2016, pp. 303–335).

36. Hacker and Pierson (2016, pp. 63–69, 100–101, 126), Stiglitz (2013, s. 116, 144, 293–295, 354). Mann (2013, pp. 150–151) considers the market fundamentalism and anti-statism of American neoliberals to be hypocritical in view of American military spending and farming subsidies. In 2012, Republican presidential candidate Mitt Romney claimed that 47% of the population do not pay income tax but are instead supported by the government (ultimately by hard-working taxpayers). He forgot to mention, however, that even those who do not pay federal income tax pay indirect taxes and usually state and local taxes and those among them who work also pay payroll taxes, which, on top of it all, are regressive. Romney, if anyone, cannot afford to judge freeloaders, having paid from his large income and wealth only 14% in taxes in 2011, i.e. relatively less than citizens much poorer than himself. Stiglitz (2013, pp. xviii–xxi, 143, 370–371), Noah (2013, pp. 181, 201–206). According to Mann (2013, p. 163), the complex American tax system involves numerous allowances and exemptions, serving as veiled redistribution to the middle and upper class. The French economist Piketty states more bluntly than American researchers that Americans are more strongly prejudiced toward the poor

than Europeans and that these attitudes have a partly racist background. Piketty (2013, p. 765).

37. Skocpol and Williamson (2012), Hänninen (2014, s. 158); http://en.wikipedia.org/wiki/Death_Panel. Accessed March 18, 2017. Palin, who criticizes excess federal government power, was the governor of Alaska from 2006 to 2009. Alaska receives more federal support per capita than any other state in the union. Hacker and Pierson (2011, p. 54). Most of the Republican Party (and a number of Democrats lobbied by the coal and oil industries) also deny global warming. Mann (2013, pp. 374–377, 391–393). President Trump removed the United States from the Paris Climate Agreement in early June 2017.

38. Hacker and Pierson (2011, pp. 109, 285), Stiglitz (2013, pp. 184–185); https://www.nytimes.com/2017/02/07/upshot/one-third-dont-know-obamacare-and-affordable-care-act-are-the-same.html?_r=0. Accessed March 18, 2017. See also Bartels (2008, pp. 162–196), Gilens (2012, pp. 229–232).

39. Stiglitz (2013, pp. xliv–xlvi, 60–61, 76, 88, 93, 149, 209–215, 225–226, 241, 248–257, 290–296, 305–318, 322–323, 458–459, 468, 471–472, 483–484), Weik and Friedrich (2014, pp. 146–165); http://en.wikipedia.org/wiki/American_Recovery_and_Reinvestment_Act_of_2009. Accessed March 18, 2017. Unlike in the banking crisis of the turn of the 1980s and 1990s, fraudulent conduct led to indictments in only exceptional cases. The government retroactively collected compensation from the leading banks for their abuses of trade in mortgage-backed securities. The banks did not have to admit wrongdoing.

40. *Helsingin Sanomat*, November 4, 2014 (Laura Saarikoski, "Obamaa ei kiitetä piristyneestä taloudesta"). The article cites the *Washington Post*'s statement that 90% of American households were poorer in 2014 than in 1987.

41. *Helsingin Sanomat*, January 10, 2015 (Paavo Teittinen, "Heikko palkkakehitys varjosti USA:n työllisyyslukuja"); http://www.lemonde.fr/economie/article/2015/01/09/les-creations-d-emplois-au-plus-haut-depuis-quinze-ans-aux-etats-unis_4552828_3234.html. Accessed January 9, 2015.

42. Charity Navigator (Giving Statistics), http://www.charitynavigator.org/index.cfm?bay=content.view&cpid=42#.VCT5cxA09m6. Accessed April 20, 2017.

43. Alesina et al. (2001). Alberto Alesina, the most prominent of the three is not an American but an Italian economist, who has greatly influenced the creation of the "expansionary austerity" theory in economic terms and its adoption as a guideline in the European Union in 2010. Blyth (2015, pp. 167–179, 205–207). Expansionary austerity sounds as convincing as pro-life death sentence.

44. Stiglitz (2013, pp. xiii–xiv, 12, 17, 87, 93, 121–122, 204, 229, 345–346, 384, 386–387, 481, 500), Wilkinson and Pickett (2009, pp. 73–87), Hacker and Pierson (2011, pp. 30–31, 274–277, 281–286, 291–294; 2016, pp. 87, 226, 273–281); https://data.unicef.org/country/ (the data on infant and child mortality is from 2016). Accessed July 5, 2018.

45. Stiglitz (2013, pp. xxxiv, 21, 93, 283–287, 347 and *passim*), Mann (2013, pp. 56–66). Neoconservative economic thinking is based on neoliberalism.

46. Richard Hofstadter's article "The Paranoid Style in American Politics" from 1966 (pp. 3–40) is an excellent description of the historical roots of extremist thinking in America. According to press reports, Steve Bannon, the extreme right wing White House Chief Strategist of the first months of the Trump administration declares himself a Leninist: "Lenin wanted to destroy the state and that's my goal too. I want to bring everything crashing down and destroy all of today's establishment." https://www.theguardian.com/commentisfree/2017/feb/06/lenin-white-house-steve-bannon. Accessed March 2, 2017. Most Americans, however, do not support the Mexican wall or measures against illegal immigrants of such a radical nature as proposed by Trump in his presidential campaign. Betsy DeVos, Trump's choice for Secretary of Education, singled out education reform already several years ago as a way to "advance God's kingdom." According to the *New York Times*, the Christian right shares the "apocalyptic conviction that extreme measures are needed." Trump put together what will be the wealthiest administration in modern American history, and DeVos is one of its richest members who will promote private and charter schools. Following the appointment of pro-creationist DeVos, it has been asked if classroom globes in American schools will be flattened. *Helsingin Sanomat*, February 9, 2017 (Elisa Rimaila, "Trumpin opetusministeri Betsy DeVos"); https://www.nytimes.com/2016/12/13/opinion/betsy-devos-and-gods-plan-for-schools.html?_r=0; http://www.independent.co.uk/topic/betsy-devos; http://www.spiegel.de/lebenundlernen/schule/usa-krise-im-bildungssystem-der-kampf-der-schulen-a-1136040.html. Accessed March 19, 2017.

47. http://www.gallup.com/poll/204191/putin-image-rises-mostly-among-republicans.aspx. Accessed March 7, 2017. It appears almost certain that Putin's Russia helped Trump win the election with the aid of the Democrats' hacked and published emails and a propaganda campaign on Facebook. This matter, however, and above all the possibly related collusion of Trump's assistants with Russia are for the time being under investigation by former FBI director Robert Mueller as special counsel appointed by the US Department of Justice. See Harding (2017).

Trump starting a new arms race may ultimately be a worse alternative for Putin and the Russian economy than Clinton would have been, while on the other hand Trump has damaged the international image of the United States and is undermining procedures of collaboration among the Western nations.

48. See https://www.huffingtonpost.com/entry/russian-facebook-ads-examples-election_us_59fa16d1e4b01b474047d7a5?ncid = inblnkush-pmg00000009; https://www.politico.com/story/2017/11/01/social-media-ads-russia-wanted-americans-to-see-244423. Accessed November 2, 2017.

49. *Le Monde diplomatique*, Décembre 2016 ("Dossier États-Unis"); http://www.bbc.com/news/election-us-2016-37889032; https://www.the-guardian.com/us-news/2017/dec/21/us-life-expectancy-down-for-second-year-in-a-row-amid-opioid-crisis. Accessed March 1 and December 21, 2017; Case and Deaton (2015, 2017), Kranish and Fisher (2017, pp. 309–366), Saarikoski and Saarikoski (2016, pp. 79–276). Europeans find it hard to understand the antipathy felt by many Americans toward Hillary Clinton. She would have been exceptionally well prepared and qualified for the office of president. Clinton's use of a private email server while secretary of state was not worth the scandal that it led to. But Trump's tactics were to make Clinton even more objectionable and unpopular than he himself was. Trump acquires information from the "alt" sources of the far right and is surprisingly ignorant and blasé about facts.

50. http://www.cjr.org/analysis/breitbart-media-trump-harvard-study.php. Accessed March 7, 2017. A group of young people in Macedonia produced false news on the US presidential election for social media. Their only motivation was to get Americans to share the news as much as possible on social media and to get rich from the related advertising revenue, in which they were successful.

51. https://www.cbo.gov/publication/52752; https://www.cbo.gov/publication/52849; https://www.cbo.gov/publication/53300; http://www.huffingtonpost.com/entry/gop-health-care-bill-congressional-budget-office_us_5924e896e4b00c8df29feb68?ncid=inblnkushpmg00000009. Accessed December 16, 2017.

52. Report of the Special Rapporteur on extreme poverty and human rights on his mission to the United States of America, http://undocs.org/A/HRC/38/33/ADD.1. "The new policies (under President Trump— AK and MD): (a) provide unprecedentedly high tax breaks and financial windfalls to the very wealthy and the largest corporations; (b) pay for these partly by reducing welfare benefits for the poor ..." (p. 4).

53. https://www.theguardian.com/politics/2016/dec/15/poorer-voters-worries-immigration-fuelled-brexit-vote-study-finds; https://www.theguardian.com/politics/2016/dec/17/socially-isolated-voters-more-likely-to-favour-brexit-finds-thinktank. Accessed March 4, 2017.
54. https://www.chathamhouse.org/expert/comment/what-do-europeans-think-about-muslim-Immigration. Accessed March 7, 2017. The survey did not include any of the Nordic countries.

References

Aaberge, R., and A.B. Atkinson. 2010. Top Incomes in Norway. In *Top Incomes: A Global Perspective*, ed. A.B. Atkinson and T. Piketty, 448–481. Oxford: Oxford University Press.

Akateeminen talousblogi. http://blog.hse-econ.fi/?p=6897. Accessed 4 Mar 2017.

Alesina, Alberto, Edward Glaeser, and Bruce Sacerdote. 2001. Why Doesn't the US Have a European-Style Welfare System? NBER Working Paper Series, http://www.nber.org/papers/w8524. Accessed 26 May 2017.

Atkinson, A.B. 2007. Measuring Top Incomes: Methodological Issues. In *Top Incomes Over the Twentieth Century: A Contrast Between Continental European and English-Speaking Countries*, ed. A.B. Atkinson and T. Piketty, 18–42. Oxford: Oxford University Press.

Atkinson, Anthony B. 2015. *Inequality: What Can Be Done?* Cambridge, MA and London: Harvard University Press.

Bartels, Larry M. 2008. *Unequal Democracy: The Political Economy of the New Gilded Age*. Princeton and Oxford: Princeton University Press. http://www.bbc.com.

Blyth, Mark. 2015. *Austerity: The History of a Dangerous Idea*. Oxford and New York: Oxford University Press.

Bourguignon, François. 2013. *Die Globalisierung der Ungleichheit*, trans. Michael Halfbrodt. Hamburg: Hamburger Edition.

Case, Anne, and Angus Deaton. 2015. Rising Morbidity and Mortality in Midlife Among White Non-hispanic Americans in the 21st Century. *Proceedings of the National Academy of Sciences of the United States of America (PNAS)* 112 (49): 15078–15083. https://doi.org/10.1073/pnas.1518393112. Accessed 25 Mar 2017.

Case, Anne, and Angus Deaton. 2017. Mortality and Morbidity in the 21st Century. *Brooking Papers on Economic Activity*, March 23. https://www.brookings.edu/bpea-articles/mortality-and-morbidity-in-the-21st-century/. Accessed 25 Mar 2017.

Charity Navigator (Giving Statistics). http://www.charitynavigator.org/index.cfm?bay=content.view&cpid=42#.VCT5cxA09m6. Accessed 20 Apr 2017.

http://www.chathamhouse.org/expert/comment/what-do-europeans-think-about-muslim-Immigration. Accessed 7 Mar 2017.

http://www.cjr.org/analysis/breitbart-media-trump-harvard-study.php. Accessed 7 Mar 2017.

Congressional Budget Office. https://www.cbo.gov.

Dunkerley, James. 2007. *Bolivia: Revolution and the Power of History in the Present, Essays.* London: Institute for the Study of the Americas.

http://ec.europa.eu/eurostat. Accessed 5 July 2018.

http://www.gallup.com/poll/204191/putin-image-rises-mostly-among-republicans.aspx. Accessed 7 Mar 2017.

Gilens, Martin. 2012. *Affluence and Influence: Economic Inequality and Political Power in America.* Princeton and Oxford: Princeton University Press.

http://www.theguardian.com.

Hacker, Jacob S., and Paul Pierson. 2011. *Winner-Take-All Politics: How Washington Made the Rich Richer—And Turned Its Back on the Middle Class.* New York: Simon & Schuster Paperbacks.

Hacker, Jacob S., and Paul Pierson. 2016. *American Amnesia: How the War on Government Led Us to Forget What Made America Prosper.* New York: Simon & Schuster.

Hänninen, Jyri. 2014. *Veroparatiisit ja Suomi: Eli kuinka liituraitamafia pyörittää varjotaloutta ja laskun siitä maksamme me.* Helsinki: HS-kirjat.

Harakka, Timo. 2014. *Suuri kiristys: Tie ulos eurokriisistä.* Helsinki: Schildts & Söderströms.

Harding, Luke. 2017. *Collusion: How Russia Helped Trump Win the White House.* London: Guardian Books and Faber & Faber Limited.

Helsingin Sanomat.

Hofstadter, Richard. 1966. *The Paranoid Style in American Politics and Other Essays.* New York: Alfred A. Knopf.

Horn, Gerd-Rainer. 2009. *The Spirit of '68: Rebellion in Western Europe and North America, 1956–1976.* Oxford and New York: Oxford University Press.

http://www.huffingtonpost.com.

http://www.independent.co.uk.

International Monetary Fund. 2015. Power from the People. Finance & Development, March, vol. 52. no. 1. http://www.imf.org/external/pubs/ft/fandd/2015/03/jaumotte.htm. Accessed 22 May 2015.

International New York Times.

Jacobs, Lawrence R., and Theda Skocpol. 2005. American Democracy in an Era of Rising Inequality. In *Inequality and American Democracy: What We Know and What We Need to Learn*, ed. Lawrence R. Jacobs and Theda Skocpol, 1–18. New York: Russell Sage Foundation.

Jäntti, Markus. 2006. Income Distribution in the 20th Century. In *The Road to Prosperity: An Economic History of Finland*, ed. Jari Ojala, Jari Eloranta, and Jukka Jalava, 245–260. Suomalaisen Kirjallisuuden Seuran Toimituksia 1076. Helsinki: SKS.

Jäntti, M., M. Riihelä, R. Sullström, and M. Tuomala. 2010. Trends in Top Income Shares in Finland. In *Top Incomes: A Global Perspective*, ed. A.B. Atkinson and T. Piketty, 371–447. Oxford: Oxford University Press.

Kabaservice, Geoffrey. 2012. *Rule and Ruin: The Downfall of Moderation and the Destruction of the Republican Party, From Eisenhower to the Tea Party*. Oxford and New York: Oxford University Press.

Keeley, B. 2015. *Income Inequality: The Gap Between Rich and Poor*. Paris: OECD Publishing. http://dx.doi.org/10.1787/9789264246010-en. Accessed 21 Feb 2017.

Klein, Herbert S. 2011. *A Concise History of Bolivia*. New York: Cambridge University Press.

Kranish, Michael, and Marc Fisher. 2017. *Trump Revealed: The Definitive Biography of the 45th President*. London: Simon & Schuster UK.

Kujala, Antti. 2013. *Neukkujen taskussa?: Kekkonen, suomalaiset puolueet ja Neuvostoliitto 1956–1971*. Helsinki: Tammi. http://labour.fi. Accessed 14 Sept 2017.

Mann, Michael. 2013. *The Sources of Social Power. Globalizations, 1945–2011*, Vol.4. New York: Cambridge University Press.

Mann, Thomas E., and Norman J. Ornstein. 2012. *It's Even Worse Than It Looks: How the American Constitutional System Collided with the New Politics of Extremism*. New York: Basic Books.

Milanovic, Branko. 2016. *Global Inequality: A New Approach for the Age of Globalization*. Cambridge, MA and London: The Belknap Press of Harvard University Press. http://lemonde.fr. *Le Monde diplomatique*.

Noah, Timothy. 2013. *The Great Divergence: America's Growing Inequality Crisis and What We Can Do About It*. New York: Bloomsbury Press. https://www.nytimes.com.

OECD. 2014. *Focus on Inequality and Growth*. December. http://www.oecd.org/els/soc/Focus-Inequality-and-Growth-2014.pdf. Accessed 5 Mar 2017.

OECD. 2015. *In It Together: Why Less Inequality Benefits All*. Paris: OECD Publishing. http://dx.doi.org/10.1787/9789264235120-en. Accessed 21 Feb 2017.

OECD. 2017. Income Inequality (Indicator). https://doi.org/10.1787/459aa7f1-en. Accessed 24 Mar 2017.

Patomäki, Heikki. 2013. *The Great Eurozone Disaster: From Crisis to Global New Deal*, trans. James O'Connor. London and New York: Zed Books.

Piketty, Thomas. 2013. *Le capital au XXIᵉ siècle*. Paris: Éditions du Seuil. http://politico.com.

Riihelä, Marja, Risto Sullström, and Matti Tuomala. 2010. *Trends in Top Income Shares in Finland 1966—2007*. VATT Research Reports 157. Helsinki: Valtion taloudellinen tutkimuskeskus.

Riihelä, Marja, Risto Sullström, and Matti Tuomala. 2015. Veropolitiikka huippu-tulojen ja –varallisuuden taustalla – onko Pikettyn kuvaama kehitys nähtävissä Suomessa? In *Hyvinvointivaltio 2010-luvulla – mitä kello on lyönyt?* ed. Heikki Taimio, 144–169. Raportteja 30. Helsinki: Palkansaajien tutkimuslaitos.

Roine, Jesper. 2014. *Thomas Pikettyn Pääoma 2000-luvulla: Kooste ja pohjois-mainen näkökulma*, trans. Maarit Tillman. Helsinki: Art House.

Roine, Jesper, and Daniel Waldenström. 2010. Top Incomes in Sweden Over the Twentieth Century. In *Top Incomes: A Global Perspective*, ed. A.B. Atkinson and T. Piketty, 299–370. Oxford: Oxford University Press.

Saarikoski, Laura, and Saska Saarikoski. 2016. *Trump*. Helsinki: HS-kirjat.

Schlozman, Kay Lehman, Sidney Verba, and Henry E. Brady. 2012. *The Unheavenly Chorus: Unequal Political Voice and the Broken Promise of American Democracy*. Princeton and Oxford: Princeton University Press.

Schlozman, Kay Lehman, Benjamin I. Page, Sidney Verba, and Morris P. Fiorina. 2005. Inequalities of Political Voice. In *Inequality and American Democracy: What We Know and What We Need to Learn*, ed. Lawrence R. Jacobs and Theda Skocpol, 19–87. New York: Russell Sage Foundation.

Skocpol, Theda, and Vanessa Williamson. 2012. *The Tea Party and the Remaking of Republican Conservatism*. Oxford and New York: Oxford University Press.

http://www.spiegel.de.

Statistics Finland. http://pxweb2.stat.fi/Dialog/varval.asp?ma=270_tjt_tau_117&-path=../database/StatFin/tul/tjt/&lang=3&multilang=fi. Accessed 20 May 2015.

Stiglitz, Joseph E. 2013. *The Price of Inequality*. London: Penguin Books.

Stiglitz, Joseph E. 2016. *The Euro: And Its Threat to the Future of Europe*. London: Allen Lane/Penguin Books.

http://www.taxpolicycenter.org/. Accessed 20 Dec 2017.

Therborn, Göran. 2013. *The Killing Fields of Inequality*. Cambridge and Malden: Polity Press.

UNICEF. https://data.unicef.org/country/. Accessed 5 July 2018.

United Nations. http://undocs.org/A/HRC/38/33/ADD.1. Accessed 3 June 2018.

http://vasemmisto.fi. Accessed 10 Sept 2017.

Weik, Matthias, and Marc Friedrich. 2014. *Der grösste Raubzug der Geschichte: Warum die Fleißigen immer ärmer und die Reichen immer reicher werden*. Taschenbuch 60804. Cologne: Bastei Lübbe Taschenbuch.

Wikipedia.

Wilkinson, Richard, and Kate Pickett. 2009. *The Spirit Level: Why Equality Is Better for Everyone*. London: Penguin Books.

CHAPTER 9

Reciprocity Past and Present

The human tendency for reciprocity and collaboration is an innate trait that has developed through a long process of evolution. The ability to assess the acceptability or reprehensibility of actions is also part of human nature. Retributive (rewarding and punitive) moral feelings make people reward behavior going beyond obligations and punish behavior that they regard as sub-standard even when the punishment conflicts with the economic or other interests of the punishing party.

Early human communities and individuals organized their internal and mutual relations through the gift form of exchange, based on reciprocity and retributive moral feelings. It involved the exchange of commodities and services, but the exchange did not primarily serve economic goals. The community was under the obligation to accept gifts from other communities and to respond to them with counter-gifts, since breaching the obligation of reciprocity would lead to a breach of relations, and at worst to war. The same obligatory requirements applied to individuals exchanging gifts. The exchange of gifts thus maintained good relations between communities and internal solidarity. As hierarchy increased in communities and rulers and elites raised themselves above the rest of society, the redistribution of the resources of society to benefit the elites often imitated the reciprocal gift exchange. It was also worthwhile to present redistribution as reciprocity to subjects, although equality was no longer present.

A system of mutual expectations and obligations existed between rulers and subjects which, according to Barrington Moore, also placed

© The Author(s) 2019
A. Kujala and M. Danielsbacka, *Reciprocity in Human Societies*,
https://Doi.org/10.1007/978-3-319-96056-2_9

obligations on the former. By paying taxes and rent and providing troops, the common people expected their rulers in return to refrain from raising taxes without compelling reasons, to provide emergency assistance in times of crop failure and to protect their subjects against external enemies. While the system of mutual obligations was only partly defined in law, reciprocity obligated rulers just as much even with no formally confirmed rules. History, and modern history in particular, is full of examples of rulers who neglected their obligations and were deposed through outright revolution or rebellion, or merely the tacit disobedience of their subjects.

Reciprocity is the glue that holds society together, but breaches of its obligations can lead to social instability. Reciprocity can be defined as a system of rights and obligations that all parties concerned regard as fair. The system of mutual relations between rulers and subjects described by Barrington Moore has existed in one form or another in practically all societies with hierarchies. The historical examples cited above are from South America, India, Japan and the Nordic countries, but we could have selected different ones.

The tensed relationship between rulers (or those giving orders) and subjects (or those following orders) is most clearly evident in conscript armies based on a strict hierarchy. Armies of conscripts established in connection with the emergence of nation-states became a two-edged sword for governments. They increased the military power of states, but at the same time made all males "citizen-soldiers," thus exposing rulers to the power of the masses and its underlying expectations of reciprocity and fairness.

Reciprocity structured, and continues to structure, relations between groups of people of that are mutually more equal than rulers and subjects. The examples discussed here are the village servant system that functioned in places in India and indigenous communities of the Andes which have tried to maintain their own pre-conquest culture of reciprocity under the pressure of an originally European state, population and culture. In Peru and Bolivia, the centuries-long oppression of the indigenous population became a burden on society as a whole, because the economy did not progress toward sustainable improvement, democracy took root poorly, and welfare for the whole population was not achieved.

Although exchange via the gift institution lost all its former significance in relations between communities, the exchanging of gifts still influences relations between individuals. Reciprocity in the form of the gift institution, however, laid the basis for the emergence of a contractual society. This was the core idea of Marcel Mauss's essay on the gift. The present-day welfare state is based on a social contract between the state and the citizens. The latter pay taxes to the authorities and expect in return education, healthcare, and social welfare services in times of emergency. Reciprocity is also present in employer-employee relations. Retributive moral feelings also shape and define the activities of present welfare states and the behavior of people in them.

Gøsta Esping-Andersen's well-known typology of welfare states classes them into three systems: liberal, conservative and social democratic. The norm of reciprocity is associated in different ways with the respective principles by which these states operate. In liberal welfare states such as the United States and Great Britain, individuals have the main responsibility for their own livelihood and welfare. The freedom of the individual is emphasized at the cost of the role of the state. The ideal is a night-watchman state that protects its citizens against external and internal threats but offers only marginal and highly means-tested social security for risks such as unemployment, illness and other problems of livelihood. Owing to poor or non-existent public services, differences in health and education between various sectors of the population in the United States are generally greater than in West European countries. American medical research is the best in the world, but the standard of public health in the United States, analyzed with all metrics, is clearly lower than that of other developed countries, in other words of a good Belarusian standard. In liberal welfare states, the requirement of reciprocity is associated above all with punitive morality and the so-called free-rider problem, which concerns the poorest sector of the population.

In conservative welfare states, the operational logic of the system involves reciprocity in its purest form: the insurance-based model provides what is paid into it. Germany has been called the prime example of the Continental European social insurance state.

The social democratic or Nordic model, on the other hand, underlines the responsibility of the state to provide social security of last resort and comprehensive public services. The Nordic welfare state is based on the notion of universalism, i.e. that everyone is both a payer and a recipient of services. This ensures that, at least in principle, the system can be felt to be fair. The Nordic model also has the feature that the care of the weakest members of society is considered to be the duty of the state.

Both aspects are included in the social contract between the state and its citizens.

Comparisons of these welfare-state systems using various metrics of social well-being almost always give the highest places to the Nordic countries. A background factor of the success of the Nordic model appears to be that by reducing class and gender-based inequality the state generates trust both between it and its citizens and in relations between citizens, reinforcing in turn the feeling of being "on the same side." It is also possible in the Nordic countries to rise from the social status into which one is born. In these countries, social mobility is possible in a completely different way than, for example, in the United States, where it is highly limited, despite what is claimed by the myth of the American dream.

The state of being disadvantaged, however, also accumulates in the Nordic countries. The example of Finland shows that these countries are not a social utopia. An important indicator of accumulating disadvantage is Finland's homicide rate, which is high in comparison with the other Nordic countries. In Finland, both victims and perpetrators of capital crimes are mostly marginalized middle-aged men with drinking problems. Disparities in health and life expectancy between classes and especially between men, but also women, are disproportionately high in relation to social well-being in other areas. As Göran Therborn points out, the otherwise egalitarian Nordic countries have not been able to get rid of inequality in matters of life expectancy and health.

Both the liberal and social democratic welfare state systems support equality and an equal distribution of resources, because the idea of reciprocity and fairness appeals to everyone universally. In all settings, however, people are prone to punitive morality, which means that free riders are viewed in negative terms everywhere, the only difference being the distance between classes (or groups) in society. This influences who, and how many people, are felt to be free riders. The greater the social distance, the more the elites and upper middle class emphasize opportunities for abusing the system, generally exaggerating the problems of free riders to a great degree.

The destruction caused by the world wars, progressive income tax adopted by states and the Great Depression of the 1930s particularly reduced the largest amounts of wealth and leveled income distribution in the developed industrialized countries, where it was at its most even level in the 1970s and 1980s. The modern welfare state came about through the democratization of societies and in response to the challenges of wars and communism.

Since the 1980s, neoliberal economic theories have been a guideline for economic policy especially in the United States, but also in many West European countries. It was believed that the freest possible operation of the markets would lead to better economic development than their regulation. The shift of focus in economic activity from real production to financialization and rent-seeking, however, has not only led to an immense redistribution of wealth but also reinforced the economic cycles that are a normal aspect of capitalism. The world economy was in danger of collapse when the American mortgage and finance bubble burst in 2008. The banks that had recklessly financed the bubble economy were bailed out by governments with money from taxpayers. The laws of the market economy now apply only when profits are made. Losses are compensated from public funds. In this situation, the responsibility of investors and shareholders to bear the possible losses of investments mostly ceases to exist.

While the American economy has now mostly recovered, the risk factors by which the financial markets can create a new crash of the economy have only been addressed nominally. Europe had its own banking and debt crisis largely due to its financial system based on the common currency. The European and Finnish economies are now in their early stages of recovery.

Over the past 30 years, governments have believed that reducing taxes will reinforce economic activity. The progression of income tax can be reduced, or even eradicated, making the system of taxation regressive for the earners of the largest incomes (often capital income), i.e. they will pay tax according to a lower rate than the average wage earner. This economic theory claims that wealth will trickle over time down to the middle class and the poor to benefit everyone. In reality, however, income disparity has increased over the 30 years in almost all developed industrial nations. This has happened to the utmost degree in the United States, where the richest 10%, and richest 1% in particular, have grabbed the lion's share of economic growth. In the early 1980s, there was exceptionally low-income disparity in Sweden and Finland, but over the past 25 years differences of income have grown sharply, which has been above all a result of capital income being taxed at a clearly lower rate than earned income. Owing to their starting point of low disparity, Finland and Sweden are still far behind the American or South European level of income inequality. On the other hand, many Continental European countries which originally had higher income disparity than the Nordic countries have managed to slow its growth relatively well. Norway reduced special preferential treatment for capital income in taxation and now has lower income disparity than Finland.

Wealth has thus not trickled down to the middle class and the poor, but definitely into tax havens. International corporations use tax havens to avoid paying taxes even according to the prevailing corporate tax rate, although tax competition between countries has led them to lower their corporate tax rates. With decreasing tax revenue for public authorities and its use for subsidizing banks, public services are at risk. In the United States, where social security for young people and the working population is poor compared with Western Europe, times were hard for people who lost their jobs in the last recession.

When the last economic crisis of the Eurozone broke out, Germany and France saved their banks, which had financed the economic bubble of the South European countries. Operating in an unregulated financing market, the banks had become even more bloated than their American equivalents in relation to GDP. The debts were transferred to be the liabilities of EU institutions, individual Eurozone countries and the International Monetary Fund. Originally private debt now became public debt, with the money of the taxpayers of the Eurozone countries as security. Profits were private; debts were socialized. Just as previously in the United States, the financial system was rescued, but investor responsibility, i.e. personal liability for the materialized risks of investments, was swept under the carpet.

The European Commission, the European Central Bank and the International Monetary Fund awarded assistance packages and other support to Ireland and the South European countries in crisis. Aid was contingent on these countries fixing their own government finances and this condition was laid down in the name of strict European budgetary rules. This led to unprecedented austerity policies creating an unemployment rate of approximately 25% (in Spain and Greece), large-scale social and health problems and fostering violent extremist movements. It is understandable per se that North European politicians could not be generous to the citizens of other countries without demanding sacrifices from them, because the citizens of their own countries, upon whose favor their position depended, had already become concerned about the sufficiency of their own services. Nonetheless, the result in the countries beset by the crisis was a shock therapy that both impoverished their citizens and halted economic development and often just increased their public debt. The simultaneous drop in purchasing power in several countries exacerbated a downward spiral that weakened the economies of all countries of the European Union. No doubt, there were no easy solutions to the problem, but the means that were now chosen only made the situation worse.

It was imagined far too long in Finland that the economic recession that began with the American mortgage bubble was mainly an import. It was believed that the recession could be weathered by temporarily raising taxes and taking on more debt. This would allow the stimulation of the economy to prevent the mass unemployment that Finland saw during the recession of the 1990s. Unfortunately, the Finnish forest and electronic industries encountered major problems around the same time owing to their own short-sighted decisions. State finances have suffered from growing debt and reduced tax revenue. Finland's present government claims that its main goals are to reduce public debt and to balance state finances, but this does not appear to be the case. The government's implemented tax cuts are counterproductive to these aims. Tax reductions apply in principle to everyone, but cuts to benefits apply only to the unemployed and other disadvantaged people. The classes of society to which the prime minister himself belongs have not had to give up anything.

Austerity policies carried out in the United States and Western Europe over the past decade, with focus on saving banks and major investors at the cost of meeting the needs of ordinary citizens aroused widespread dissatisfaction. As moderate left-wing and centrist parties in governments were in many cases involved in implementing this policy, dissatisfaction became channeled into support for right-wing populist movements. These movements, however, acquired their actual impetus from opposing immigration. The Brexit position won in the British referendum held in the summer of 2016. Right-wing populism's greatest victory came in November 2016, when Donald Trump won the US presidential election. It will be interesting to see to what degree Trump's nationalistic and isolationist policies which also serve the interests of the super-rich will satisfy the white blue-collar workers who voted him into power.

Reciprocity, mutual obligations and retributive moral feelings have belonged to the relations between rulers and subjects in both past and present societies. The neoliberal economic policies of present welfare states, tax cuts for corporations and the rich, and forgetting the responsibility of investors in the care of the economic crisis all serve to erode the social contract between governments and the people. Social welfare services are highly popular among citizens even in countries where they are more limited than in Finland, the Nordic countries or Continental Europe, which means that the end of the welfare state is hardly in sight. We must, however, remember the strong and deeply ingrained human tendency to expect and demand that the authorities follow the obligation of reciprocity. A society that also takes care of its weakest members and is therefore regarded as fair in a general sense, is a better alternative than the winner-take-all model, in which social stability has to be maintained with armed guards, barbed wire and disciplinary policies.

INDEX

© The Editor(s) (if applicable) and The Author(s) 2019
A. Kujala and M. Danielsbacka, *Reciprocity in Human Societies*,
https://doi.org/10.1007/978-3-319-96056-2